C0-ATX-094

THE KILLING STONES
Two Years in a Papua New Guinea Jungle Village

Margel Lee Craig

THE KILLING STONES
Two Years in a Papua New Guinea Jungle Village

by Margel Lee Craig

Wyndham Hall Press is an academic imprint
of the Cloverdale Corporation.

Library of Congress Catalog Card Number

92-050346

ISBN 1-55605-209-X

Printed in the United States of America

Cloverdale Corporation
Bristol, IN   46507-9460

DEDICATION

To my husband, Bill, who shared
in the joy and adventure.

TABLE OF CONTENTS

CHAPTER 1

"My country is the world, and my religion is to do good." - Thomas Paine

The first question asked by our family and friends, when we announced that we had applied for a two year assignment in the Peace Corps was, "Why? What gave you the idea?" Peace Corps had sounded fascinating to me from its very beginning. My conception was that it was designed to help third world countries by delegating young college graduates to serve in these areas for two years. It was only after we Americans were introduced to Miss Lillian, mother of President Carter, that I realized that Peace Corps used senior citizens. Her enthusiasm, as she told small excerpts of her two years in India, was contagious-I caught the infection!

My first husband and I had built a successful metal fabrication company manufacturing gravity beds and augers used in agriculture and containers for the solid waste industry. It grew from the original small operation in Indiana to a sizable enterprise with factories in Indiana and Iowa. Finally we sold the company and we each went our own way. I was fifty-four; my marriage had failed. What would I do with the rest of my life? Would Peace Corps want me? On second thought I decided to do some world traveling.

The many years I had worked in our company never gave me time enough to visit many of the countries I longed to see, so I toured much of Asia, South America, Africa, the Caribbean and Europe. An introduction to new cultures and foreign lands was a learning experience. In some third world countries I saw a lot of poverty but it didn't repulse me; instead, I simply yearned to help those people improve their living standards.

Time passed and through fate I met a wonderful man who won my confidence and finally persuaded me that the two of us could have extremely happy years as husband and wife. We were married on

January 26, 1980. For a while I worked as a real estate broker, then we both decided it was time to retire. However, we could never accept the normal retirement, but it would give us time to pursue the enjoyments and hobbies we had never found time to include in our busy lives.

Bill and my leisurely early mornings were an enjoyable daily ritual. Our morning pattern was always the same. We started our day by sitting in our favorite chairs in the family room/ kitchen and drinking many cups of coffee while we talked and planned and reminisced. On one such morning, one of us said, "If we hadn't married, I would have seriously considered joining the Peace Corps." And the other replied, "Really? Why I'd thought about a term in Peace Corps too!" So we both agreed that would be a good project for our retirement. There was one problem. My Mother was 84 and in a nursing home and I was her only child. I felt that I must remain near her. She was growing senile and sometimes failing to recognize close friends and relatives. Peace Corps would have to wait, but the idea never left our minds. We did contact the nearest Peace Corps office to see if they could use two people our age. Their answer was affirmative, providing we could pass the physical and other requirements.

Mother died quietly in January 1985, some two years later. She was 86. Her passing was a blessing because she was paralyzed, unable to talk or to enjoy life. A few days after the funeral I asked Bill if he was still interested in joining the Peace Corps. We phoned them for two applications. Ten days later we had their acknowledgement of our applications and we had a package of forms to complete. We were on the first lap of a new adventure.

The next few weeks were busy ones. We must have complete physicals, obtain oral x-rays from our dentist. We both visited our optometrist and got new eyeglasses and copies of the prescriptions. All the questionnaires had to be completed and returned. These were my task. We must send our school records and list all our skills and qualifications. Bill listed farmer, veterinarian skills, cattle feedlot management, livestock which included cattle, hogs, sheep, goats, chickens and ducks. He also listed gardening, grains and hay crops and repairs, welding and fabrication skills. My skills were different-gardening, food preservation, sewing, all types of needlework, but my life work had been bookkeeping, advertising, public relations and real estate. I wondered how these types of work could be used in an agricultural setting which Bill was qualified to do.

The summer months seemed to drag by as we anxiously waited for the next mail, the next word from Peace Corps. In August we were notified that our papers had been accepted and our names were being processed for assignment. We couldn't wait to learn the name of the country where we would be living and working. We had asked to be sent to a politically safe country and we requested the South Pacific area, specifically Papua New Guinea. Each week I used the toll free number to telephone the Washington D.C. office to ask if we had been assigned. In desperation I wrote a poem about going to Peace Corps and sent along with a photo of us, which we had had taken recently to leave for our children. Bill has four children and I have two.

Our Dream
One day soon we'll be leaving the U.S.A
For at least two years or more.
Hopefully we'll be accepted and assigned
By the U.S. Peace Corps.

It's a dream we each had
Before we joined our lives;
A dream to help those in a strange country.
Are you really surprised?

There will be times of frustration,
Yet mostly happy days
As we struggle to teach the people
Higher standards and better ways.

One can't force happiness,
For happiness one must give.
We'll be indebted to this Peace Corps adventure
For as long as we live.

They will give to us the challenge
That Bill and I need to experience.
Our new host country and its people
Will, to us, make all the difference.

When I phoned again on September 16th, Peace Corps told us we would be sent to Papua New Guinea as Community Development Extensionists. We were to report for a week of training called Crest in San Francisco on November 11th. There were many preparations to make before we could leave our home and farm. We must sell all of the livestock, find someone to farm the ground, find someone to house-sit, find a person to manage our apartments and someone to generally oversee, file taxes, sort mail, etc. My son agreed to be our power of attorney, his father-in-law took the responsibility of the apartments, our neighbor agreed to do the farming and lastly, we found a young lady to live in our house. Our next task was to decide what items to take with us for our next household in a foreign country.

We were informed that we could each take eighty pounds of luggage. We should take light weight clothing, but we should also take some warm garments in the event we were placed in the Highlands which sometimes has quite chilly nights. A good supply of hobby items was also recommended and a short wave radio and tape player would provide some entertainment should we be in a remote area. We would need sleeping bags and backpacks for patrols. There were many decisions to make!

When we first told our children of our decision to join Peace Corps, none of them objected as long as we promised to write them often. They said we were old enough to live our lives as we saw fit, yet they wondered why we wanted to leave the comforts of our home for some unknown place. Friends were not always so understanding, especially when they learned we were headed for Papua New Guinea. Some of them had served there during World War II and had experienced the heat and humidity, the daily tropical rains, the swamps and the uncivilized conditions which existed then. Others expressed their admiration for our courage to face the unknown. There were many farewell parties given for us by our families and friends which were evenings of group discussions about the challenges we might face in our new environment. They were concerned that we were making the right choice!

From the moment we learned our destiny was to be Papua New Guinea, we searched the libraries for books to read about our new host country. Most books related to stories and history during and just after

World War II. Bill read every one of them. I sorted and packed and stored our personal belongings to get ready for the house sitter. While I worked, he read excerpts to me and disclosed bits of information. Finally my daughter, Suzanne, found a publication on travel in Papua New Guinea called "Papua New Guinea, a Travel Survival Kit" by Lonely Planet, compiled by Mark Lightbody and Tony Wheeler, which had been published in April of 1985. It gave us a lot of current statistics, facts, maps and travel tips. We immediately ordered a copy to take with us. This country was not the same Papua New Guinea of World War II. Later as we traveled over many areas of Papua New Guinea the Lonely Planet handbook provided much information. We carried it with us always.

We left home on November 3, 1985 with eight pieces of luggage. My son and wife drove us to the South Bend, Indiana Airport. At last we were on our way! Our first stop was in Spokane, Washington to say goodbye to my daughter and family. From there we flew to San Francisco where Bill's youngest son and family met us at the airport and drove us to their home in San Jose. On the 10th they drove us to San Francisco and we ate our farewell dinner at Fisherman's Wharf. Later they dropped us at the Hotel San Francisco where we would receive a week of training from Peace Corps before our departure for Papua New Guinea.

After we registered at the hotel, we looked around the lobby for other possible volunteers, but no one seemed the right type for such an adventure. We did see a middle aged couple in the coffee shop where we ate our evening meal. We saw them again on the elevator. "Those two are Peace Corps Volunteers," I remarked. And we saw them again in the coffee ship next morning at breakfast. This time they smiled and nodded.

When we walked into the meeting room and approached the registration desk, a young man called, " Hello Bill and Margel!"

"How do you know our names?", I inquired.

"Well didn't you send us a picture and a poem?" It was Roy Lester. I remembered talking with him on some of my many phone calls to the Washington, D.C. office. And there was the same couple we had seen before in the hotel coffee shop. I'd guessed right. There were forty-nine people attending Crest, forty-nine hopeful candidates. We all must pass this training course before we would be certain that we were actually going to be accepted. Nine of us were forty-five or older - three couples and three single ladies. All of we older ones had grey hair showing or were already solidly white. But most of the candidates were young college graduates in their twenties. They were going to have an adventure before they settled into a job. And we oldsters were also seeking an adventure!

After the introductions, we learned that of the forty-nine aspirants, only eighteen were going to Papua New Guinea. The larger group would be sent to Western Samoa. Bill and I were the only older ones assigned to Papua New Guinea. It was a big disappointment for us.

During the training we discussed our individual aspirations for joining Peace Corps. We were told some expectations we should incorporate into our goals, how to find needed information, frustrations we might encounter and a re-evaluation of ourselves. We divided into two groups so that we could meet with a recently returned volunteer from the country where we would be living. Our speaker had worked for two years with the forestry department in Mendi located in the Southern Highland Province of Papua New Guinea. She spoke to us first in Tok Pidgin. We heard our first sounds and music of the country and she told of the cultural differences we would experience. It was an exciting revelation.

In another training session we split into teams for a closer examination of our individual motives. It soon became evident that Crest was a week of re-commitment. Peace Corps was trying to discourage us from embarking on a two year term unless we were totally confident that we were making the correct choice as individuals. To introduce us to the idea of cultural shock, we played a game, Bafa Bafa, where we had to communicate with actions. No words could be spoken. We were also given medical instructions about diseases we might encounter. Finally we received our first shots and oral malaria prophylaxis which we were instructed to take once a week for the duration of our assignment.

Bill and I had spent many hours at home discussing the challenges we would face in a new culture. We repeatedly ask one another if we could live in a bush village, bathe and wash our clothes in a river, cook our meals over an open fire, give up all the comforts we now had and live in a totally different fashion. Neither of us had any reservations. Why bother to leave our country unless we could learn a new culture and lifestyle. We were ready to meet the challenge.

After individual interviews with the Peace Corps staff, it was time for each to write his or her commitment. Bill wrote, "I, William P. Craig, commit the next two years of my life and knowledge to the benefit of others to the best of my ability. My goal is to give something of lasting value or skill to Papua New Guinea and to make many friendships and promote goodwill."

I wrote, " I pledge to Peace Corps and the country of Papua New Guinea the next twenty-four months of my life to give my skills, abilities and time to the people. My goal is to leave something of lasting value and skills to the people of Papua New Guinea and to make friendships and promote goodwill between the two countries."

On late Sunday afternoon on November 17th, 1985 we volunteers collected our mounds of luggage and boarded the airport bus. The importance of a week at Crest became evident when two young women decided to return to their homes. One was to have traveled with us to Papua New Guinea. During the seminar they both discovered that they weren't ready to accept the challenge and the unknown. Our group of seventeen flew from San Francisco via Los Angeles, Sidney, Australia to Port Moresby in Papua New Guinea. Those going to Western Somoa flew via Honolulu to their island. We waved farewell to our new friends of one week. Would we ever meet again?

CHAPTER 2

"You can cover a great deal of a country in books."
- Andrew Lang

Papua New Guinea is an independent nation with a population of over three and one-half million people and has a land area of 176,289 sq. miles, a little larger than the state of California. On September 16, 1975 it was granted its independence from Australia. It is a member of the Commonwealth, so the Queen of England is the Head of State represented by a Governor-general. The nation, following the Parliamentary system, is governed by a Prime Minister, a single House of Parliament and a cabinet chosen from elected Parliament members. Port Moresby is the national capital, population approximately one hundred-fifty thousand. This new nation is located in the South Pacific in the eastern half of the largest tropical island of the world. The western half of this island is called Irian Jaya, which is a province of Indonesia.

There are nineteen provinces in Papua, New Guinea. Each has its own elected provincial government headed by a Premier and an Assembly to handle certain affairs within the province. Some provinces are smaller islands or groups of islands off the coasts of the mainland. Each province is divided into districts, similar to states and counties.

There are over seven hundred tribes and tribal languages. Often in remote areas neighboring tribes cannot understand one another. These people are now called "Nationals"; to refer to them as natives is considered an insult. It is interesting to note that when these people speak of two or more members of a tribe, the tribal name remains singular such as Bari, Yumi, Musa, Huli, Kukukuku. It is symbolic of the oneness which still exists throughout Papua New Guinea. However, they use the plural form when they refer to more than one National. These primitive people, whose lives are ruled by strange customs, live in a land that "time nearly forgot." They have, for the most part, only heard of more advanced civilizations since World War II. For them

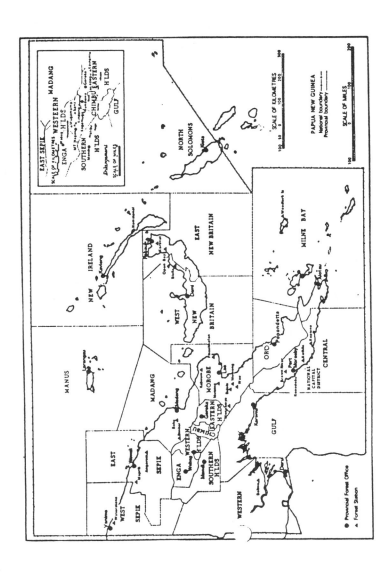

time is meaningless; there is always tomorrow and tomorrow. Their needs and wants are few - some food to fill empty bellies, the camaraderie of the village people and "wantoks" (relatives and close friends) and the wealth of pigs, good yam crops and sea shells.

The official language for government and education is English. There are two other principal languages which were developed in the early days of European contact. They are Motu, used in the most southern part, and Tok Pidgen, the more popular, which has been called "baby talk" or "broken English." Some examples of Tok Pidgen are: mi liak biam (I want to buy), lukautim gut (be careful), mi no klia (I don't understand), mi liakim sampela kaikai (I want something to eat), tok isi (speak slowly).

It is a beautiful land, a place filled with dramatic contrasts and surprises. There are towering mountains covered with dense jungle growth; others are bare except for rocks and grass. Mighty rivers flow from these mountains down to the sea. There are mangrove swamps fringing the coasts, vast prairies of grassland, lowland forests, rain forests, deep gorges, coral reefs, volcanic islands, majestic palms, acres of Arabica and Robusta coffee gardens, cocoa, oil palms and coconut plantations, fjord-like terrain and picturesque native villages augmented with colorful tribal dress.

To further enhance this wonderland are the unusual fauna and flora. There are thirty-eight species of the exotic bird of paradise. The most beautiful, the Raggiana, is used on the National emblem and flag. There are more than six hundred species of birds, including colorful parrots, white cockatoos with yellow plumage, the Victorian Crowned pigeons, hornbills, eagles and the impressive cassowaries which are unable to fly and resemble the ostrich. Reptiles range from tiny lizards to crocodiles, not to mention the many varieties of snakes. There are many kinds of marsupials, which carry their young in a pouch, such as tree kangaroo and cuscus. Fruitbats often darken the sky as they swarm above the tree tops. It is also the land of beautiful butterflies. The largest butterflies in the world live here.

The forests are glorified with white, yellow and pink frangipani, red bottlebush, brilliant red flame of the forest vines, white angel trumpets, giant red poinsettias, red, yellow, and pink hibiscus, colorful crotons, the African tulip trees with bright orange blossoms, the red flowering poinciana trees, blue jacarandas and the golden wattle trees and many more varieties of flowering shrubs, trees and plants. It is truly an untamed paradise!

Archaeological excavations have found evidence of human activity dating back to twenty-six thousand to thirty thousand years. The first known outside contact was in 1528 A.D. when Alvaro de Saavedia sailed along the northern coast of the mainland on his return trip from Moluccus to the Spanish territories in North America. Other ships passed along the eastern coast of the mainland and outlying islands some time later. There was little contact with Europeans until the 19th century. About 1870 laborers were recruited, especially from New Britain, New Ireland and the islands of the Torres Straits, to work in the sugar fields and pearling industry in Queensland, Australia. Others were sent to the Samoa Islands to work on the copra plantations. It was the search for and discovery of gold in Papua New Guinea that finally opened the country to foreign contacts. In the early 1930's Michael Leahy, an Australian, and his brothers penetrated the Highlands. The natives watched with awe as a giant bird landed on their soil and beings with white skin emerged from its bowels. The terrified natives at first assumed they were dead ancestors returning to earth. Later they watched these strange creatures defecate, smelled their feces and then understood that they must be humans. But it was not until after World War II that progress was made in education, industry and mission development.

The people of Papua, New Guinea are know as Melanesians. They have dark skins and fuzzy black hair. In fact, Papua means the "land of fuzzy hair." Some tribes are very short, under five feet, while others are five to five and one-half feet and still other tribes are as tall as six feet. Some Nationals, especially the people of New Ireland, have blond hair and bronze skin. They are often called the "ginger people." In contrast, the people of North Solomon Island have extremely dark skins and are considered the darkest skin people in the world. Most Nationals have broad flat noses and spayfeet. It is easy to discern the type of terrain where they live by looking at the calves of their legs. Those living in mountainous areas have enormous calves due to the constant travel up and down the slopes.

Dress differs with each region. Those living in or near town or cities have abandoned their tribal dress for western attire. The men usually wear trousers or shorts, shirts or T-shirts; some professional men wear suits and ties. The women wear simple dresses or skirts and blouses or a "laplap and meri blouse." There are many used clothing stores supplied by shipments of used clothing from Australia. For special celebrations or holidays, the people usually revert to their traditional tribal dress.

Each tribe has its own traditional dress code. In some provinces, such as New Britain and New Ireland, the women and men wear a "laplap" which is a straight piece of cloth wound about the waist. Often the women wear a "meri blouse", a loose maternity type blouse. The laplap may be a printed cotton material imported from China or "tapa cloth", the ancient cloth-like material made from the inner bark of the mulberry tree. The inner bark is soaked in water, then laid on a flat surface and beaten with a flat paddle until the bark becomes thin and cloth-like. Oro Province is noted for tapa cloth which is painted with intricate geometric patterns using dyes made from plants and berries from the jungle. Each unique pattern reveals the tribal area where it is made. The men cut strips of tapa to wear as loin cloths; the women wear tapa laplaps. The rest of their bodies are bare.

In the Highland Provinces women wear grass skirts or skirts of unpainted tapa cloth and are naked above the waist. Their men wrap vines around their waist and hang small twigs of leaves or grass from the vine bands to cover their front and backsides. This apparel is called "arse grass." The most unique dress is found in Western Sepik and the extreme northern part of Western Province where the men wear a "penis gourd" especially grown in their gardens for this purpose. The long narrow hollow gourd is used as a sheath to cover the penis only, held in place by a woven string attached to a vine about the waist. The rest of the body is naked. A few of the older men still wear the gourd as daily dress. The women wear short grass skirts which cover their fronts and backs while exposing the sides of their thighs. However, across Papua New Guinea simple western style dress is gradually becoming the daily wearing apparel.

No tribal dress would be complete without beads, feathers and shells draped about the chest. These adornments are know as "bilas."

Feathers from the beautiful birds, fur and sea shells are also combined into colorful headdresses. The men of the Huli tribe, who live in the highlands of the central mainland, are famous for their headdresses fashioned from human hair and decorated with everlasting flowers - we call them straw flowers. Their women folk keep their hair cut very short so that the men can use the cut hair to weave into headdresses. The men paint their faces and bodies with red, yellow, white and black patterns for special events. Many people of Papua New Guinea, especially the men, have holes through their noses and ear lobes so that pig tusks and small bones can be inserted as decoration. Tattooing the arms, face and often the entire body is another common practice. Although these traditional clothing customs and body decorations may sound extremely primitive and unusual, the people look spectacular and attractive.

It is quite common to see groups of people walking along a road or trail carrying spears, bow and arrows, axes and bush knives because these are their hunting weapons and only means of protection. Very, very few own a gun. They could be on their way to another village, to settle a dispute, to attend a celebration, to their gardens or a hunting trip. Usually they wave to an occasional passing vehicle hoping to hitch a ride.

The currency of Papuas New Guinea is named for the shells originally used for barter, the "kina" and "toea" shells. The kina is made in denominations of 1.00 (a coin with a hole through the center) and 2.00, 5.00, 10.00, and 20.00 paper notes. The toea comes in coins of .01, .02, .05, .20 and .50 denominations.

Airplanes are the principal means of travel. Many Nationals have seen an airplane long before they see a vehicle, because the foreigners could penetrate the interior land only by foot or aircraft, therefore development was begun before there were any form of roads. The rugged terrain, the remoteness and the heavy tropical rainfall makes road construction and maintenance costly and often impossible. Now there are some seven hundred sod airstrips which often provide the only available means of transportation and trade, except for walking, for many of the rural villages. The most extensive road system had been developed from the Highlands to Lae, a major seaport on the eastern coast, because there was an urgent need for a road to transport the large coffee crops grown in the Highlands to Lae for processing and exportation. Even around the national capital of Port Moresby the roads only extend approximately sixty kilometers from the city. Coastal shipping handles most of the country's incoming freight and exportation of copper, gold, timber, coffee, copra, cocoa and palm oil. From the ship docks incoming supplies are carried inland by planes.

****

Oro Province, where we lived, is located in the southeastern portion of the mainland, sandwiched between the Solomon Sea on the east and the Owen Stanley Mountains to the west. Popondetta, population eight thousand, is the provincial capital and only city/town in the province. Besides the provincial government offices, it offers banking and postal facilities, an agricultural college, high school, both a private international- al and a public grade school, a vocational school, coffee and cocoa buying companies, truck sales and rentals, two hardware stores, wholesale and retail food and supply stores, a hospital, a doctor, sea freight companies, a construction company, Air Niugini and Talair airline offices, a theater and a hotel. The Higatura Oil Palm Develop- ment Company, located a few kilometers from town, is the major commercial/agricultural industry of the area and it is the largest palm oil company in the southern hemisphere.

Popondetta is truly the cultural and life support center of the province because it is here that all the now necessary items of refinement and a civilized society are found. Oro Province, originally know as Northern Province, experienced the incursion of the Allied and Japanese troops in 1942, particularly in the Oro Bay, Buna, Kokoda and Higatura areas. The Battle of Buna is said to have been the bloodiest battle of WWII. Soon the spark of a kinder, more civilized society began to smolder. For example: the Nationals often carry a small smoldering stick of wood from their recent fire with them as they travel to their gardens or as they walk from village to village. Later they can blow on the stick and it will begin to burn again so that they can light another fire or a cigarette. As this stick burns very slowly, like punk, so has this new contact with other cultures from distant lands. Before the military encounter the Nationals were content to make clothing from the inner bark of a tree and to use vines from the jungle to lash poles together to build their huts. They made salt by scorching taro leaves and then pulverizing them or by evaporating sea water. They carved their tools from stone and wood. Now it is different. They are learning to grow crops of coffee, palm oil, cocoa, copra and chilies to sell for cash. They need money to buy salt, sugar, coffee, tea, rice, canned fish, canned corn beef, biscuits, tobacco, clothing, blankets, towels, bush knives, axes, cooking pots and nails.

The land surrounding Popondetta and eastward is relatively flat; south and to the west there are mountains. A road leads from Popondetta south and west to Kokoda where it ends in the Kokoda valley. Here is the beginning of the famous Kokoda Trail of World War II, the trail across the Owen Stanley Mountains to Port Moresby. Traveling westward on this trail, the Japanese troops attempted to reach Port Moresby to capture MacArthur's headquarters. It became a journey of death and disaster as hundreds lost their lives in the dense jungle infested by leeches and slippery mud, and even their commander, General Horti, fell to his death while crossing a river.

There is a sealed road from Popondetta eastward, past the Garui Airport and south to the seaport of Oro Bay, a distance of thirty miles. Ships bring the majority of all supplies and equipment sold in the area to the Oro Bay docks where it is transported by trucks to Popondetta. Often there are long delays in replacing inventory stock. The excuse is, "Sorry! The boat has not come yet." It might be weeks before the items arrive.

The highway from Popondetta to Oro Bay turns west at the entrance to the harbor and continues some seventy miles to end at Itokama, the village where we lived for two years. The sealed road surface ends at Oro Bay and becomes a narrow dirt road, which soon becomes two tracks with grass growing down the center most of the way. There are eight bridges, some are Bailey bridges while others are loose planks laid across a crude foundation, plus there are seven rivers to ford. During the rainy season sections of this road become almost impossible to travel due to the slippery mud, deep ruts and chuck holes, shifting boulders and the mountainous terrain. With good road condition it requires from five to eight or more hours to make the trip from Popondetta to Itokama in a 4 wheel drive vehicle. It is called the Pongami-Afore highway. The Pongami-Afore trail would be a more realistic name. It is a beautiful journey over mountains with breathtaking views of the sea and coastline, through valleys and dense rain jungle where the vegetation crowds the narrow road and scrapes against the vehicle, past native villages, through flat plains of kuni grass and coffee gardens. It is an unbelievable experience!

Talair airline has a regular passenger and freight service from Popondetta to Itokama each Tuesday and Thursday morning, weather conditions permitting. A direct flight takes only fifteen minutes and costs 25.00 kina ($25.00). The Itokama airstrip is one of the largest sod strips in Papua New Guinea. It was on this airstrip that we landed to begin our work. We were assigned to live in Itokama, the principal/head village of the Barai tribe, comprised of fifteen villages and over two thousand people. The Barai tribe live in Afore District of Oro Province, in the upper Managalasi Plateau, along the southern slope of the Owatama range at an elevation of 2,500 feet. The Sibium Mountains are to the south.

The soil of this area is well drained and derived from volcanic ash, which could best be described as a sandy loam. It is low in nutrients, especially nitrogen, potassium and potash, and suffers the leaching of nutrients so typical of tropical countries with heavy rainfall. During the six month rainy season, it usually rains every afternoon or early evening, but the water soon disappears. The ground is dry again by the next morning. Often it rains four inches in two hours or less. The remaining six month period is known as the dry season, the time to plant gardens. Then it only rains every week or two.

The Barai people use the "slash and burn" method of gardening, which is prevalent over all of Papua New Guinea. Their gardens are located a considerable distance from the villages in jungle area and they are used for one year, never more than two years. Then the garden site is abandoned and reverts quickly to jungle growth again, not to be cleared for another garden for fifteen to twenty years. This practice of continual shifting of gardens provides a more fertile soil. Chemical fertilizers are unknown in most rural areas and far too expensive to buy. They raise snake and winged beans, yams (totally different from our American yams), taro, pumpkins, corn, aibiki (greens), lowland pitpit, sugar cane and a few tomatoes. They also grow pineapples, bananas, papayas and melons. Cash crops are Arabica coffee and birdseye chilies. Pigs are considered as wealth and are allowed to roam freely through the villages. They may not be harmed or killed except for feast and special ceremonies. Pigs are a constant nuisance and create a problem around the school grounds and airstrip.

In 1958 Anglican Bishop Hand came to Itokama and planted a cross which still stands near the present church. The Itokama Anglican church was established in 1964. It continues to be an active religious influence. Father Daniel also travels periodically to far villages to conduct church services.

As early as 1965 a few young boys attended a grade school located at Sakarina, about twenty miles to the east. They were the first educated Barai. An American couple, Dr. and Mrs. Chip Larson, came to the Barai people in 1968 for the purpose of studying the Barai language and putting it into its first written form. The man was working on his doctorate in linguistics. They also organized a first grade class at Itokama and each following year added another class until 1974 when all six grades were functioning. It is the only grade school in the Barai land.

A small medical clinic, sometimes called a sub-health center, opened in Itokama in 1984. Medical treatment and medicines are provide free by the national government. This was a step forward to combat the existing problem of malnutrition and disease treatment. Protein and high energy foods are not available in sufficient quantities among the Barai. They have no meat except for wild birds, rodents, snakes, insects and canned meat, which they must buy, so they suffer from malnutrition. Other illnesses are malaria, tuberculosis, venereal diseases, tropical ulcers, fungus, conjunctivitis and scabies. These people still first consult the"Shamam" (medicine man) to treat their illnesses. They go to the sub-health center only after the Shaman's rituals fail to heal them; then once they begin to feel better, they stop going to the clinic for treatment.

Nahara Coffee Growers, Ltd., Pty., located at Itokama, was organized in 1976 for the purpose of buying coffee beans from the local farmers. It has 831 shareholders from the Barai, Musa and Orokiva tribes and is quite an impressive organization for such a primitive setting.

Another organization, the Barai Non-Formal Education Association, better known as BNEA, formed in 1980 as a pilot project, the first in Papua New Guinea. It was initiated by an Australian couple, Paul and Betty Evert working part time with the Barai under the Summer Institute of Linguistics, usually called SIL, in conjunction with the Provincial Non-Formal Education Office at Popondetta. The project was funded by grants. Their main goal was to enable the Barai people to find his or her place in the community. The emphasis was not only education, but on spiritual, social and material development.

CHAPTER 3

"People must learn to gather adventures and experiences rather than things or possessions. Possessions will burden you; adventures become memories which will enrich your soul and last forever." - Anom.

We were flying at five thousand feet over virgin forest that spread like a mottled green carpet as far as the eye could see from the window of the plane. Sometimes there were splashes of red and yellow, which must have been flowering trees and shrubs. We were on our way to our new home at Itokama, where we would live for the next two years. It was normal that both of us were very excited and apprehensive.

Three days earlier we had received our final briefing from the Peace Corps office in Port Moresby, and had flown to Popondetta to buy supplies and to travel on the Tuesday morning air flight to our final destination. While we were staying at Popondetta's only hotel, the Lamington, the manager and his wife, both Australian citizens, were very helpful in familiarizing us with the places to shop for our supplies and general information on business facilities. They also told us the original town, known as Higatura, laid at the foot of Mt. Lamington. In 1951 the volcanic mountain erupted, totally burying the town and killing over two thousand people. The new rebuilt town was named Popondetta and it was relocated a distance away from the volcano; however Mt. Lamington dominates the landscape like a threatening enemy, as the continual smoke emerges from her crater.

The Garui airport, large enough to accommodate jet planes, is about twenty kilometers east of the town on the road to Oro Bay; it is adjacent to the old Dobadura airstrip built by the Allies during World War II. At the entrance to the terminal are two war relics, a B-25 bomber resting vertically on her nose and a Japanese Zero fighter parked on the grass. Both planes are riddled with bullet holes, grim reminders of the past terrible conflict. There are still over three hundred downed aircraft missing. As a hobby, groups of expiates and Nationals continue to search the jungles for these missing planes.

The Talair plane wound its way between the rolling mountains, much like the Appalachian mountain range. Suddenly, below on our right, was a tiny sod airstrip bordered by native huts along the length of the strip, surrounded by mountains. Our pilot told us that this was Gora and that the airstrip was only 1,400 feet long. He told us that a pilot must spiral down between the mountains to lose enough altitude to land. As we flew on, another airstrip on a mountain ridge appeared. The pilot started preparations to land.

He taxied to the end of the sod strip. People lined the one side, waving and smiling. Bill and I were elated that so many people were on hand to welcome our arrival. There were five other passengers aboard, a couple and their three small children. Our plane was an Islander, a propeller driven aircraft, which had four seats to accommodate twelve passengers and a small area in the tail section for cargo. Our twenty one pieces of luggage and cartons of supplies, enough to last us for the next four months, made it necessary to remove the rear seat. The other couple were also traveling with considerable cargo; most of it had been left at the Garui airport with the promise that it would be sent on the Thursday Talair flight. The Islander's load capacity is about 2,000 pounds, give or take a little.

We were the first two off the plane. People began shaking hands with us and speaking to us in a strange language. One young man approached us, and in good English, asked us what we were doing in his village. "We are Peace Corps Volunteers and we have come here to Itokama to work with the Barai people for the next two years," I explained.

"Then you'd better get back on the plane because this is Tetibeti! Itokama is the next stop," he replied.

By this time the couple and children had left the plane and collected their small amount of baggage. Now another couple with a small daughter and twin babies had boarded in their place. We thanked the young man, waved goodby to the crowd and quickly re-boarded.

Approaching the Itokama Airstrip. Kuai village in the foreground.

Itokama Airstrip

In another six minutes we landed at a large sod airstrip seemingly on a plateau. This time our pilot told us we had arrived at Itokama. He taxied the plane to the end of the runway, which was bordered by native huts and an old, long building, which we learned later was the Nahara Coffee Growers, Ltd., Pty. coffee storage and trade store. "You have just found your first challenge," Bill told me. "Look, there is a ditch between the airstrip and the village. You will have to walk across those four poles." I have always been terribly afraid to walk on narrow bridges with no railing, planks or seawalls. This time I knew I must, because this was the first impression I would make. Somehow, hanging onto Bill and moving at a snail's pace, I inched my way across the five foot chasm. The small gathering of villagers roared with laughter.

Simon Savieko, his wife and baby, and about a dozen others were waiting to greet us. We had met Simon the first week of our arrival in Papua New Guinea, when he came to Port Moresby enroute to Japan for a Non-formal Educational Seminar. Peace Corps had already assigned us to work in Itokama with an organization called BNEA, which stood for Barai Non-formal Educational Association. Simon was the administrator for this pilot project, the first of its kind in the country. He was probably in his late twenties. Few Nationals know their age or birth date. He was about five foot three inches, a pleasant man with a winning smile.

We shook hands with everyone, and told them we were so happy to be working with them and looked forward to our two years in the village. By then the younger boys had brought our baggage from the plane. Everyone picked up a piece of our supplies and placed it on their shoulder or on top of their head and we started through the village. It was a twelve minute walk to the far end where we would live. Each house along the way was built on poles, some higher off the ground than others, but an average of about three to five feet. The sides of the huts were made of bamboo strips woven in many different geometric patterns. The roofs were made of leaves bound together on long sticks overlapped in rows. We would see them make these strips of roofing many times and watch the men patiently weave the bamboo siding during the next two years.

Houses lined each side of the village. The ground between the rows of huts was completely bare. Simon pointed to the area ahead where stood a house on the east surrounded with grass framed by a bamboo fence. Coconut trees, red and yellow hibiscus, colorful crotons and some unfamiliar pink flowering shrubs lined the fence. What a beautiful setting. The village councilor lived here. He was regarded as the lawyer. It was his duty to hear all the complaints such as fights between clans, husband and wife and small crimes. He decided the punishment. To the west side stood a small narrow building which was the BNEA trade store. The entire area was in grass. In an adjacent large grassy lot was the big two story BNEA community building, which contained offices, printing rooms, tool shop and a large community meeting room. It was quite uncommon for a jungle village. Ahead of us was another housing section, much like the first one we had passed. It also had bare ground. Simon told us a separate clan lived at each end of Itokama. At the far end, beyond the last hut was a grassy yard and the house we were to occupy.

The house was larger than the other village dwellings. It had a tin roof and a 2,000 gallon metal water storage tank to save the rain water from the roof. The big yard had banana, papaya, betal and o'kari nut trees and a nice shade tree. Two edges of the yard, the west and the south, were lined with red hibiscus, pink and white frangipani, crotons and two St. Thomas orchid trees full of lavender flowers. A path to the next village, called Neokananee, was between the west row of flowering shrubs and the jungle. The east edge of the lot overlooked dense jungle that dropped abruptly to a small obscured stream. A tiny guest house stood at the back of the yard next to a huge granadilla passion fruit vine and a citrus tree. Both buildings were made of native poles and woven bamboo and rested on poles above the ground. We couldn't wait to see inside.

We climbed up three pole steps onto a roofed open sided porch, with crude benches along three sides and a firebox in the center of the floor. A firebox is made with four small logs, two to three feet in length, laid to form a square which is filled with sand, so a fire can be made for cooking or warmth. The people deposited our baggage on the porch, and most of them filled the benches to watch the two strange looking arrivals get settled.

Simon opened the screened door and unlocked the dutch style door. It opened into a kitchen which had a plank floor, a small apartment size

Itokama village

BNEA Tradestore on the right and
BNEA Community building on the left

Our village house

Our porch and firebox

LP gas stove, an antiquated, rusty, kerosene refrigerator, crude base cabinets and a double stainless steel sink with water faucets. The house had been built by a missionary, with the help of the village men, for his wife and seven children. They were members of SIL, which stands for Summer Institute of Linguistics. They had worked for a few months each year for a period of eight years with the Barai people to teach them to translate books of the Bible into Barai language, and to teach them to read their native tongue. Finally they felt their work was ended. They gave the use of the house to BNEA, provided they applied for a Peace Corps couple to continue with some of the projects already started.

There was a living room with a small nook furnished with a table made from a round piece of plywood nailed to a short length of log to serve as a dining area. The living room was bare except for two shelves made of poles and woven bamboo nailed to the wall and two small crudely fashioned end tables. There were four small bedrooms and a tiny room at the end of the hallway which had four shelves made of native material across one wall. Beneath the shelving was a strip of plywood to serve as a desk. Another tiny room contained a flush toilet, bucket shower and a lavatory. At the back of the hall was a ladder to climb to a large loft bedroom. All the bedrooms had a cot frame made of poles and a small side table. We chose the larger bedroom which had two cot frames, four small stacked shelves and a rod for clothes. All of the interior walls were also woven bamboo. The underside of the tin roof was covered with a rolled foil insulation. The pole rafters and braces were exposed. All windows were covered with screen, but no glass. The flooring was strips of black palm laid about two inches apart and covered with pandanus mats.

Simon had told us during our meeting in Port Moresby that the house was completely furnished and there were linens, dishes and cooking pots, so we need not bring any. Where were they? We found them packed into a small storage off the kitchen. The inventory was:

4 thin tired foam mattresses
6 metal folding chairs
1 old rattan rocker
1 broken lawn chair
2 kerosene lanterns

1 steel drum which contained 3 plastic plates, 6 cups, 1 tiny sauce pan, 4 badly stained dish towels, 1 griddle, a few pieces of silverware and utensils, 4 pillows and slips, 2 double sheets, 6 cot blankets and drapes.

We also found a dust pan and dust brush, but no broom. The house had been empty for a year. No wonder it was filthy and smelled of mold.

The people began to leave the porch. Simon's wife and niece offered to help us unpack. We thanked them, and said that we were tired and wanted to rest before unpacking. Before they left they pumped water from the storage tank to fill the two fifty-five gallon drums at the top of the house so that we could have water. There was not time for resting if we intended to have a place to sleep. We had simply told a little white lie so that we could be alone to clean and unpack at our own pace. What a big price I would have paid for a broom! Bill has an unbelievable talent for solving problems and improvising with materials available. He wired the dust brush onto a stick. I started sweeping our bedroom. He brought the four thin mattresses and placed two on each cot. The bedding was musty, but we would probably be too tired tonight to notice the odor. While I swept the living area, Bill brought the folding chairs and rocker. He tied the broken lawn chair together with rope from our supplies. Then he wiped off some of the shelving in the storage room, which we would use as a pantry, and began unpacking cans of tinned food. We had brought several large plastic containers from home. These would be used for storing dry packets of soup, crackers and anything that bugs or rodents might attack. One hardly knew what to unpack first and then where to put it. We were both thinking how lucky we were to have such a nice place to live because at home we had visioned living in a hut with a dirt floor. Running water was farthest from our dreams.

I couldn't wait to get our books unpacked and placed on the book shelves. Somehow it would make it look like a home. We had brought a good supply of books from home; we both enjoy reading. Also Peace Corps had supplied us with many books and pamphlets on subjects such as tropical gardening, raising chickens, coffee, medical information, language, marketing, general country information, etc. Where were the three cartons of books? I looked everywhere. About this time Simon's niece came onto the porch carrying a heavy box of books on her head. She had discovered three boxes were left at the airstrip and had already fetched two of them. My panic ended. Then I remembered a saying I'd learned long ago on my first trip to Europe. The tour guide was always saying, "Slowly, slowly! Not to worry," when he needed to calm a frustrated tourist.

That evening our first meal in our new home was cheese and crackers, a can of cold pork and beans and hot instant coffee. We were famished because we had not eaten except for coffee and cookies for breakfast in our hotel room. Bill hung a wire from the pole rafter to hold a kerosene lantern, but the lantern leaked and the kerosene slowly dripped to the floor. We gave up and went to bed early. We were exhausted.

Neither of us could sleep. Our cots were hard and uncomfortable. I could count every pole supporting the foam mattresses. In the darkness I heard something running back and forth in the bedroom. Bill had told me that when he first walked through the rooms, a big lizard scurried from our bedroom. One of the men told him it was probably a pet of the former occupants. I turned on my flashlight, but there was nothing I could see. Maybe it was a rat running between the inside and outside walls.

This first night in our new home was New Year's Eve. During our five weeks of training at Wau Ecology Institute in Morobe Province, we had learned about some of the basic traditions. The training staff told us it was the custom to celebrate New Year's Eve and Day by smearing and throwing mud on houses and people. Usually the young men and boys roamed the villages on New Year's Eve carrying mud and sticks or tin cans, anything to make noise. About 10:00 PM we heard voices and someone pounding on our kitchen door. Some were banging on the storage tank and there was shouting. We had no intentions of answering the door and have a gob of mud thrown at us. Finally the group left and their voices faded into the distance. They returned again and again. It was 3:00 A.M. before we could finally go to sleep. We were both up at daylight.

Our first job was to finish cleaning and to unpack all of our supplies and clothing. The kitchen cupboards, stove and refrigerator need scrubbing inside and out to get rid of the mold. The kitchen equipment must be washed. I aired the bedding and drapes on our new clothes line, finished unpacking the books, hung pictures of our family, and a world map and a map of Papua New Guinea on the walls. Later I hung the drapes. Bill cleaned the pantry thoroughly and stapled plastic in front of our clothes storage area to keep out the mold. Our new home was beginning to look comfortable.

Time for a break. We decided to walk to the BNEA trade store to buy sugar, flour, coffee, a cooking pot and tea kettle. They had none. They said their stock was very low. We were told during our training that the village trade stores carried basic staples, so we only brought a small sack of flour, sugar and coffee, because we wanted to patronize the village store.

The village seemed empty - no one was in sight. Later in the afternoon Simon brought his wife, Theresa, and their four month old baby boy named Sonny to see how we were getting along. They brought us a pumpkin and some kaukau, a type of sweet potato. He told us most all the village people were at their garden sites and probably would not return for several days. He promised to bring us a kerosene pressure lantern the next day so we could see to read at night. Also he would bring us a list of local fruits and vegetables with the price we should pay for them to the Barai people.

After they left, we wrote a letter to the managers of the Lamington Hotel. They had told us we were crazy to work in such a primitive place and made us promise to write them if we needed supplies when we reached Itokama. We included a check for 100 kina (Approx. $100) and ordered 2 dinner plates, 2 cereal bowls, 2 soup spoons, 1 tea kettle, 1 cooking pot, 2 dish towels, a broom, a container to hold boiled drinking water, 2 bottles of orange cordial (a concentrate to add to water), flour, sugar, coffee and a plastic garbage can for storage. Then we wrote letters to our family because tomorrow the Talair plane would come.

The old refrigerator refused to cool. We had been warned in training that kerosene refrigerators could be quite a challenge to keep running. They gave us some remedies. One was to rock or roll it. We even turned it end over end in our small kitchen. It still did not cool.

"Slowly, slowly! Not to worry," again I thought of the words of my first European guide. That problem could wait until later.

Before we could plant a garden, the yard fence had to be rebuilt with bamboo poles to keep out the pigs that roamed through the village. A few days after we arrived, BNEA called a council meeting. Simon asked us to come to the community building so he could introduce us to the members, who had returned from their gardens for the meeting. The council told us they would have some young men build a new fence the first time and after that we would be responsible for keeping it repaired. They would also have the boys cut the tall yard grass. It was our job to rake the cut grass and our responsibility to keep it mowed thereafter. BNEA had a lawn mower we could use but it was broken. They wondered if Bill could fix it? He did. Also they gave us two weeks to get settled before our work with the people would begin.

We kept busy. I hemmed ten napkins by hand from material we had purchased in Popondetta, because we knew we couldn't afford the luxury of paper napkins after pricing them in the store. They cost 2.00 kina for a small package. Paper toweling was 2.50 kina for a roll. Bill made a wire hanger and hung a roll of toilet paper on the kitchen wall to use as paper toweling. We had bought a carton (100 rolls) in Popondetta to bring with us.

Bill put pole handles on the big Chinese hoe and rake we received at our training. He sharpened his new bush knife and repaired some small tools for BNEA. He made a small room off the dining area into his workshop. We took walks through the village and found our way to Neokananee, which was about a twenty minute walk from Itokama. Occasionally someone would stop at our porch to visit or sell us some fruit, pumpkins or kaukau.

One day two girls, Susan and Agnes, came with a huge pamelo which is like a giant grapefruit. We asked the price. The girls giggled and whispered and finally said they wanted 2.00 kina. "We can't pay that much," I replied; our price list from Simon said 40 toea each. So the girls ate it on the porch and threw the peeling on the floor. Pamelos have a very thick skin, sometimes three-fourth inch thick, and the meat is coarse and not very tasty.

On our first Sunday we attended the Anglican church. Father Daniel gave the mass in English for our benefit. The church was made of native poles and woven bamboo sides and floor. The seats were sawed planks resting on wood blocks about two inches off the floor. Women and children sat on the right side, while the men and boys sat on the left side. The service lasted over two hours; it seemed we were up and down all the time. Later Bill told me he had counted twenty two times. At the close of the service, Father Daniel welcomed us and told us he considered us just as black as they were. "Thank you, Father," we replied. We considered that as a great compliment!

Barai Villages

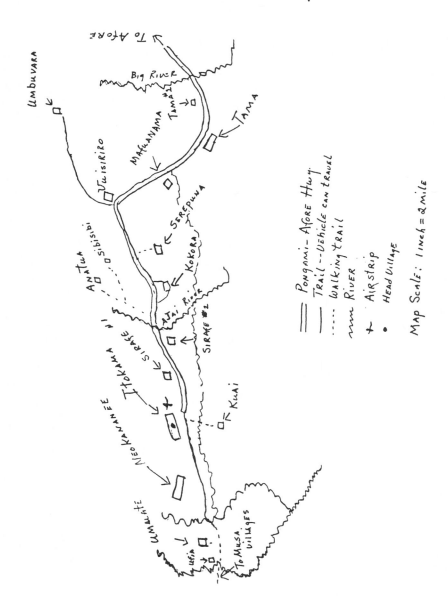

CHAPTER 4

*"I pity the man who can travel from Dan to Beersheba,
and cry 'tis all barren - and so it is, and so is all the
world for him, who will not cultivate the fruits it offers."*
- Laurence Sterne

The third weekend we were at Itokama, Simon asked us to go with him
and his family to the church at Serepuna on Sunday morning. It was a
one hour and a half walk east on the Pongami- Afore highway. We
were to leave at 7:00 AM from his house. When we arrived, no one
was at home. His neighbor told us that they had left before daylight in
a truck. We felt a bit rejected. We decided to walk there alone.

It was not easy hiking for a sixty year old person because it was up hill,
down hill all the way. We passed Sirafe #1, a tiny village with about
eight houses, and past Sirafe #2, a smaller village, and came to a river.
Bill walked across on a long fallen log. I took off my shoes, held up my
skirt and waded across the slippery rocks to the other side. Next we
passed by several coffee gardens and past Kokoro village, which was
almost obscured by the dense jungle growth. Finally we came to a
house and another building. A young boy who spoke good English told
us that it was a pre-school and that Serepuna was just down the hill
behind the school. He would show us the way. The path was a sharp,
slippery, down hill descent, but we made it without falling, only to learn
that Serepuna was at the top of a much steeper tricky climb. The
Nationals usually go barefoot; they are accustomed to the terrain. Their
feet are very wide and flat, and they dig into the ground with their toes.
They think it is quite hilarious to watch "white-skins," their name for
Europeans, struggle to traverse the trails, yet they are always eager and
helpful to show the way.

We had to stop and rest on our way to the top. The villagers were
gathered in an open shelter which served as their church, talking and
chewing betel nut, a small intoxicating fruit from the Areca palm tree.
They chew it with a mustard bean and a little lime made from charred

sea shells; the combination turns the saliva bright red and eventually the teeth turn black. The service had ended before we arrived. Simon was there and he was thoroughly surprised and pleased to see us. He explained that a truck had come to Itokama village and the driver offered to take them to Serepuna. Some women brought us slices of fresh pineapple and offered us a green coconut, "kulau," good for drinking. It was quite apparent that they felt honored that we had come by ourselves to their village. Most of them spoke only Barai, and so Simon interpreted for us.

Earlier in the week Simon had told us that beyond the eastern most Barai village of Tama, a big river crossed the highway, and often during the rainy season it become too deep and swift to ford. He wished that the provincial government would build a bridge across it. Bill volunteered to check it out because there was a good chance that he could engineer a bridge of native logs and rough sawed timber, providing the Barai men would agree to do the work and BNEA would use their new walk-about-sawmill to cut the sawed planks for the surface covering.

Visiting with the village men, Bill asked how far it was on to the big river. "Oh it is just on the far side of Tama."

"And how far is it to Tama?" Bill inquired.

"There is a short way through the bush from Serepuna. It only takes a little while to walk there," Simon replied.

We decided to go. Simon sent for three young boys to guide us through the jungle. They took us down another steep hill at the back of Serepuna. Bill called to me, "Margel, you are going to encounter your second challenge. Look ahead!"

There I saw a stream spanned by a single narrow log, about fifteen feet above the water. "I can't walk across that!" I exclaimed. The boys burst into a fit of laughter. One said that he would walk in front and another boy would walk behind me and so that it would be easy. "Not for me," I replied. "The only way I can ever get cross on that log is to sit straddle and scoot across." But Bill told me my clothes would be in shreds by the time I reached the far side. He was right. I should explain that it was no short distance: the log extended thirty feet to the other bank of the stream. "And how much longer does it take to reach Tama by walking on the highway, the long way?" I inquired.

"Oh, twice the time," they replied.

"Well, I am going back to the road. Wait for me at the big river, Bill." One of the boys, Newton, volunteered to go with me. We started to retrace our steps upward to Serepuna. There was another round of laughter when the villagers learned of my malady of pole walking. By the time we reached the highway, I was exhausted and trembling, but I kept walking. Each time I asked how much farther Newton would tell me Tama village was just over the next hill. Finally we saw a village ahead of us. He told me it was his village, Vuisiriro. We had been walking almost an hour. "How much farther to Tama and the big river?"

"Oh, we are about half way," he replied.

My legs were shaking and my heart was pounding. I thought that once I got there, I would have to walk all the way back to Itokama. The sensible thing for me to do was to return to the pre-school at Serepuna and wait there for Bill. So I told Newton to go on and find Bill and tell him that I had turned back and would wait for him. I know Newton was relieved to be able to travel at his own speed.

After resting a while along the roadside, I walked back to the school and sat down on the ground in the shade of an overturned water storage tank. It wasn't long until two women found me. They couldn't speak a word of English and I couldn't speak any Barai. I knew they were curious about why I was there. I smiled a lot at them as they sat staring at me. Finally one woman took a papaya from her string bag and gave it to me. Soon a small boy came; the women talked to him and he left. About a half hour later he returned from Serepuna accompanied by a young man. His name was Gordon and he lived in the village of Neokananee. He could speak English, and he came to visit us nearly every week. We had enjoyed talking with him very much. I told him why I had returned to wait for Bill. He repeated my story to the women who were relieved that I was not unhappy with their people. Shortly a truck drove into the school yard. Gordon talked with the driver and came to tell me I was to go with this man. He would not tell me the man's name, saying only that he was his "tambu" (relative). Later we learned that it was taboo to say the name of any relative acquired by marriage such as in-laws. I did not want to go, but Gordon insisted. After I had gotten into the truck and the driver had headed in the direction of Tama, I learned that his name was Benson. He was a member of the Oro Provincial Assembly. He was from Tama and had passed Mr. Bill on the road and learned I was walking to meet him. Benson said that I was too old to be walking so far if I was Bill's age, so he would come and take me to him. It was a long drive to the river which was at the bottom of a steep hill with a steeper grade on the opposite bank. The river was at least a hundred feet wide. We picked up Bill on our return trip near Tama. Benson insisted on driving us back to Itokama.

Before the village "big men" (leaders) called a meeting two weeks later to decide if they wished to help construct a bridge at the big river, the Oro Provincial Department of Roads began hauling truckloads of big stones and dumping them into the river to form a raised course across it. The problem was solved; there was no need to build the bridge. Now we must find another task that would help the Barai people. They seemed so slow to involve us in their development.

The average life span of the Barai people is about 46 to 48 years. When they first saw us and saw our grey hair, they were amazed that we had come to work in Itokama. Seldom do you see any Nationals with grey in their hair. People do not live that long. Older people are highly respected everywhere in Papua New Guinea. The Barai name for old people is the same as grandparent in Barai, "tato." Families are extremely important throughout PNG. Older people are fed and pampered by their children, grandchildren and relatives. Once we understood their extreme respect for the elderly, we realized why they seemed so reluctant to allow us to start our work.

With extra time on our hands, we tried to learn as much as possible about the lifestyle and customs of the Barai people and their village structure. We learned that the school teachers, the Father of the Anglican church and the medical staff were not members of the Barai tribe. Therefore, the villagers referred to the area where the teachers, the medical staff and the Father lived, including the school grounds, the church grounds and the medical clinic, as the Mission Station. These people came from other tribes and parts of Papua New Guinea, so they must live apart. The Mission Station was located on the far side of the airport across from Itokama. We decided to visit this section.

When we walked to the Mission Station to see the medical clinic. Martin Lukes, the Officer in Charge, welcomed us and proudly showed us his new building, a sawed timber, modular design, constructed by the government. It stood on steel poles, about three feet above the ground. There was a veranda, or porch, across the entire front with benches for waiting patients. Several doors lined the porch area. One led to the delivery room where the only equipment inside was a delivery table. Another door opened in to the hospital ward which was absolutely bare. We asked, "Where are the beds?" His answer was, "They bring their own." The next door opened to a small office with a kerosene refrigerator for medicine, and then Martin Lukes took us into the examination room. There were two rows of benches, like bleachers, a counter with open shelving and a sink. He shooed four chickens out the back door. He led us to his "injection room." It was a tiny four by six foot empty room, which was probably originally designed for a restroom. At one end was a huge cardboard box completely filled with dirty swabs and empty viles. He was so proud of this special room. He introduced us to his staff which was his wife, Dorcus, who was the nurse and a young man named Lucian. Next, he wanted to show us his nutrition gardens at the back of the clinic. The government wants the medical clinics to demonstrate better gardening practices to teach people ways of combating malnutrition. He also had about a dozen laying hens but he had no success in getting the villagers to raise them for eggs (protein); instead they would kill and eat the chickens before they began to lay. He gave us some green onions, snake beans and a pineapple, and promised he would come to visit us soon.

The next day, Doctor, as we called him although he was actually a medic, knocked at our door bringing more vegetables and accompanied by his two sons, Kingsley, age ten, and Iloi, age three The boys were very shy. Kingsley could speak English, but Iloi could speak only Tok Pidgin. They were fascinated with our house and particularly our bathroom. Later Kingsley asked if he could go to our bathroom. After they left Bill discovered feces running down the back of the lid and seat. Kingsley evidently stood on it. They were accustomed to an outside toilet with only a hole in the ground and no seat - an Asian type which is simply a hole to squat over.

The Luke family adopted us as Mom and Dad, and every day the boys would come to see us for a few minutes. Usually they brought some fruits or vegetables but they would never take any pay for them. Sometimes Kingsley would pull an egg from his shirt pocket and eggs from each pocket of his shorts. We usually had cookies and an orange drink called cordial for them. Their visits filled the emptiness in our lives. Doctor also had two daughters, Philipa and Judy, who were away at school in Port Moresby and Milne Bay. I can't remember any of their four children calling us by our names. They always called us "bubu," which is grandparent in Tok Pidgin. Doctor and Dorcus called us Mom and Dad. What a joy we found in this family and from Doctor we learned more about the local medical and hospital facilities.

The Itokama medical clinic is in touch with the hospital in Popondetta by short wave radio Monday through Friday, so it is best to become ill during the week! Hospitals in PNG are quite unusual. When a patient goes to the hospital for treatment, some of the family go along. The patient must take a pillow, sheets and towel, and the family are responsible for bathing and feeding the patient. The family may sleep under the bed of the patient or sleep outside of the hospital. Sanitary conditions are varied, but certainly not up to the standards of European or American medical facilities. Another reason for the family to accompany the patient to the hospital is the fact that they have committed their loved one to a foreign type institution to be healed, much against the will of their "shaman," who advocates that many illnesses are caused by evil spirits who cast spells or by magic and sorcery. For example: when a person dies, a bit of hair or a cutting from fingernails, a bit of clothing or any personal substance produced by the person, like feces, cigarette butt, betal nut spatel, a photo can be used to cast a spell on that person's relatives.

In Papua New Guinea a man may have multiple numbers of wives. The first marriage is usually arranged by the parents; additional wives must be approved by the village council. About three months after we had arrived in Itokama a married man in the village of Anatua saw a young girl in the village of Kokoro and wanted her for his second wife. The village council rejected his request because she was also desired by some parents as a bride for their young unmarried son. The man from Anatua was outraged at being denied the girl. Later he found her and her young husband working in their garden quite some distance from Kokoro. He killed her husband with his spear, hacked her in the side and skull, and cut off her left arm with his axe; then he returned to his village and speared his wife, son and daughter and hanged himself in a tree. This happened on a Friday. The injured bride was carried to the medical clinic at Itokama and kept alive until the plane arrived on the normal Tuesday morning flight; then she was flown to Popondetta and transferred to the hospital. Miraculously she survived!

We made friends with the teachers. They and their families came to visit us often. One teacher's wife, Rose, came to ask if I could fix her sewing machine. The bobbin didn't work. She told me to come to her house at 1:00 PM. the next day. As I walked up the crude steps to her door, I heard her say, "She is here already! But of course, she is European." I had forgotten about PNG time which was one of the more difficult adjustments we had to make. In Papua New Guinea time is not important. There is always another day, or week. People would tell us they were coming at a given time, but seldom did they arrive. It might be a day or two or even a week or more before they came. They were arriving on PNG time. It was equally as difficult for the Nationals to understand why we were sometimes disturbed that they did not come to work as they promised on American time (pre-arranged).

We wanted to learn the Barai language because the older men and women could not speak English or Tok Pidgin. Our neighbor, George, who had some schooling, was appointed to be our teacher. He came to our house for the first lesson and said he would come for our second lesson exactly one week later, Monday morning at 8:00 AM.; he didn't arrive until five weeks later. We finally gave up trying to learn Barai because he was so unpredictable. We did manage to learn very basic words. Most of the young men and boys and some of the young girls speak English because they have attended school. Only English is spoken at school.

We were sent to work in Itokama at the request of BNEA (Barai Non-Formal Educational Association), who wanted a volunteer couple to work with the organization. We were to:

1. Set up suitable bookkeeping systems for the trade store, sawmill and BNEA bank.
2. Train BNEA Administrator, Simon, how to apply for funding requests and how to follow up with reports.
3. Train the BNEA trade store manager in purchasing and merchandising.
4. Teach a manager and crew how to operate the walk-about-sawmill and find a market for the sawed timber.
5. Help BNEA with communications and any of it's other projects.
We were to report to and work under Simon Savieko.

Bill's first job was to repair the two lawn mowers owned by BNEA for the purpose of keeping the airstrip mowed. They, BNEA, were paid by the national government to maintain the airstrip. My first job was to make a sewing project for the women's group which met each Wednesday morning at the BNEA community building. Simon wanted me to teach them some basic embroidery. His niece, Doreen, was the leader. They had no needles, no material and no embroidery thread, but I had brought a supply from home for my own hobbies. Doreen and I made eighteen kits for the meeting the next day. Not one woman came to the morning meeting, and the following Wednesday morning, no women came. When I began questioning the village women, I learned that they were having a disagreement over who should be the leader. They thought Doreen was much too young to teach them. Eventually Doreen resigned, and the BNEA womens organization ended.

Much later a few women began coming to use the sewing machines, which operated with a handcrank. Some of the village women could sew simple gathered skirts and ripped or torn clothing. None seemed interested in increasing their sewing skills. Most of those who came to use the machines simply played at stitching. It was a place to come to visit. Six of the nine machines were broken, so Bill repaired five using the sixth one for parts. It is sad that parts which came loose or became broken on equipment were thrown away.

Mail delivered by the Talair pilot comes to Itokama by private mailbag. We had been there four weeks without any mail. Also we had been in transit for two more weeks after we left our training site. We knew our families had written to us. Every Tuesday and Thursday we waited for the plane to arrive with mail, but no mail came. One day we saw Simon and his wife and baby boarded the plane with lots of baggage. We asked Doreen where they were going. She said they were going to Ukarumpa to attend a SIL literacy training class and would be gone for two months. Simon, whom we were to work under, had never mentioned it to us. We felt like abandon children.

We intended to find something to do. Bill had heard that the Nahara Coffee Growers' truck would not run so he asked William Suremo, the manager, what was the matter. "The tire is broke," William replied. Bill looked at the tire. It was OK, and then William told him the wheel would not go round. Bill soon found the trouble. It was 4-wheel drive Toyota and it had a broken rear axle, but they had continued to drive it in front wheel drive until the rear axle froze. Bill said he would repair it if William could buy a used axle in Popondetta; William went to town on the next flight. He found an axle at the salvage yard. But the owner refused to sell it to him until someone knowledgeable in repairs would check the truck and confirm that the used axle would fit. William asked Bill if he would fly to Popondetta on the next Tuesday and see if it was the right axle. Nahara would pay the plane fare and would send cash for the axle.

It was the opportunity for us to find the reason for the mail delay. We had heard that Nahara was responsible for the mail bag fee each year and had not sent the money to the post office. I decided to buy a ticket and go with Bill. Even after receiving our supplies we had ordered through the hotel managers, we still wished for a few more things. Going to Popondetta would be fun. William said he had sent the money to the post office and he would give me a letter so that I would be able to get a mail bag.

When I showed the letter to the postmaster, he told me the post office had waited a year for payment, so he decided to make Itokama wait a while for mail. He said he did not know that there were "white skins" in the village and he promised to send it regularly. We spent our first night in Popondetta reading our fifty-six letters! Bill bought the axle and brought it back with us to Itokama on the Thursday flight. Mission accomplished! Most of the villagers came to watch him replace the axle. Then he discovered the brake fluid was leaking, so he repaired the hydraulic line by making a mold with wet clay, laying the tubing in it and covering the break with melted lead. He drove it to Popondetta to have it repaired properly. Using his own ingenuity, Bill had been able to solve a mechanical problem without the proper tools. The next task was to get a garden planted.

The young boys completed the new bamboo fence around our yard and then dug up the soil for a garden at the back corner. We were both excellent gardeners at home, but we had learned in our Peace Corps training that tropical gardening was done differently by planting in ridges. We decided to plant our seeds as we did at home. People lined the fence watching us, some laughing and others shaking their heads to warn us we were doing it all wrong. They were fascinated at our little packets of seeds with the picture of the plant on the front. We could hardly wait to have lettuce, carrots, green onions and cabbage to eat. To be quite truthful, neither of us were fond of yams and kaukau and pumpkin. Nor did we like using the tips of the pumpkin vine for our greens. We wanted to introduce some good American types of vegetables to the Barai people.

It seems we were the first to learn. We soon understood the importance of planting in ridges. With the daily rains, our garden was sometimes under water and the seeds washed out of the row. Also we noticed what few plants did come up turned yellow. We never thought about testing the soil with the soil testing kit we carried from the states. The soil looked rich enough. Bill found this beautiful black dirt contained almost no nitrogen and potassium and only a trace of potash. This meant we must start a compost pile at once, but composting takes time and our plants looked critical; we were desperate. We started saving our urine and mixing it with ten parts of water and putting it along the rows. It helped immediately. Our composting was progressing and then we experienced the problem of roaming pigs.

Neighbor George had some very wise, stubborn and persistent pigs who liked the grass and other delicacies in the Craig yard, so they simply stood at the fence and gave a big jump. Our garden was their target. Bill strung wire above the bamboo fence and attached it to higher posts, which added another foot for the pigs to clear. Then we sat back and listened to their squeals as they were knocked to the ground by the unsuspecting wire. We planted a second, bigger garden in another area of our yard surrounded also by a fence and gate to protect it from the devastating pigs. We even planted it in ridges. Our tomatoes were big, beautiful and ripe. Our corn was ready to eat. This was sweet corn - not the field corn used by the Barai. We had peanuts, eggplant, kale, green onions and winged beans. I had also planted twenty-six pineapple plants in other parts of the yard.

One day there was a BNEA council meeting in Itokama. People came from other villages and many brought their small pigs with them, much as we might travel with a pet dog. All day there was a small black pig in our yard. Time after time we caught him and put him over the fence, yet time after time he was back in our yard. Finally Bill came home and told me he would take care of the situation. He took a club and hit the pig and threw it over the fence! There was a young boy sitting on our porch watching Bill. He seemed quite upset at the fact that Bill hit the pig. I tried to explain to the boy but no way could he understand. A few hours later we had visitors, Gilford and John Michael from Neokananee. They brought a letter from the Itokama Councilor which read:

> Dear Bill:
>
> We thank you for your cooperation with us in the BNEA Programme: We are sorry you didn't know some of the laws which our council has made in the villages: Nobody cannot kill the pig for nothing unless you must have good reason. Who ever comes to the programme must get to know our laws and follow it.
>
> Your charge to pay 5.00 kina or if not you will another charge for 10.00 kina.
>
> Many thanks,
>
> Councilor James

Neither of us could make change for 5.00 kina but we did have a 10.00 kina note, so we gave it to the deliverers, John Michael and Gilford, and had John Michael sign a receipt for it. Many months later Simon questioned why we had only paid 3.00 kina for the pig to a widow woman. We showed our receipt for 10.00 kina and asked what happened to the other 7.00 kina? We never found that answer.

The pigs came again! This time they dug under the fence. Our beautiful garden #2 was destroyed. We replanted with garden #3. Again the pigs devoured our garden. I was furious with neighbor George"s pigs. I yelled, and chased pigs and said nasty words to George who made no effort to control his pigs. I replaced the third ruined garden with garden #4 which was also ravished by George's pigs. For the fifth time I planted a garden. The tomatoes, peanuts, corn, turnips, greens ,onions, beans and kaukau were starting to produce at the time that we must travel to Lae to attend a Peace Corps All-Volunteer Conference. When we returned our garden was in ruin. George came to apologize as soon as we reached the house from the airstrip. In past times I had yelled and said some big words, not good for children to hear. This time I spoke to him in a hushed tone, "George, do not worry about the pigs getting in our garden. If I am going to work in this village and help your people, I can't accomplish anything when I am angry. We just will not have a garden. We will buy our vegetables from the Barai people. I will never get angry again when the pigs come into the yard and rout, unless it gets to be so muddy that my shoes come off as I walk across the yard."

The pigs now roamed our yard day and night. Earlier BNEA had decided we must pay them 5.00 kina for the use of the mower each time we mowed our grass. We quit mowing our yard. Now remember it was Bill who kept the two BNEA mowers in repair. Sometimes the Head Master of the grade school would send some of the older children to cut our grass with grass knives because the teachers were ashamed of the way BNEA treated us. He refused to accept any payment, so we provided the students with cookies and orange drinks. However, the pigs kept the grass badly routed and so there was not much left to cut. The pigs had a nice place to sleep under our house. It did not matter that they bumped into the posts and shook the house at night or squeaked and fought, which awakened us. The village people could sell their extra yams, pumpkin and kaukau. And we had more time to work on our assignments. "Slowly, slowly, not to worry!" How often I repeated this catch phrase to myself. I now understood its full meaning.

CHAPTER 5

"Adapt yourself to the things among which your lot has been cast and love sincerely the fellow creatures with whom destiny has ordained that you shall live." - Marcus Aurelius

The Summer Institute of Linguistics gave a "wokabaut somil" and a chain saw to BNEA about a year before we arrived at Itokama. A wokabaut somil is a portable saw mill that can be disassembled and carried to the location of the next logs to be sawed. It was invented in the midwest United States and is used by many third world countries where the terrain makes it impossible to transport the logs to a central sawing location. It was designed for easy maintenance and transportation. Currently there are about twelve different models used throughout the world as a result of one man's ingenuity.

The sawmill consists of a track about 30 feet long and a carriage unit that travels the length of the track, which includes a 16 H.P. gas engine, a battery for an electric start, a fuel tank, a transmission, a hand crank to propel the saw and both a 30 inch vertical and a 12 inch horizontal insert tooth blade cutting unit. The carriage assembly has places to insert a pole at each of the four corners so that four men can carry it on their shoulders to the next sawing site. The track can be unbolted into five separate sections. Each section requires two men to transport it. The basic sawmill weight about 359 kgs. (770 lbs.) and costs approximately $5,000.

The sawmill rests on uniformly cut blocks of wood. Each time a cut is made, the thickness of the cut is controlled by removing four blocks of the same thickness. For example: If a 1 inch thick horizontal cut is to be made, four 1 inch blocks are removed, one at each corner. These many blocks are carried to each new sawing site. The saw can cut up to a 16 ft. log making both a horizontal and vertical cut on each trip of the saws down the length of the log. The carriage unit moves on 4 tiny wheels along the length of the track, propelled by a hand crank. The

30 inch vertical saw is a direct drive, while the horizontal blade is gear driven by 4 V belts.

BNEA also has a tiny storage shed, about 4ft. x 6ft., where the tools, winch for moving logs, chain saw and the drum of gas (it is called petrol in PNG) are stored and locked for security. This tiny structure can be unbolted so that each section can be carried to the next mill location.

The Nationals have much knowledge on the various trees, bushes and vines. They understand which wood is suitable for their fires; they know which poles are strongest to use for axe handles or digging sticks, which they use to till their gardens; they know which wood is the best to use to make spears; and they know which vines are suitable to tie together the poles for the framework of their houses. They are adept with their bush knives and axes. They know how to travel through, and survive, in a dense jungle. They know which plants and berries to eat and where to find water, should there be no stream close by. However, they can't comprehend mechanical machinery or equipment made of metals. They can't hear the hard pull of an engine or the unusual stress vibrations. Because they are extremely curious about what is inside the machine, they love to take motors and equipment apart to satisfy their curiosity, and then they can't assemble it again. When they remove a bolt, they have no idea if they should turn it to the left or to the right, and when they tighten a bolt at what point it is snug.

Bill was asked by BNEA to teach a crew to operate their strange new sawmill. In fact, BNEA council decided that he must work with a new crew of four men each fortnight. He tried to explain that it was more logical to train one crew to become accomplished sawyers, so that after he left Itokama their expert crew would be able to train other men to work on the sawmill. However, the council insisted he must train new crews each fortnight, therefore more men could receive some money; each man was paid 35 toea per hour. Bill thought, "I'll go slowly. Later maybe I can make them understand."

A few days before he met the first crew, Gordon, the man who had previously been in charge of the chain saw, and another man, came to our porch. They brought the chain saw parts carried on a banana leaf

The Wokabaut Somil system

and the empty chain saw case. "Bill can you fix the chain saw? It is broke," Gordon asked.

Bill said he needed the instruction manual, because he had never worked on a Japanese chain saw. No one knew what had happened to the instructions, so for weeks, during his spare time, Bill struggled with all those parts, nuts, springs, washers and bolts, testing where each piece must fit. He was a triumphant man, when he pulled the starter rope and it finally roared into action some two months later.

All the land is owned by individuals or families; therefore, before a tree could be cut, BNEA must negotiate the purchase price with the owner or owners. Usually the royalty fee paid for a tree was 30 to 50 kina. Sometimes the Nationals argued over the actual ownership, so it was a lengthy process and could take several weeks. After the royalty was paid, the workers cut a trail through the jungle to the tree and the surrounding ground was cleared of undergrowth so that the crew would have an open area to work around the fallen tree and space to assemble the walk-about saw. It took about three weeks of work before they fell the first tree.

The trees in Oro Province are enormous like the giant Kauri trees of New Zealand. Many are up to 300 feet tall and measure up to 28 feet in circumference. The first branches start at 65 to 75 feet. Most trees have huge brace roots, so many are cut from 10 to 20 feet above the ground. A scaffolding of poles is constructed around the base to hold the men who cut down the tree. Sometimes parasitic vines are wound around the tree and these must be cut or pulled down before the actual cutting of the tree begins. Some vines contain a sticky sap, almost like wood glue. If they use the chain saw to cut then, the chain has to be cleaned before the saw can be run again.

Finally a group of four men took turns chopping down the tree with axes, two men working together. It took about 5 hours. The men were experts at determining the direction and place the tree would fall. When the giant timber crashed to the ground, it brought down four or more other smaller trees. It was an awesome sight to behold. Next the log was cut by axes into sections for sawing. Finally a cut section of log was winched to the sawmill site. Using a nearby tree as a dead pivot, one end of the log was pulled then blocked, and then the opposite end pulled and blocked. This procedure was repeated again and again until the log was positioned under the carriage and track of the walk-about sawmill.

Once the sawmill was set, the men made a framework of poles and covered the frame with a blue plastic tarp to protect them from the hot sun. They also made a small lean-to of poles and leaves so that they would have a shelter from an afternoon rain, a place to sit and talk and chew betel nut and cook some food.

The crew members were Reggie and Clemens from Neokananee village, James from Kuai and Martin from Sirafe #1. Clemens started the motor and when the engine responded, he continued to hold his hand on the starter. His first lesson was to remove his hand from the starter switch as soon as the motor ignited! Clemens also operated the carriage and saw. As he cranked the assembly down the length of the log, time after time the saw stalled. He could not apply uniform, rhythmic pressure to traverse the log. The cutting blades were belt driven, direct drive; when the blades were forced under excessive pressure it would wear the belts. Over and over Bill cautioned Clemens to listen to the motor and ease up when it began pulling hard. He should also watch the flow of the sawdust. Bill put his hand over Clemen's hand and turning the crank tried to gently guide him along the log. There was another problem. They were cutting 1 x 4 inch boards. At the one end the board would be 1 inch and at the far end it tapered to 3/4 inch. Either the men controlling the cut were not doing their job or else there was too much room for error. Bill returned home at the end of the first day completely exhausted.

The previous year SIL had sent a man to teach this same crew to operate the saw. He had worked two days with them and sawed one log. They gave the sawed boards to the church to use for seats. It is easier to form a habit than to discard a habit, and, so it was with the Barai people. Once they thought they knew how to do a task, they found it impossible to accept a new or better method.

After dinner, we sat and talked - rather Bill talked and I listened. He knew these four men were so proud to be the sawmill crew. It was a status symbol for them; it gave them importance in their villages. He felt they wanted to do good work. How could he teach them to change

Felled tree

Log in position to saw

their ways? His game plan was, "You know how the saw works. You can cut logs. Wouldn't you like to learn even better methods of operating the sawmill, so you can be more productive?" It sounded easy. But these men spoke limited English which was Australian English. One man spoke only Barai and Tok Pidgin. They were skillful working with wood, but they were infants in knowledge of machinery. It would take time and patience to teach them. He must never reprimand them because they then would feel shame and lose face to their people.

Bill felt he knew the reason the boards were not uniform. He devised a different method of control, and he asked the men if they would be willing to try it to see if he was right. They agreed. The choice was theirs. When they did good work Bill always gave them praise. It took many days and an abundance of patience. Before he could teach them, he had to gain their friendship. Each day after work he would bring them to our porch and give them cigarettes or tobacco to roll a cigarette. It was an honor for them.

Many of the people grow tobacco, because it is costly to buy from the trade store. They hang the tobacco in their houses to dry. Sometimes, if it isn't quite dry enough to smoke, they hold a leaf over hot coals to dry it a bit more. They tear strips of newspaper to roll up the tobacco. Nahara trade store buys bundles of old Australian and New Zealand newspapers and sells them to the people for 10 toea per sheet. The newspapers printed in Papua New Guinea are heavier paper and do not burn as well. When they have no paper, they use a leaf of tobacco or a certain leaf from a wild bush which is rough on the back. Tobacco can be bought by the pouch for 80 toea, a tin for 1.20 kina or a twist for 45 toea. The most popular brand is Spears. Bill always kept tins of Spears to share with the Nationals. He soon discovered it was best to have a supply of cut newspaper rather than to allow them to tear their own strip of paper. One man tore a strip from the newspaper and rolled a twelve inch cigarette!

One Sunday one of the crew, James from Kuai village, stopped at our porch. Bill went immediately to visit with him. He gave him "smoke," the term the Barai people used. James spoke no English, only Barai and Tok Pidgin. In fact, he was the only Barai to speak to us in Pidgin. He said, "Bill, yumi brata" meaning you and I are brothers.

Bill replied, "Mi amamas tru" ("I am very happy") and then he added, "Yumi blut brata tru " ("You and I are blood brothers") then he opened his pocket knife, nicked his wrist and handed the knife to James, who did the same. They held their bleeding wrists together. From that very day they always called each other Brother. They became very close friends.

The sawmill crew was making great progress. They could saw uniform boards and they were making one hundred-ten cuts a day. After work, the crew carried the day's production on their heads to the BNEA timber shed near the community building. Usually they stopped at our porch to rest and smoke before walking home. Often they would come to visit us after church on Sunday, sometimes bringing their wives and children. We sometimes gave the children cordial which is much like Kool Aid and cookies or crackers and Bill passed out cigarettes to the women also.

Simon, the BNEA administrator, had asked Bill to find a market for the cut timber. That was an easy task because the manager of Nahara Coffee Growers wanted to build a new trade store and office. He was interested in using sawed timber for the framework and he wanted to use plank flooring. That would take all the production for several weeks.

Martin, of Sirafe #1, one of the crew, brought his small son to the porch and asked for Bill. The men talked a while and had a smoke. Then Martin took Bill's hand and placed his son's small hand in Bill's saying, "I give you my son to take home to America. Educate him, please! Now he is no longer my son. He is your son."

Bill was shocked. He knew that his answer might offend but that was a risk he had to take. He replied, "Martin, you have shown me a great honor by offering your small boy for me and my wife to raise. You are my very good friend. I am grateful for your friendship, but I can't accept the responsibility of raising your son, for I am getting old. I'm sixty-six years old. I am an old man. He is just a little boy. I may not live until he grows to be a man. Besides it would take a long time to get the proper papers from the government of my country to allow him to live there. I will always remember this honor you have offered to me. If I were a younger man, I would be glad to take him. Thank you, my friend." Martin bowed his head and was quiet. Then he took the boy's hand and left the porch. The subject was never mentioned again. Martin and Bill remained good friends.

At the end of the first fortnight, BNEA appointed an entire new crew for the saw mill. Bill suggested that they include Gordon, who had brought the chain saw to Bill to put it together. They refused. Gordon was in disgrace and would not be allowed on the BNEA payroll. It was because of the chain saw incident. He was blamed for taking it apart. Gordon was one of the better educated young men and some were jealous of him. The four new workers were there to draw 35 toea an hour and nothing more. Bill had set production quotas for the first crew as a challenge, and they met every one. This second crew didn't seem to care. If Bill left the mill to go elsewhere to repair a coffee pulper or a lawn mower at the airstrip, he would return to find them sitting in the lean-to shelter chewing betal nut and the saw motor would still be running. The petrol had to be trucked one hundred miles by hired vehicle, or by a chartered plane. Gas and kerosene are not allowed on passenger flights. It is a priceless commodity in a remote village. It is not to be wasted.

All the people use betel nut. The saliva turns bright red and stains anything it touches. After chewing several betel nuts, the person breaks out in perspiration and the eyes become glassy. Returning to a crew in such condition, Bill would say, "Better go home. Come back tomorrow and we'll try again."

He was glad when the second fortnight ended and he got a third group to train. They were no more productive than the last crew. The only part that seemed to excite them was operating the chain saw. They insisted on using it rather than their axes to cut the tree logs into lengths, regardless of the fact that the chain saw blade was too short to cut through the large trunk. They dug the ground out from under the felled tree and attempted to cut around the huge tree trunk and run the cutting chain into the earth. Bill had to clean the chain before the chain saw could be used again. Then they did the same thing the second time. Bill was getting desperate. He went to Simon and begged him to give him the original crew at the end of this fortnight. Simon called a meeting of the BNEA Council. Bill pleaded with them, and finally told them he was wasting his time working with men who didn't try. Finally the new crew was selected by the council. They were Clemens, Reggie, and Martin from crew #1 and Lester, who was to be the manager. He would keep the books, figure the metric board feet and pay the men their wages. He would also work on the saw. They would not allow Brother James to work on the saw. We never knew why. Bill asked for a fifth man to bear the sawed boards away from the saw area and stack them. They added Parmius, another young boy. Both Lester and Parmius were among the favorites of the BNEA organization. That didn't mean they were good workers.

This crew could meet the quotas. They cut and sawed several trees. Twice Lester brought the chain saw to Bill to repair. The first time he had taken the starter rope off. The second time the chain saw arrived in pieces. Bill questioned Lester. He said he took it apart to find out why it didn't cut. Bill threatened to take the chain saw to Simon and tell him to sell it, if he ever took it apart one more time.

Sometimes the sawmill was set up near a trail. Then the children on their way home from school and also women would line up around the clearing and watch the men saw. The noise of the motor fascinated them. It was a new sound, something different. They never got in the way of the crew.

The men usually cut a type of cedar tree. The wood was coarse, but it repelled wood eating insects. They also sawed tulip, okari and black palm, which was the hardest of all wood. It was from the black palm that the men made their hunting spears. It was also used for flooring strips. Once it dried it was impossible to cut with a bush knife. When sawed timber was sold Bill taught Lester how to figure the board feet for each piece. Papua New Guinea uses the metric system, therefore board feet were figured in meters. Board sizes were stated in reverse such as 3" x 2" (75mm x 50mm), 6" x 4" (150mm x 100mm), etc.

When trees were cut down the crew members often found large grubs around the base of the cut tree and under the bark. They collected every grub worm. It was like children finding chocolate candy. They would eat them for their evening meal. Sometimes they would find large beetles around the sawmill area. Often the insects were two to three inches long. The men pulled off the legs so they could not crawl and put them in their pockets. We often saw women, going past our yard along the trail to Neokananee, clutching a beetle in their hand. Meat on the table?

The sawmill didn't operate every day. Sometimes the men went to their gardens for three weeks. We wondered why. Since Lester became the manager, Bill seldom worked at the sawmill site unless there was a serious problem because Lester refused to follow Bill's instructions and suggestions and so his presence was of little use. Finally some of the crew members came to Bill and asked why they were not getting paid? Bill had no idea, but he certainly intended to find out the reason. Lester said he did not have any money left in the sawmill account at the BNEA bank. He said BNEA had taken the money from the sawmill account to use elsewhere. Bill went to Simon. He did not seem too concerned. Eventually some of the funds were replaced in the account so that Lester was able to pay the back wages.

Lester was in charge of buying the trees to be cut; he was in charge of telling the men when to work. Bill had no control over Lester. Soon after Lester was appointed the manager, we got him enrolled in a school for wokabaut somils in Lae because he had never worked with a sawmill. BNEA was glad to send him and pay the cost. While Lester was away for three weeks, Bill kept the saw running. When Lester returned, he was a changed person. He strutted through the village with the sawmill ledger under his arm. He now was an important man. Knowledge for him was dangerous, and for the sawmill operation it was a disaster. Production stopped. Bill tried to talk with him to see what was the problem. He smiled and walked away. Lester stayed out of sight. He refused to get the mill operating. The crew kept coming to our house to ask when they could work. Bill sent them to talk to Lester who gave them no answers. Bill went to Simon. He said it was against Barai custom to tell or demand a Barai to do a certain job. Then we got a letter from the sawmill school. One of the teachers had given Lester 20 kina because he did not have enough money for his airfare back to Itokama. We gave the letter to Simon. He was upset. Lester had been given ample money. He had spent it foolishly.

Finally Lester told Bill that the sawmill could not operate because he could not settle the royalty payment for the next tree. After the royalty fee of 40 kina was set, four more men claimed part ownership, so there were five men involved, and no one could agree on what portion each should receive. Bill told him it was easy to solve. He told Lester to call the five men together, and then throw down 40 kina coins and walk away. The royalty would have been paid; the tree could be cut.

Eventually they cut the disputed tree. It was within sight of our house. Lester failed to assemble the crew to start the sawing. Weeks went by. One day the wife of Augustus set fire to the area around the tree. He had originally claimed to be the sole owner of the tree. We figured she did it for spite. When they finally sawed the log sections, there was quite a lot of burn damage to the wood. Only one more tree was cut and sawed. By this time Bill had generated a lot of interest in building with sawed timber; there was a constant demand. People in other Barai villages expressed their desire to purchase boards, but BNEA had sold all the timber and the sawmill was not operating.

We read and were told by expiates of several different villages purchasing a walk-about sawmill for 5,000 to 6,000 kina and making 10,000 to 12,000 kina the first year, which was enough to pay for the mill and still have a profit. That amount of profit may not seem like much to expiates, but for the people of Papua New Guinea it is unbelievable! BNEA was given a wokabaut somil by SIL. It was free. They had been taught to rely on yearly grants to fund their expenses; therefore, they did not feel the need or have the desire to use the sawmill to make kina for their organization. We firmly believe we can best help these people by transferring skills. "Give a man a fish and you feed him for a day. Teach a man to fish and you feed him for a lifetime."

CHAPTER 6

*"You will find, as you look back on your life, that the
moments that stand out are the moments when you
have done things for others. " - Henry Desmond*

Douglas Tumai operated the BNEA trade store. Simon had told me
that I would be working with Doug teaching him a better bookkeeping
system and correcting some of the problems at the store. Douglas was
an amiable young man in his early twenties and single. He was our
close neighbor and the middle brother of George, who owned the
clever pigs that ravished our gardens. He spoke good English and
seemed a promising chap. He was the leader of his clan's boy house
and he played guitar in their small string band. The group often played
their instruments and sang in evenings, entertaining their clan and
lulling us to sleep with their music.

I had talked to Douglas about working with him. He did not appear to
have any reservations about working with a woman instructor since I
was a foreigner. Traditionally the Barai women have no voice in village
work or business. He said he would send for me when he was ready to
start. Several weeks passed with no word from Doug. Finally Simon
intervened and told me to take an inventory of the BNEA trade store.

When I arrived at the store, Douglas seemed glad to see me. I
questioned how he arrived at a selling price. He said that he marked
up all the items 10%. "But first you must add the freight charges to the
cost of each carton. Do you?" I asked.

"There are no freight charges," he replied.

"You do pay money to Talair to bring the merchandise to Itokama by
plane!"

"Oh, they only charge 25 toea ($.25) per carton, which would not be
enough to bother adding on to the carton cost. It would only be about

1 toea or less per item." I dared not argue, because I had no information on air freight rates. Later I talked to the pilot; the freight rate from Popondetta to Itokama was 25 toea per kilogram. After we had finished taking the inventory and had arrived at the total amount of stock on hand, I told him we must take an inventory each month on the same day, keeping records of all purchases and daily sales so that we could determine if the store operated at a profit or loss. He agreed, but on the date of the next inventory, Douglas was absent from the village. He did not return for several days; he had been to his garden. During his absence the store remained closed. When he did come back to the village, he was too busy to bother with taking another inventory. Finally I talked to Simon about the problem. He just shook his head and did nothing.

It was Simon, the BNEA administrator, who had applied to Peace Corps for a mature couple to work in Itokama at the suggestion of the SIL workers, Peter and Betty Evert. They had created the BNEA organization and had funded the operation with yearly grants from SIL and from Compassions of Australia plus a yearly grant from the Oro Provincial Non-formal Education Department. Now BNEA had no free monies except the 5,000 kina ($5,000) given by the Oro Non-formal Education Department because SIL and Compassions had withdrawn their assistance. There were not enough funds to continue paying the employees to translate the books of the Bible from English to Barai and to teach the Barai people to read their own language.

Bill and I could see several ways that BNEA could make money to support their work. The sawmill offered the most potential for revenue. People wanted to buy sawed boards to make doors and steps for their houses. Before sawed wood had been available, steps had been made with poles or by leaning a log from the ground to the doorway of the hut and cutting notches for the steps. Doors were fashioned by tying sticks together with vines. Benson Garui, a Barai living in the village of Tama, wanted to buy timber to build a new house. He was the Speaker for the Oro Provincial Assembly in Popondetta. Father Daniel, pastor of the local Anglican Church, wanted timber to build a new parish house. People from other tribes came to Itokama to purchase timber. Lester, the sawmill manager, failed to keep the sawmill running, and Simon, the administrator of BNEA, and the council did nothing to solve this problem.

The BNEA trade store could have made money, if the store had been operated properly. Simon was in charge of ordering goods for the store. Much of the time the stock was all but depleted, or the store was closed, so the villagers bought from the Nahara trade store. The villagers brought their crop of dried chile peppers to the BNEA trade stores to sell. Often the bags of peppers were not shipped by plane to the market in Popondetta and the chilies spoiled. The store needed supervision. I offered to help, but they didn't use me.

Periodically Simon came to our house to talk. One day he told us that an old man had a large coffee garden near Kokoro Village. He would like to sell it for 4.00 kina ($4) per tree. Simon's family owned approximately seventy-five hectares of land that could support ten-thousand coffee trees adjacent to the garden. They would be willing to lease the ground to BNEA at no cost for fifteen to twenty years, providing BNEA planted the land to coffee. The gardens would be given to the family at the end of the lease period. We could see that BNEA could accumulate some revenue with the purchased coffee garden while the new garden was being cleared, planted and grown to production in three years. Laborers would be paid to pick the coffee crops and this would stimulate Barai incomes.

Bill had offered to measure and stake the land corners. I was to write a contract to be signed by the Savieko family members. It was rugged jungle, so Simon got some boys to accompany them to cut a trail for him and Bill to walk the perimeter of the land. One area had a steep, deep ravine with a river; the boys fell a tree over the gully so that Bill could walk across. When the tree toppled, the boys spied a cuscus dropping from the tree. It is a small marsupial animal valuable to the Nationals for its meat and fur. They scrambled down the precipitous slope, grabbed the cuscus and killed it with their bare hands. The boys would have a feast that night and the fur would be used to decorate headdresses and necklaces. Although Bill was very tired by the time the group returned to Itokama, he felt the day of work had proved to be a most interesting experience.

Bill had worn shorts that day. Usually he wore long pants when he walked through the jungle. He returned home with scratches on his legs and bitten by mosquitos. They were tiny mosquitos unlike any he had ever seen. Two days later he had severe chills and fever. He started taking fansidar for malaria; then his left leg swelled tight and the skin was covered with red blotches and a red streak started up his leg to his groin. I went to the medical clinic in the village and got penicillin. In a few days he felt fine, but the swelling in his leg remained for two months. We sent a slide to the Peace Corps nurse to check for malaria. It was negative; he had reacted to some plant in the jungle.

For a few weeks Simon was full of enthusiasm for the coffee project. He often came to our house to talk and plan the next steps to be taken toward making the coffee garden a reality. Then one day he went to plant his family yam garden near Tama and was away for three weeks. When he returned, he never mentioned the coffee plantation project again. Later he asked Bill and me to work on another venture called the O'kari Nut Project.

O'kari nut trees grow abundantly in the forests of the Barai lands, especially around Itokama, Neokananee and Umuate. The nut shells measure from four to six inches long by two to three inches in diameter. The shell is very hard and nearly a half inch or more thick so it has to be split open with a bush knife or ax head. Inside is a large, long, slender nut meat, much like a Brazil nut, creamy white and very tasty.

The American man, who had lived in Neokananee while he worked on his doctorate in linguistics and now headed the linguistic department at the University of Papua New Guinea, had obtained a 4,000 kina ($4,000) grant for Neokananee from the government for the purpose of making tests on the feasibility of marketing the nuts and to pay villagers to count all the okari trees in that area. The village had selected an O'kari Nut Council, and Brian Kasari was the president. The council had built a storage and had paid people to pick fifty bags of the nuts the year before we had arrived at Itokama. The nuts still were in the storage.

One day Brian brought us a letter to read from the American, Dr. Chip Larson. He wanted the three of us to fly to Port Moresby as soon as possible to meet with him and the head of the Department of Primary Industry. We were to bring a bag of shelled nuts so that he could have tests made to determine how long the nuts should be processed for shipment and their food content.

We spent a week in Port Moresby. Dr. Larson had found a man in Oregon who was interested in packaging and marketing the nuts in the States. He wanted 24,000 pounds in the first shipment. Dr. Larson had arranged a meeting with DPI (Department of Primary Industry) to discuss getting a loan from that department. He had already made a rough draft of the budget for the first five years. He wanted to ask for a 100,000 kina ($100,000) loan. We contacted shipping lines and got prices for containerized, climate controlled freight to Oregon, reworked the estimated budget to 86,000 kina ($86,000) and filled out the loan application. The nuts would be shipped from the Oro Bay dock to Hong Kong, reloaded on another vessel and sent to San Francisco. The buyer would pay the transportation cost from there to Oregon. The people would receive 80 to 90 toea ($.80 to $.90) per kilo of shelled nuts. The buyer would pay $1.63 per pound. Brian was to get an approval for the new endeavor from his council as soon as he returned.

Many months passed before we learned that the loan had been turned down. Bill and I felt that it would have been much wiser to have requested only 10,000 kina ($10,000) to operate for the first year. The sale of the nuts would be able to finance the next year's operation. Also Brian could not explain to the head of DPI just how the 4,000 kina ($4,000) grant had been used. Later the manager of the Agricultural Bank visited Itokama. He offered to loan the O'kari Council 10,000 kina ($10,000) providing Brian would sign the note. He was upset that he must sign for the money. He felt the banker did not trust him and so he would have to think about it. Brian never made a decision. The O'kari project was dropped. Nearly a year later Peace Corps disposed of the bag of nut meats we had taken for Dr. Larson to pick up from the Peace Corps office and have tests made, because the nuts were full of maggots.

The manager of the Nahara Coffee Company, William Suremo, asked Bill and me to attend a meeting of the Board of Directors. After introducing us to the Directors, he told us that Nahara did not have enough cash available to buy coffee from the farmers and stockpile for shipments to Popondetta, so they had asked the Westpac Bank for a loan. The manager refused because William was not able to provide records showing any net worth or profit made by the trade store and coffee division. He suggested that William find a person to teach him bookkeeping and how to make profit and loss statements. Would either of us help him? Bill replied, "That's Margel's type of work. She will help you."

William was probably the best educated of all the Barai. He had graduated from high school and had taken additional schooling in Australia. Finally he studied two years at Mount Hagen Vocational School for the coffee industry located in the Highlands where most of the PNG Arabica coffee is grown. (Oro Province is the second largest coffee producing area.) He was about five feet tall, possibly twenty-eight to thirty years of age. He was a very quiet, gentle man, but he managed to cover any shyness with wide smiles. Directly behind the Nahara coffee storage stood an old sprawling tree that shaded the little hut from the hot sun where William and his wife, two small boys and a baby girl lived. He had a small office in one corner of the coffee storage. It contained a table made of native poles to serve as his desk, a safe, a shelf that held his coffee and trade store records, three metal folding chairs, a red plastic bucket for waste paper and betal spit and a portable typewriter. He was the Talair airline agent for the Itokama sod airstrip and he handled the mail.

I explained to William that we must first take an inventory of the merchandise in the trade store, check the pricing procedure, record all of the purchases and sales. On exactly the same day each proceeding month, we would take another inventory so that we could arrive at a profit figure for the previous month. Then I would type a P&L statement to give to the Westpac Bank manager. He was willing to cooperate. He wanted me to write a letter to the bank manager advising him that I would be helping Nahara with the records, and he asked me to please visit the bank manager on my next trip to Popondetta.

Trade Store is the name given to small enterprises that sell basic needs such as flour, sugar, rice, instant coffee, tea, dried milk, canned milk, tinned fish, canned meats such as corned beef, duck, chicken and goose, biscuits (a hard type of large soda crackers), sweet biscuits (cookies), soap, tobacco, cigarettes, new and used clothing, bush knives, grass knives, razor blades, size D batteries, umbrellas, cooking pots, blankets, towels, baby oil and baby powder. The two trade stores in Itokama, as in most bush villages, stocked only the bare necessities of rice, tin fish, corned beef, coffee, tea, soap, biscuits and bush knives. The scarcity of stock can best be emphasized by the first inventory taken at the Nahara trade store. The total inventory was 287 kina ($287). Edwin Noaka was the store keeper. He was from another tribe and had married a Barai woman. Originally he was from Tetibeti, in fact, it was he and his wife, small daughter and twin babies, who boarded the plane in Tetibeti when we stopped on our first trip to Itokama.

At first I tried to keep a perpetual inventory system. I gave up at the end of the third month, because we came up with shortages each inventory. Edwin vowed he wrote down all the sales. Then I remembered the "wantok system" practiced in all of Papua New Guinea, which means relatives and close friends are never refused if they wish something belonging to another wantok. Edwin and William would feel compelled to give out store items to their wantoks and they would never willingly admit it to me. Always the missing stock was the most sought after items such as rice, tin fish, biscuits and PK gum. Also Edwin often left the store open and unattended while he went to help his wife care for the twin baby daughters, Mona and Teddy. Sometimes he left the store to sit with the men and chew betal nut under the big poinciana tree at the side of the store.

Several times I had gone to the stores and found Edwin absent and six or eight small boys inside all chewing PK gum. They would giggle and run outside as soon as I entered. Many times I cautioned Edwin and William that they must lock the trade store door, if they needed to leave the building. They always smiled and nodded in agreement, but nothing changed. One day I walked to the store to buy a tin of butter. Edwin was nowhere in sight, and as usual, the door was open. I looked outside and saw there were no people in view. The store had a U shaped counter about forty inches high. To enter behind the counter one had to go through the door to the coffee storage. I decided to teach Edwin a lesson. I hoisted my derriere onto the counter top, swung my feet across to the back of the counter and dropped to the floor. Quickly I put six tins of butter into my bilium (woven string bag) and scrambled back over the counter and walked directly to William's house. I figured he would be taking his afternoon nap, for he seldom missed taking at least a two hour break. "William, William," I called, "I need to speak with you!" He emerged from the doorway rubbing the sleep from his eyes. Wende, his wife, came outside too. "Look William," I whispered loudly, "Edwin's gone again from the store. I came to buy butter. No one was around so I helped myself. See, I stole six tins!" I placed them on the step in front of him and laughed.

Sweet, shy William didn't know what to think or say, so he gave me a broad grin, exposing his red betal juice stained teeth. Wende gasped and threw up her hands. "Now William you know I intend to pay for them. I took them off the shelf to prove to Edwin that even an old"white-skin" woman can get behind the counter. If I can do it, the village people and the children can accomplish it much quicker." Then I went to search for Edwin, told him the same story and paid for all the butter. It didn't solve the problem completely, but he seemed to leave the store unattended less frequently.

I emphasized if you want to make a profit in the store, you must have an ample amount of merchandise and keep the store open on a regular schedule. Often the store was closed. I asked William, "Do you want to make a profit? Do you understand the word profit?" I wasn't sure he comprehended so I continued. "I enjoy working. I like to be busy, but I want to see results from my effort. I want to make money. Do you?" He acknowledged that he did. "Then let's work hard in the trade store and then we will have a profit to show to the bank manager."

The first part of April we left Itokama to attend the Peace Corps' four month conference for our group of seventeen volunteers. Since the plane came to Itokama only on Tuesday and Thursday mornings, we had to take the Thursday flight which was four days before the scheduled meeting. This gave us a three day layover in Popondetta. I made an appointment to meet the Westpac Bank manager, Jerry Toboda. He was delighted that I was working with William and would send him monthly reports on earnings. Also I promised to furnish him with a financial statement. He implied that this would be impossible to compile, because he doubted that Nahara has any substantial assets.

Bill called on the Mainland Coffee agent and learned that Nahara sometimes delivered coffee beans which were too wet to receive top price. He said Nahara made very little profit after paying the sea freight to the Mainland Coffee Mill at Lae.

We happened to meet Mr. and Mrs. Ted Koy, an Australian couple, who operated a wholesale-retail business in town. When they heard we were working in Itokama, they asked us to come to the store office to talk. They told us the SIL representatives in Itokama had begged them to extend a line of credit to the BNEA trade store, promising to see that the account was paid within a reasonable amount of time. Later they learned that the couple had left the village without notifying them. BNEA owed the Koys over 3,000 kina ($3,000) which they had not been able to collect. Would we help them? Maybe this was the reason that Simon didn't keep a stock of goods in the store.

Our week of conference at the Jais Aben resort north of Madang was a breath of fresh air. Neither of us had realized how much we had missed the comforts of a modern society and good American food. The resort owner was an American lady married to a German. They pampered us with delicious meals. The rooms were newly furnished and comfortable. We could walk along the beach, swim in the spacious pool, or go snorkeling in the coral reefs. They drove our group to Madang about ten kilometers from the resort, where we could explore the huge native market filled with vegetables, fruits, fresh fish, clothing, artifacts, native beads and bilums.

Each volunteer had a personal interview with the Peace Corps Director. There were group discussions and job related group meetings. Most of the volunteers were apprehensive that they were not progressing fast enough with their job assignments. Everyone was anxious to make a difference. It was already apparent that progressive changes came slowly in Papua New Guinea, because the Nationals moved at a sluggish pace. Perhaps the hot steamy climate contributed to their complacent ways. After visiting with other volunteers, Bill and I realized we were accomplishing more than we had surmised. The problem was we Americans were accustomed to the fast tempo of a competitive world. We must learn to adapt to the momentum of the Nationals.

When we got off the plane at Itokama, we were met by a large group of villagers. They shook our hands and slapped us on the back and greeted us with smiles and tears. Evidently they wondered if we would actually return as we had promised. Suddenly we both realized we were extremely happy to be back in this primitive place among the Barai people. We belonged here. This was our new home. These people were our friends, our very special friends. It wasn't an important negative happening that the mandarin orange tree in our yard had been stripped of all the fruit during our absence, or that the bamboo poles we had hired cut to keep our fences in repair were missing from under the porch along with two bags of clay and all the wood for our firebox. We had paid the boys to collect the poles, clay and wood for us. Clay could be used for many things such as to caulk a drum oven and for making wet molds like Bill made for the hydraulic line to repair the crack in the hydraulic line so that he could drive the Nahara truck to town. Another time someone broke off the handle of Bill's screwdriver, so Bill made a wet clay mold, placed the screwdriver shaft vertically in the mold and filled it with melted lead. In the Barai culture these items belonged to them, if they wanted them. This practice we must learn to accept.

My first task was to start gathering a list of Nahara's assets. I was quite surprised when William explained that the 4-wheel drive Toyota truck was loaned to them by the Mainland Coffee Mills, providing all the Nahara coffee was sold to that firm. In exchange, Nahara could use the truck to haul coffee to the Mainland shipping station in Popondetta and was allowed to haul merchandise back to their trade store. He told me that Nahara owned another trade store, which had a metal roof, in the village at Tetibeti. "Does the store make a profit?" I asked. He shook his head and admitted they were not making enough to pay for new stock. He didn't want to close it because it involved a wantok of one of the Nahara directors. At least the metal roofing tins had some value. The Nahara building in Itokama also had a tin roof. Nahara trade store and the coffee division had separate checking accounts at Westpac Bank. I generously depreciated the roofing tins, small equipment such as scales, safe, typewriter, calculators, deep freeze and generator, then added the store inventory and cash. The grand total came to over 20,000 kina ($20,000).

At the end of the first month the trade store had made a profit of 28 kina ($28), small by western standards, but the average Barai family would earn under 280 kina ($280) each year. William and Edwin were happy. They deserved praise. "We can do better next month," I told them. "You have worked hard. Thank you." I gave them a Dale Carnegie sandwich - praise, challenge and more praise -, and mailed a copy of the profit statement to the Westpac Bank manager. The following month the profit was 98 kina ($98). This time William paid my airfare and accompanied me to Popondetta to personally present the profit statement and the financial statement to Mr. Toboda, who was visibly impressed. William was listening to my suggestions and implementing them as best he could. In the ensuing months the profits slowly increased to 600 kina ($600) for the month.

My work with the BNEA organization progressed at a snail's pace. Simon asked me to total all the money which had been deposited in the tiny BNEA bank. Actually is wasn't a bank by western standards, but rather a place of safe keeping. People brought their meager earnings from the sale of coffee beans and chilies and gave it to BNEA to hold until such time they wished to withdraw cash. Meanwhile BNEA deposited the money, except for a small cash reserve for future withdrawals, in a certificate of deposit at the Bank of New Guinea at Popondetta and used the derived interest money for operating expenses. The depositors received no interest. The BNEA bank was located in a room at the rear of their trade store. Banking was transacted through a walk-up window. Many times Douglas, who was in charge, failed to open the store and bank. He was noticeably absent. The villagers complained.

The bank provided each depositor with a homemade deposit book, which usually remained at the bank. When I compared these with the bank ledger entries of deposits and withdrawals, I found many inaccuracies between the amounts entered in the deposit book and the entry into ledger. Next I checked each depositor's account from the first entry in the ledger to the last transaction. Again I found errors in addition and subtraction. For example, the church was shorted 100 kina ($100), the sawmill account was short 300 kina ($300), Simon's wife should have 10 kina ($10) instead of showing zero balance. Always the mistake was a shortage to the depositor. I made notations and a list of mistakes for Douglas and a copy for myself, then I took the ledger to Douglas and instructed him how to make a corrected entry after the last entry. He didn't seem concerned over the discrepancies between ledger and deposit book figures. And a few days later, when I checked his corrections, he had used correction fluid and obliterated and smudged the figures until, without my own notes, it was impossible to arrive at the correct final balance. A bottle of white liquid correction fluid is like a bottle of magic to the Barai people. I was furious and appalled! When I gave the grand total of monies on deposit to Simon and advised him of all the mistakes Doug had made, he simply shrugged his shoulders and walked away. It was several months before I was again allowed to work with any BNEA records.

Simon did ask me to teach a two week bookkeeping class. He said several young men were interested. I agreed to teach, although it seemed strange that they would want training in record keeping, because BNEA and Nahara were the only organizations in all the Barai villages. There were no opportunities for employment. I sensed the competition between Nahara and BNEA. They were jealous because I spent most of my time working with Nahara.

Fifteen young men enrolled in class, including Douglas and Lester, the manager of the sawmill. Class was from 8:30 to 12:00 with a ten minute break at 10:00. The second morning of class the BNEA community room door was locked. Simon had kept the key and he had gone to his garden. Everyone seemed to accept the locked door except me. I was furious! The following morning the door was unlocked. The men listened intently as I explained very simple, basic bookkeeping procedures. In Papua New Guinea, credit is known as "in," debit as "out," and accounts receivables are"bookings." At the end of the first week I gave them a test, a problem dealing with credit and debit and balance. They were to copy information and figures from the black-board and make the proper entries on columnar paper and arrive at the correct balance. Three of them filled their papers with fictitious figures that made absolutely no sense. Most of the students failed to arrive at the correct ending balance. When I graded their papers I made corrections and wrote encouraging notes with red ink. On Monday morning everyone beamed as they were handed the graded test sheets. They loved the red ink. They felt special. No one acted concerned over a low grade. I felt defeated and confused. Actually I was learning more than my class. I was learning the simplicity of their culture and concept of education. If they attended a study course they felt educated whether they comprehended the lessons or not.

Bill had been working with a young man named Boudwin, who brought Bill a diploma he had received from a vocational school. He had studied carpentry and graduated with the classification of a joiner, which indicated he was an interior finisher, skilled in moldings, stairways and cabinets. But Boudwin could not make a straight cut with a hand saw, nor could he read a measuring tape, or drive a nail without bending it. Often he came to work smelling so strong of feces that Bill demanded he go to the river and "waswas" (wash) himself. Bill was trying to teach him to make simple straight chairs for BNEA. He never was able to build a chair by himself. Yet he had a certificate inscribed with his name which commanded respect from his people.

The fifth grade teacher had advised Bill that he must repeat each instruction at least five or more times to the men and boys he was attempting to teach. Recalling this, I began doing the same with my class. At the end of the two weeks three students, including Douglas, Lester, received a high grade on the final exam. Later they failed to apply that knowledge in the trade store, bank and sawmill. They chose to visit with friends and chew betal nut, which clouded their brain, or to spend time in their garden or another village.

William Suremo inquired whether Bill could draw some plans for a new store and office building for Nahara. He said they had already purchased the roofing tins and he gave Bill the count and lengths so that he could draw the plans to accommodate the tins. William wanted a porch across the entire front, with a sliding walk-up window into his office for the purpose of paying for coffee, selling Talair plane tickets and dispensing mail. There must be a large storage room for store cartons of merchandise and kerosene drums, with doors at either end of the storage for unloading trucks. He wanted a high, steep pitched roof and louvered glass windows covered on the exterior with welded wire to prevent break ins. Sawed timber would be used for the frame work and flooring. The sides would be made of woven bamboo. In a few years when the siding needed to be replaced, they intended to use wood. Bill drew the plans and presented them to the directors, who approved the plans unanimously. William hired a crew of four men. Bill was to supervise the construction.

The new structure was to set on elevated pole footings. Working with the only available tools, a roll of twine, a measuring tape and a bundle of sticks, Bill and I staked the four corners of the 36 ft. x 36 ft. building. Then we proceeded to measure and place a stake where each of the more than thirty footing poles would be set to support the floor joists and framework. The villagers gathered around to watch us, amazed at all this sophisticated approach. What were we doing? Bill explained that the building must be perfectly squared and the poles must be placed at precise intervals. They laughed and shook their heads and clicked their tongues, their way of showing amazement.

It took the building crew over two weeks to collect the poles. Victor brought a length of bamboo and asked Bill to mark how long they must be cut. Then men had to travel far into the jungle to locate the special hardwood tree whose wood resisted rot and wood-eating insects. The trees must be chopped down with an axe, cut into proper lengths, then they were debarked and carried on their heads back to the job site. When the crew began to set the poles it was our turn to watch in amazement, because each hole was carefully dug with a bush knife. They were set in sloping terrain, so Bill marked the correct height on each pole so that the floor joists would be level; then the crew cut them off with a hand saw. At the front of the structure the poles were two feet above the ground, while at the rear they stood five feet tall. The next task was to notch each pole to hold the 2 x 8 ft. floor joists.

The village dwellings are made with a framework of poles and sticks tied together with the vines from the forest. These men had never built with sawed timber and nails. Patiently Bill taught them how to use hammers and nails to fasten the joists and plank flooring and how to use a tape measure. He taught them how to put up the rafters and how to nail together the partition studding and brace work on the ground and later how to raise the entire section into place. They learned to frame windows and doorways, to build shelving and counter tops. One of the men named Emmanuel spoke no English or Tok Pidgen, only Barai, yet he and Bill communicated well with eye contact, facial expressions and touch. He always seemed to understand what Bill was trying to convey. There was consistently an audience of people watching them work.

The new building would have a steep V pitch roof, twenty feet to the peak, so Bill built a wooden ladder. He was astonished when the crew admitted they were terrified to climb the ladder. These were men that quickly climbed to the top of a thirty foot coconut or betal nut palm to pick the fruit, sometimes throwing their weight to sway the tree and then jumping to the next one. So Bill nailed the high end rafters and studs and the first two roof rafters in place. Then the men scrambled up the frame work like monkeys, feeling perfectly at ease to add the gussets and finish nailing the roof rafters. They could balance themselves walking upright on the timber.

Bill had suggested laying insulated foil between the roofing tins and rafters to keep the building cooler from the hot sun. He also suggested placing one plastic skylight over the store area. He had designed the building to accommodate Nahara's supply of roofing tins. When they began laying the tins, he found that William had not given him the correct lengths. He realized he should have measured the tins before drawing the plans. Now he had to cut one row of tins by hand. Building without proper tools was a challenge!

The new Nahara building

Margel works with William, Mgr of Nahara

CHAPTER 7

"The secret of contentment is knowing how to enjoy what you have, and to be able to lose all desire for things beyond your reach ." -Lin Yutang

Living in Itokama was never dull. Each day unfolded new experiences. Our porch became a stopping place, a resting place for Barai people traveling past our house on their way to the villages of Neokananee and Umuate. They gathered on our porch from the daily afternoon rains. Anyone was welcome as well as the Musa tribe, who lived a two day walk beyond Barai territory. Nationals and government officials traveling to Itokama often visited us. It was a respite from village routine, an opportunity for comradeship with two old "white-skins," a chance to observe our habits and learn about our customs, a place to beg a favor, "Can you help me?" And, for us, it was a priceless privilege to learn their way of life. We were so eager to know more about this complex culture. A young woman, Lelia Koki, came with a group of women, who spoke only Barai.

She said they wondered what I put on my skin to make it look different and feel so soft. I answered that I did nothing. These people were also curious about us. Our hair was a different texture and often someone would touch our hair.

Their body odor was offensive. Often we smelled them before we saw them. The men usually dressed in T shirts and shorts. The women wore skirts and a top, sometimes only a skirt being naked from the waist up. The very young children often were naked. Sometimes the small girls wore only a skirt, and young boys wore only a pair of shorts or a loin cloth. About 10% of the people were covered with white scales, a body fungus, the result of malnutrition and filth. Under the scales were patterns much like an erratic ringworm. At first I thought it would be impossible to touch them, then Lelia's son, Eddie, a small beautiful boy with enormous brown eyes, knocked at our door and gave me a small bundle of snake beans tied with a jungle vine. He spoke no English; I spoke little Barai. How could we communicate? I put my arms around him, hugged him and smiled. Then I gave him cookies. He understood. We were friends. After he left the porch I washed.

Even though our porch was a gathering place, we were selective of persons to invite into our house, not because we were bigots, but because we must be able to speak a common language, either English or Tok Pidgen. Stewart and Victoria Jada came to our porch one Sunday. We invited them inside. Stewart had been a carrier of radio equipment for the Australian and American armies in World War II. He didn't know his age, but he indicated his approximate height at the time. We assumed he must of been about eight or ten. He had kept in contact with Mr. Dick, his commanding officer from Australia. He had a few, very few, white hairs. He appeared old for a Barai because their life span is about forty-six to forty-eight years. Seldom did we see a National with white hairs. He spoke good English; Victoria spoke only Barai. She loved her smoke, so Bill gave her a cigarette. Victoria was covered with white fungus. She walked about the room looking at everything. Stewart told us that they had never been allowed inside this house before today. I brought coffee and cookies, placed them on the dining table and indicated that we would all sit around the table. Very carefully Victoria lowered her body onto the folding chair. She grasped the seat of the chair with both hands. With one hand she quickly took a sip of coffee, then grabbed the chair seat again. We understood. She was uncomfortable. The Barai people have absolutely no furniture in their houses. The rooms are empty. They sit on the floor. They sleep on the floor. Some are fortunate enough to have a pillow and a blanket or a bath towel to use as a towel and also as a blanket on cold nights. Every house has pandanus floor mats and a firebox where they can cook a meal or warm their huts. The smoke escapes through an opening at the peak of the roof. Each household has a limited number of granite coffee cups and plates, two or three at the most, a large granite bowl, a couple of cooking pots, maybe a skillet, maybe a couple of forks or spoons, maybe a kerosene pressure lantern, maybe a torch (flashlight) and a very few have a shortwave, battery powered radio. These are their belongings! They wear their clothing until it literally falls apart. Their prize possessions are their bilums, small knives, bush knives, axes and spears.

Our kitchen had two window openings covered with screen. One window faced the porch. We had no curtains, so as I worked in the kitchen, the people, men and women with children held on their shoulders, pressed against the window to watch me. Sometimes I was afraid they would break through the opening as they pushed against it to view me, their noses flattened against the screen. When Bill returned home one day. I was sewing a piece of material by hand. What was I doing! "I'm making a curtain for the kitchen window. I can't work living in a goldfish bowl any longer!" I replied.

Gordon from Neokananee often stopped at our place. One day I had just finished baking a double recipe of oatmeal cookies when he arrived. I made coffee and took the container of cookies and set it on the small table beside his chair. "Help yourself," I said. He did. When he finally left, I found an empty container. He had eaten every single cookie! Henceforth, I put two or three cookies on a plate and served with coffee. It is the custom of the Nationals to eat all the food given to you because food is not always available.

One of the colorful people who visited our porch was Sammuel Dumare. He was the Christian leader for BNEA, traveling from village to Barai village with a tape recorder with Christian messages. "Bill, can you help me? My recorder doesn't work." It was covered with dust and grime. Bill cleaned the recording mechanism and sent him on his way. A few days later he would arrive to beg a piece of writing paper to correspond with an American lady in the state of Washington. Then he returned to ask for an envelope and still later he needed a 70 toea stamp to mail his letter. He had a wife and three small daughters, one was a baby. He loved to relate how this American had enriched his life by sending him a guitar, dolls for his daughters and clothing. Time after time he repeated his needs. "Can you help me?" One day Simon told us that Sammuel had been severed from BNEA for adultery. He no longer was involved with BNEA. And Sammuel was devoting his time to running his own trade store. He had been one of my bookkeeping students. Would I help him price his merchandise? I was delighted to help him. We worked many hours together as I tried to assist him with his store. Then he would not come again for several months. Business to him, as to most Barai people, was a game.

John Willie, who lived in Neokananee came to our porch one Sunday morning. He gave me his new bush knife and said, "Have Bill sharpen it NOW. I will pick it up on my way home from church."

"Bill does not work on Sunday. He will have it sharpened by Monday or Tuesday afternoon," I replied. He was clearly upset. For that matter, so was I because I did not appreciate his demanding tone. Another day he stopped at the porch. BIll was working with Boudwin building straight chairs under a tree in our yard. "Bill," he shouted, "I want smoke!"

"So do I, so do I!" Bill replied and continued with his work. After those incidents, John Willie became a good friend. He learned to ask for favors in a more tolerable manner.

Bill was building a coffee drier in the yard. It consisted of a clear plastic covered area which would be filled with large stones to absorb the heat and an area covered by dark plastic that contained trays made of window screen to hold a layer of coffee beans. The stones absorbed the heat from the sun and the airflow drove the heat through the trays to dry the coffee beans. There was always a large group of people watching him work. They sat around him or lounged under the trees and chewed betal nuts. He built the drier for Nahara so that they could get a better price for the coffee beans, which they bought from farmers that brought wet beans that could not receive top prices. It was an opportunity to make lasting friendships with the onlookers as they sat watching this old "white-skin" work. It was a time for conversation, a time to teach them that coffee must be dried correctly before they sold their beans to Nahara. Bill noticed one man had a bush knife with old rags wrapped around where the handle should have been. "If you will leave your bush knife with me, I will make you a new handle." This was the beginning of a labor of love. During the two years we spent in Itokama, Bill made over two hundred bush knife handles. It was his way of giving kindness and friendship. Some brought old pitted knives; one person brought a rusty bayonet and Bill fashioned a handle. He never charged for the bolts or wood. He countersunk the bolts, sanded and varnished the handle and sharpened the knife blade. He was conveying to these people, "I care!" You are my friends. He taught John Willie, Boudwin and Morris, from the Kororo village, how to make bush knife handles. However, the people preferred for Bill to make the handles for their knives.

Jennifer came to our porch bringing her bush knife to get a new handle. One leg was shorter than the other so she had a noticeable limp. Her skin was like leather, her teeth were snags and she looked more like a witch than a human being. She loved her smoke and always wanted some tobacco or cigarettes. She would bring us a yam or a kaukau, or some fruit, which meant we must give her something in return. This ugly old woman became our joy. I could hug her despite of her fungus and enjoy the touch. She was Gordon's mother. Our priorities were changing. We were the fortunate ones. What an experience! Beauty is in the mind of the beholder.

Shortly after we arrived at Itokama we wrote to the Darian Book Company in Darian, Conn., USA who offer to supply free books to third world countries. We explained that the grade school at Itokama was trying to build a library and we sent a list of subject matter they could use. Several months later a shipment arrived, and since the school had no place for them, we kept them at our house until such time as the school library shelves were completed. The teachers came to borrow the books. It proved an opportunity to develop a bond of friendship. We sent a "Thank You" letter to Darian along with some photos of the village. Soon we received a second shipment of books. When the library was finished, we gave all the volumes to the school. We had subscribed to Reader's Digest and National Geographic. Peace Corps sent us Newsweek magazine. We passed these onto the school after we finished reading them. Printed material is such a priceless gift to the people.

Our favorite teachers were Eric and Mavis Sawaraba and their two small daughters, Lorraine, age five, and Connie, age two. When the girls needed to go to the bathroom, one of the parents would take them outside our house. Later we would scoop up the feces and throw it over the fence into the jungle. They were from the Popondetta area. Mavis asked me to teach her how to bake bread. She was accustomed to cooking over an open fire because no one in Itokama owned a stove. On the following Saturday she came to our house and learned to make a loaf of bread. The recipe called for 1/3rd cup of milk and 2-1/2 cups of flour. She didn't understand fractions, even though she taught school, and so I marked 1/3 and 1/2 on a plastic cup with a magic marker and gave it to her. She later baked bread by placing the bread pan inside a big cooking pot, set the pot over a small fire and also put hot coals on the lid. Eric was fascinated with a tool box Bill had made from rough boards to hold his meager supply of nails, screws, and tools. With Bill instructing him, Eric built a tool box one weekend. He was very proud of his accomplishment. Realizing that the hinges and hasp Bill provide for his tool box cost money, Eric insisted on giving Bill 1 kina, which was quite special; the villagers never expected to pay for anything given to them by either of us.

John Lucas was the grade 5th teacher. He and his wife, Bellfaith also came to visit us. To them we were "Daddy and Mom." John was in charge of keeping the school yard and soccer field mowed. The school had a gas lawn mower which was old and tired. Bill now kept it running. Bellfaith, too, wanted to learn to bake bread and she wanted to learn to knit. These hours together teaching and learning were precious moments. We were building friendships. Their young son, Francis, came regularly to borrow a volume of the encyclopedias sent by Darian. Often he brought his friends. Every book was returned promptly. Once he asked me, "What is ancient Egypt?" I knew then that he was browsing through the books. It was my privilege to explain the word ancient. Eventually several village boys came to borrow books to read.

Itokama has a weekly schedule. Monday is gardening day. Tuesday is open, free. Wednesday is community day, the time to cut the grass or clean around BNEA and also the day to cut the grass on the soccer field and around the school buildings. The Barai people had already stopped caring for the school grounds before we arrived, so it was left for the teacher, John Lucas, to do . Thursday is designated for gardens; Friday is the day the women must sweep the bare grounds in the village with their primitive brooms made from the stripped fronds of the coconut tree and bound together with a vine. As they sweep their bare breasts swing in rhythm to their movements. The ground must be cleared of pig and human feces and debris from betal nut husks, corn husks, sticks and other discarded items. Saturday is again for gardening. Sunday is for church in the mornings and soccer and basketball games in the afternoon.

Village life is one of contentment. The children play together without bickering or fighting. The older children tend to the babies and toddlers. They pull small children on a huge banana leaf. We never burned cardboard cartons, instead we placed them on our porch. Soon a young girl or boy would come and take them. They tied a vine at one end and placed a small child in the box and pulled the little one about the village. The toddler's face would be beaming with smiles. How little it took to make the children happy. Sometimes children took a pink flower, much like a double hollyhock blossom, and kicked it like a soccer ball lifting it with their instep as they walked across the village. The contest was to see which one could keep the blossom from falling to the ground for the longest time. Boys played marbles using round nuts from the jungle, when they didn't have man made marbles. Marbles sold for 5 toea each at the Nahara trade store, but often the supply was exhausted. Children made whirly-gigs from a stick and folded leaves or fashioned a tiny wagon using a flat fish tin or tobacco tin, round nuts as wheels, sticks for axles and pulled with a vine. Sometimes the children, even grown people, cut a section of banana leaf stem about sixteen inches in length and cut a V notch on top and pushed it with a long stick maneuvering it along the trail or through the village. Sometimes we bought simple toys in Popondetta for the children to play with when they came with their parents to visit us. We remembered how abundant toys were in the United States, how demanding the kids were to own every new toy seen on television. Here was a different world where children must use their own imaginations to create fun. Sometimes a group of children came to our yard which was covered with thick grass. They would sit on the ground and sing. I loved to watch them from my kitchen window as I worked. Other times children came to play under our house, which set high on pole footings so that they could walk upright underneath the building. They even put up a rope swing made of jungle vine under our house. Occasionally, if I was working on bookkeeping or typing, I would ask them to leave because I couldn't keep my concentration. "Amie java, jave," I would shout in Barai, meaning "children go, go" and they would scurry from the yard, soon to return again. Teenage and younger girls would often come to our porch with babies they were tending because it is the duty of the girls to care for their siblings and cousin babies while the mothers are working. The babies were usually naked, no diaper.

Village children

Villagers

Village scene

Children and I standing in front of our garden

Although the children get along together, they do have some terrible temper tantrums around their families. Parents never correct or punish them because they fear to provoke them, as someday they will take care of their parents when they become old. So when small children want gum or biscuits or whatever, they yell and scream and roll in the dirt until they are exhausted or appeased.

Wende was the only parent we ever saw correct or spank her children. Even then they were at times very naughty and demanding. One day Edwin asked me to tend the store so that he could spend the day working to clear a new garden site. Wende was in her house ill with an attack of malaria. William brought Micah, age three, with him while he worked in his office. Later he left and locked the office door leaving Micah asleep on the floor. When he awoke, he started screaming and jumping up and down on the floor, shaking the building. Finally I went into the office and asked him if he wanted to leave? He did. I watched him from the store window as he picked up a long length of green bamboo, which his mother had cut to use for cooking vegetables. He kept ramming the bamboo against the old woven siding on their house. When no one came to see what he wanted, he started throwing sticks of firewood against the house. I expected the siding would break with every blow. Finally exhausted, he sat down under the old tree and rested awhile and then resumed the attack. After about a half hour his mother opened the door and shouted, "William come take care of this small boy!" William walked around the corner of the coffee storage and faced Micah . He didn't say a word, but turned and walked to the store and returned to give the boy a package of cookies. That ended the tantrum.

Another time William was going to haul a load of coffee to Popon-detta. Since Wende and Mother Grace, Father Daniel's wife, were attending a provincial meeting of the women's society at the Anglican diocese in town, William was left to care for the two boys. He had arranged for his mother-in-law to stay with them while he made the two day trip. Wende and Mother Grace would ride back with him. The truck was loaded and tarped. It was nearly noon. Usually he left early in the morning because it could take all day to reach town if the road conditions were bad. Eventually he came to ask Bill to help him with a problem. He said that Micah was crying very hard because he did not want papa to leave him. Would Bill please drive the truck past the first curve, which was out of sight, and stop and wait for him? He would tell Micah that he was going to the garden, which was in the same direction; then he would walk out to the road and take the truck and Bill could walk back to the village.

It was at least a twelve minute fast walk from our house through the village to the airstrip and Nahara. We always took much longer because the children would call out "Morning, morning, morning," regardless of the time of day and they would run to us to shake hands. We would pass by groups of people sitting around a small fire and we would stop to talk. These people were important to us. They were our friends. We wanted them to understand that we were interested in the Barai people. It is a common practice for the people to sit and "story;" that is their word for visiting and relating past experiences. One of the village pastimes was picking fleas from one another's hair. Sometimes we would see three people sitting one behind the other. The one at the rear was picking fleas from the person in front, while that person picked fleas from the person in front of him or her. They would hold the fleas in their hand and occasionally empty them into their mouth. This was simply their way of life.

Jeramiah lived about five houses from us. He was an unusual character. He wore a synthetic, salt and pepper colored, curly female wig. We figured it had arrived in a barrel of used clothing. Once in a while we would pass Jeramiah and his wig was missing, his bald head glistening in the sunlight. Later we would spot some young man wearing it! He had two dogs. We often saw him picking fleas from one dog and placing the fleas on the second dog. It was a pastime! His dogs were important to him. They were hunters. Like all village dogs, they had short brown hair; they were curs, so thin you could count every rib. We never saw Jeramiah do any work. His family were the ones that did all the labor. One daughter attended high school in Popondetta.

Usually I carried a camera in my bilum when I walked through the village, perchance I saw an picturesque sight. This day I walked to the Nahara trade store to buy supplies. Standing in front of the store was a tall, very dark-skin man wearing only a loincloth and clutching a seven foot spear. His face was painted and he looked ferociously at me. Was he fierce? Or was he alarmed at seeing this strange white female?

Oh what a picture he would make, but I was too frightened to take the camera from my bilum. I simply turned and walked quickly away.

The Barai men hunt with spears and sling shots. To hunt pigs, they use a two prong spear; to hunt other game and to war against neighboring tribes they use a one prong spear. Birds are hunted with a sling shot which the Nationals call "rubbers." They often wear the rubber as a band on their heads, just in the event they spot a bird in a tree. They can kill a small bird the size of a sparrow at a distance of three hundred feet using a small round stone the size of marble. There are no stones in the soil, so they have to walk at least two kilometers to a river to gather them. The stones are carried in their bilums along with their betal nuts and lime pot.

Less than twenty years ago these people were cannibals. One man from Neokananee told us that years ago some of his people found a man with white skin asleep beside a trail. He had peculiar feet, so the people carefully took hold of these funny feet and they came off. They carried them back to their village and boiled the feet in a pot. They cooked them a long time, but the feet were too tough to eat. They boiled them again the next day. Still the feet (shoes) were too tough to chew, so they discarded them and drank the broth. It sounds like a fairy tale to entertain, but perhaps this is a true story. We waited for nearly a year to ask the question, "Do the Barai eat people?"

"Oh, my grandfather and grandmother ate people. They are good, they told me," would be the reply. They displayed no embarrassment or shame.

"Who did they eat?" we asked.

"Enemies, members of other tribes who entered our villages or they encountered on the trail. They struck them on the temple with a "killing stone" knocking them down and then they killed them, hung the body from a tree or in the house overnight and ate them all the next day."Young plump girls about twelve were considered the most delectable. One young man stroked my arm and said, "Ah, Margel, you would be good to eat!" To them it was not unusual.

We also heard war tales from several people of different tribes, who told us how the starving Japanese soldiers in World War II cut off a portion of thigh from young, stout, native girls and left them to suffer, perhaps die, in order to have food to eat. Some of the ancestors of the people we met in Papua New Guinea had been killed by a bayonet or gun by the Japs. One of the school teachers, Sylvinus, recalled how his father and grandfather had been carriers for the Allied army. His grandfather was caught and disemboweled by the Japanese.

Warring with neighboring tribes was a common practice, a form of entertainment and excitement throughout PNG. It still occurs today in many areas of the country. The tribes fight all day, and when it becomes evening, they stop and rest and resume the hostilities the next morning. Battles are fought to avenge the death of a person, a pig, a rape, a theft, an insult or to settle a land dispute.

Hunting and fishing, clearing an area in the jungle for a garden, chopping down trees, cutting the poles for and building a house, weaving bamboo siding, planting yams, these are jobs for men to do. Actually they do little else, except for sitting in groups to talk or chew betal nut or smoke. Sometimes they watch the small children while the women folk are working. However, the men and boys are willing to work for a wage. It is the women who toil daily. They are beasts of burden and breeding stock. It is their duty to tend the gardens, harvest and carry the fruit and vegetables back to the village, pick and process the coffee, pick the chilies, travel to the river to wash the clothes, prepare the meals, carry the water and wood and bear the babies, one after another. The man walks ahead with his sons, carrying his bushknife and the wife and daughters follow behind. We felt sorry for the women.

There are no wells in the Barai villages. BNEA community building has a tin roof and the water run-off is stored in a big metal tank. During the rainy season, which lasts for six months, it provides water for drinking and cooking for many of the people living in Itokama. Some of the villagers got water from a faucet under our house connected to the storage tank. We often heard people washing themselves, bathing babies and washing dishes beneath our house. In fact, we could watch them through a tiny hole in the floor. Sometime small children turned on the faucet and played in the water and then forgot to turn it off.

William's family have their own private source of water, a twelve foot section of eves spouting which drains into a fifty-five gallon steel drum, catching the afternoon rains from part of the coffee storage roof. Wende uses it for washing clothes and dishes and bathing the baby. No one ever bothers to wash vegetables before cooking them.

Along the side of the road between the Nahara building and the mission station there is a place where the people can get their water supply and wash their clothes during the dry season. The ground beside the road drops abruptly down to a deep ravine two hundred feet below where there is a spring. It is such a steep drop-off that I was always fearful to stand on the precipice to look down to the bottom. But the girls and women simply walk and slide down the embankment, wash their clothes or dishes or fill their large three to four gallon cooking pots with water, then placing the pot or plastic dish pan on their head, they climb the longer trail at the far side, which has steps formed by driving sticks into the ground to hold short sticks laid vertically to serve as a stairway. The Nationals never carry a load at their side, but rather, they carry everything on their heads or shoulders. One day Bill saw Simon's wife, Theresa, coming from the spring. She was carrying her little son on one hip and was balancing a large pot of water on her head. Mischievously, Bill spoke and nodded to her. She nodded back spilling a bit of water from the pot; she stuck out her tongue and caught the water in her mouth, wasting not one drop.

The people bathe in a river or small stream. Men and boys use one area, while the women and girls bathe out of their sight in another part of the river. Nakedness below the waist is taboo after the age of puberty, so everyone "waswas" wearing some clothing. During our Peace Corps training we women were instructed to never wear shorts or slacks in the villages because this was offensive as it showed the contour of our bodies. Our dresses or skirts must reach below our knees. If we went swimming, we could wear a bathing suit, but we must wrap a piece of cloth, a "laplap," around our waist to cover our bottom and knees.

The Nahara coffee truck was covered with mud, so Bill decided to drive it to the river to wash it. He invited a group of twenty young boys to go along. They were delighted because it gave them a chance to bathe. A truck never left a village empty; it was always filled with people riding in the rear. After the truck was cleaned, Bill accompanied the boys to their bathing area. They proceeded to "waswas" their bodies wearing their shorts. Bill stripped completely and scrubbed his body with soap. Suddenly he realized all the boys had climbed onto a fallen log and were watching this naked old "white-skin!"

The women carry their babies in a very large bilum, sometimes called a string bag, which they weave with a crude needle and twisted string. Often the needle is made from the wing bone of a fruit bat or a metal key used to open a tin of meat, straightened and sharpened to a point. In some areas of Papua New Guinea the women make the string by rolling three staggered strand lengths of fiber from the inner bark of the mulberry tree on their knee. In Chimbu Province they add fur from the cuscus as they roll the strands, giving the finished bilum a furry look. Bilums are made in all sizes, from a man's small bilum to carry his betal nuts and lime pot to the size to carry babies and small children, vegetables and fruits. Small pigs are also carried this way. The patterns vary from area to area and the Nationals can identify them by the geometric patterns, colors and fabric. We never went to town without our bilums. It was amazing how much they would hold, for they expanded immensely. They are carried by hanging the woven handle over the head. It is quite comfortable and much easier than to carry them over one's shoulder. The women carried enormous loads in them. Bill has lifted bilums of vegetables off women's heads and almost staggered under the weight.

Women nurse their babies for two to three years. After lactation period, they become pregnant again. It is not uncommon to see a woman walking along a trail and her five year old son sucking her breast as they walk. It is the only milk available. Powdered milk sold in the trade stores is used only for coffee. The first time I saw a woman nursing a small piglet, I nearly fainted. The men would locate a wild sow in the jungle and steal one of her small pigs, bringing it back to the village for his wife to feed until is was old enough to survive on solid foods. Pigs are valuable, a sign of wealth.

When young boys reach the age of puberty, they can no longer live in the house of their parents, because of the presence of a female means sex contamination. At this time they move to their clan's "boy house," which is supervised by the older young men. They may eat with their parents, but they dare not spend the night in their former home. Men can enter the boy houses; women are forbidden. Sometimes the boys cook for themselves, but more often they eat with parents or relatives. Most boy houses have a string band comprised of battery amplified guitars. During village feasts they compete against other clan boy houses from various villages for a prize. Often widows hire the youth of a boy house to pick coffee. The money is used to pay for more instruments or for any needs.

Missionaries taught the villagers to build "liklik hauses" or out-door toilets, in Itokama. If you have ever experienced an Asian toilet you will understand that the "liklik haus" is built over an open pit, with a framework of poles for the flooring and a hole in the center. At one corner is a branch of leaves to use for toilet paper. Adults use the facility, but small children often relieve themselves where ever it is convenient. Why they chose the path to our house, we will never understand, but often we would see them squatting along the way to our house and doing their thing. We scooped up their waste and pitched it over the fence.

One of the most colorful events of village life is a "mumu" or feast to entertain wantoks. The men lay a framework of logs topped with special sharp edged volcanic rocks. The logs are set fire and once the rocks become white hot, the remainder of logs and coals are raked aside. Layers of banana leaves are placed on top of the hot rocks, then yams, kaukau, pumpkin, greens and meat, when it is available, are put on top of the leaves and covered with more layers of banana leaves. About three hours later the leaves turn brown which signals that the food is cooked. Usually a pot of rice has also been prepared over an open fire. The mumu is uncovered and the cooked food is transferred to large granite bowls to cool. The Barai people never eat hot or warm food. They wait to start the feast until the food, including the rice, is cold. Guests sit down on the ground on pandanus mats or banana leaves and consume the food. Some have a fork or spoon, but many eat with their hands. Watching them eat was shocking, because they would heap the food on their granite plates and shovel it into their mouths giving no appearance of enjoying each bite, but rather, the fact that since the food was available, we must eat to fill our bellies. People did not always have a cooked meal each day.

Later, after the rocks are cold, the owner will loosen a spot of soil near his house with a long pointed pole called a "digging stick," scoop out a hole with his bushknife and bury the stones so people will not carry them away. They are precious because the owner has made many trips through the jungle to gather them near the volcanic mountain, Mt. Lamington, and has carried them back to his village, a two day journey each way.

Our neighbor George prepared a mumu for relatives to celebrate the second birthday of his first born, a daughter. He killed a pig for the feast. The Barai method of killing a pig is to club it to death which often takes as long as a half hour. During this time the poor animal squeals and moans. Many times Bill offered to kill a pig instantly by cutting its jugular vein thereby sparing the creature an agonizing death. But the Barai are adamant in using their method handed down from generation to generation. After the pig is dead they cut up the carcass into large pieces, not bothering to remove the hair and outside skin, nor do they bleed the animal. Then the bloody, raw meat is placed with the vegetables to cook over the hot stones.

At this particular feast the food cooked about three hours. After the food was cold and it was ready to serve, George discovered the meat was still very rare, so the guests ate only the vegetables. The pig meat was placed outside the house on a coffee drying table and covered with a cloth. The next day the hot tropical sun beat down on the partially cooked meat. Later in the afternoon George made another mumu fire and finished cooking the meat for the guests who had remained in the village. We expected many would become ill from food poisoning, but not one person complained of indigestion.

Knocks on our door sometimes was the prelude to a common question, "Can you help me?" Usually the inquiry could have been better stated as, "Will you give me?" Generally we did. James Pangare frequently came to ask for kerosene. He knew we always bought twenty liters each trip we made to town. There the cost per liter was from 48 to 52 toeas, while in the village we paid 1.10 to 1.30 kina for the same. At times both trade stores were out of kerosene, and since our old refrigerator burned over a liter a day, we tried to keep an ample reserve supply. One day he came to ask for kerosene. We knew that he had returned from a trip to town the previous day. "Why didn't you buy some while you were in Popondetta? We have very little on hand." We refused to share with him. The next evening his little son, who was such a cute boy, knocked at the door and handed us a piece of paper. It read:

> A friendly day to you and your wife from James Pangare. Bill nothing much to inform you but only one thing. I would like you to help me with a bit of kerosene, Bill I will pay you for it if you ask. That is all I want to let you.
>
> Yours faithful
>
> James Pangare
> Neokananee Village

We had told him the day before that we were low. That day we had bought two liters from BNEA store, so we wrote a reply that Nahara was out, but BNEA trade store still had kerosene. Sorry, but we could not send him any tonight.

Sometimes in the evenings young men would stop to beg a torch (flashlight) so that they could see the path to walk to Neokananee. We had three, one for each of us to use and one for a spare. For a while we loaned them a torch, requesting that they return it in the morning. With luck they would return the torch in a week and each time the batteries were spent. After someone entered our kitchen while we were away from the house and stole the extra torch from the counter, we refused to loan a torch and explained the incident. The people often carry a lighted bamboo pole when they travel at night. The Barai are afraid of the evil spirits after dark!

There were frequent council meetings held in Itokama. It was a prestigious honor to be a member of the BNEA Council. Only men could serve, but the day of the meeting all the women and children and all other men filed to the meeting place and sat on the grass outside the BNEA community building to eavesdrop. Some brought along their small pigs, calling "muck, muck" to the pigs so they would stay close by. Often the women would build fires and prepare some food. Council meetings lasted all day. The Secretary took down the minutes. There were many speeches and heated arguments until finally the members reached a decision. After the meetings were dismissed, men filled our porch to relate to us all the major decisions that had been made, because the meetings were conducted in the Barai language. At first Bill and I were elated that changes would be forth coming; finally we came to realize that the resolutions made by the council would never become a reality. Perhaps the meetings could best be described as, "a council is a group of people who individually can do nothing, yet collectively can decide that nothing can be done." Also, "a council is a group of people who discuss minutes that take hours." -Anon.

James Noble, the eldest brother of William, was the Barai councilor or lawyer. Each time there was a small crime, a fight, someone killed another person's pig or any village problem, he would hold a meeting in his yard and arrive at some type of settlement. He also negotiated a suitable amount for "bride price" with the parents of the young girl and her future husband because all brides must be bought. Serious crimes, such as murder, were handled by the Afore District police.

Peter, a handsome, educated man from Itokama, married Susan from Neokananee. About six months later we noticed a huge gathering on the councilor's lawn. The meeting was to decide how to punish Peter for severely beating his young wife. Councilor James ruled that she must return to the house of her parents for six weeks and Peter must pay a fine to her papa.

Gordon, got a girl pregnant. Sex before marriage is strictly forbidden. He was from Neokananee and she, from Kuai village. All the people from the two villages and crowds of curious people were present to hear councilor's decision. Of course they must marry and a penalty must be paid to her parents besides the normal bride price payment. What excitement and entertainment! Tongues were wagging for weeks.

Simon invited us to his house for an evening meal. We sat on the pandanus mat floor. The room was lighted by a lantern. Theresa spread a luncheon cloth on the floor in front of us and filled it with food from her small, smoky kitchen. There were bowls of rice, boiled yams, kaukau, pumpkin, greens (leaves picked from the tulip tree) cooked with coconut milk, a small bowl of tin fish and a small bowl of cassowary meat. There was a granite plate and a fork for each person because Simon was able to provide well for his family; he had several coffee gardens and a salary as the administrator of BNEA. Bill had baked fresh bread to take to them. This was served as a desert with coffee. The Nationals put two to three teaspoons of sugar, a heaping teaspoon of dried milk and a slight half teaspoon of instant coffee into a cup and fill it with hot water. It took several months to learn that the people served us coffee. At first we thought we were drinking weak tea. Theresa's food was always very tasty and well prepared compared to most of the Barai women. We were especially grateful to be able to taste cassowary for the first time.

The cassowary is a large, flightless bird, about half the size of an ostrich. The eggs and meat are considered a delicacy by the Nationals. The meat is very dark and stringy, but edible. The men go deep into the jungle to hunt the birds, who are extremely vicious and may attach humans when stalked. One man from Sirafe #1 village was wounded by a cassowary when he was a boy and, without medical aid, he was left a cripple. For many years he dragged himself over the ground. Now he uses two crude crutches made from tree branches with a Y at the top to hold his armpits. Both legs are useless but his torso is muscular. He can travel several kilometers on his crutches and he can also propel his body along the ground and cut as much grass with his grass knife as any other National.

CHAPTER 8

"What shadows we are, and what shadows we pursue!"
- Burke

The Barai people have been exposed to and taught christianity by the Anglican churches at Itokama and Tama villages and by the Seven Day Adventist in the village of Anatua. The churches were nearly filled for each service, but separately the people retained their former pagan beliefs. Reverently they obeyed the instructions of the church. Privately they preserved their traditions and culture.

This tribe believes that when a person dies the spirit becomes a "barome," which bears the form or likeness of a human. Baromes live in certain tall trees in the forests. If a barome, appearing in human form, is speared and killed, that spirit will immediately take the form of a dead pig or dog or a cassowary bird. Baromes are impossible to destroy, for they continue forever. Usually baromes are helpful to the living and playful, but if they are provoked, they can become harmful. They have the ability to direct a spear to make a perfect hit. They can guide a relative to the spot to find wild pigs, wallabies, cuscus, cassowaries or any wild game. They can also cause the gardens of a relative to excel and they can protect gardens from intruders and any harm. They are especially protective of yam gardens. Sometimes they may tease their relatives by making noises such as whistling, breaking sticks and pulling vines. Now if they are angered by a human, they can enter gardens and devour the food, but such revenge is a rare occurrence. They like to lounge in small quiet pools, and are quite upset when the pool is disturbed by humans. For this intrusion their revenge is to cause that person to become ill. The living relatives appease the baromes with offerings of food and the Barai avoid quiet pools and do not enter other gardens without the consent of the owner.

One day we were walking with Simon Savieko from Tama village to Itokama, a distance of about fifteen kilometers. We spied a huge clump of bamboo, an unusually strong, thick variety. Bill said, "Let's cut a couple lengths to take back to Itokama. I can make ash trays or bowls."

"No No!," shouted Simon, "My grandfather lives in that bamboo." Often people would point to certain trees as we walked through the jungle and tell us that a relative lived there.

Some baromes excel in wisdom and become a "kine" spirit. It is the kine that aids, instructs and converses with the shaman by talking in whistles. He advises the shaman on the cause or source of the his patient's illness and which treatment to use to cure. It is the common belief that most illnesses are caused by magic spells or sorcery, and so the kine advises the shaman how to overcome the spell.

Eventually a barome may become an "ubaibogi," which is an ancient ancestor. This spirit occurs only from males. They, too, assume the forms of humans; however, they are extremely large and are so quick and agile that they can never be killed. Ubaibogi spirits are very troublesome. They instigate sorcery and often attack humans as they walk through the forest by distorting their eyesight or hearing and they are able to capture their spirits. If a person feels threatened by an ubaibogi, he must plead with a shaman to contact a kine to persuade the ubaibogi to leave the person alone. That is the only way to placate that type of spirit.

When a Barai dies, the relatives are quite protective of his body and possessions. Should a nail clipping, a lock of hair, a feces, a piece of clothing, a cigarette butt or a wad of discarded chewed sugar cane pulp of the deceased be taken by someone with evil intent, sorcery could be made against the dead person or the family because these items would carry the expired person's "udi" (body odor). Such protectiveness of a dead Barai's possessions we learned through our personal experience.

Bill had been working with a young man named Simieon from Neokananee, teaching him carpentry. He was a moody person; some days he scarcely talked or tried to learn. One Sunday he came to our house and begged me to "snep mi," meaning to take his photo, and I did. Tuesday morning we learned he had committed suicide by drinking tea made from the poisonous root of the derris vine growing in the jungle. His family said that a curse had been placed on him by a member of the Musa tribe. Several weeks later we walked to Neokana-nee to give his parents a copy of his photo from the developed roll of film. His older brother came outside the hut to see what we wanted. He told us his mother was too sad to take the picture at this time. We should wait a few weeks longer. Then he followed us out of the village and whispered to us to please never allow anyone to look at the photo or to touch it. At the time neither of us knew about these strange beliefs. When we realized, we never mentioned the photo again to the family.

For at least two months after Simieon's death no Barai walked to Neokananee and beyond without carrying an ax or spear perchance they met a Musa on the trail. Bellfaith, the wife of John Lucas the fifth grade teacher, told me some hair-raising stories about the Musa people, how some Musa men met some members of another tribe on a jungle trail. Two of the Musa men attacked and killed two of the other tribe, yet the rest of the Musa men acted peaceable. Another time a Musa came into a Barai village and kidnapped a woman. "Never have any contact or dealings with a Musa. Some of them are good, but many of them evil. They have bad tempers and love to provoke fights!" She never called it sorcery.

My first experience with a Musa came one day when a stranger, who had very different features from the Barai tribe, walked into our house and asked to see Bill. I was terrified because I knew he was a Musa. I ushered him to the porch to wait while I fetched Bill. He had come to ask for help in bookkeeping. He had talked to William Suremo about starting a trade store. William told him to first ask Margel to teach him some bookkeeping. No National man would ever approach a woman to ask for help, so this Musa had come to ask Bill to have his wife assist him . Actually Walter was above the average intelligence, a handsome young man. Later I tried to teach him and his cousin brother, Sampson, how to figure costs of trade store merchandise and how to arrive at a selling price. Walter often came to our house but, after the first visit, he knew he must knock before entering our home. He must not walk inside unannounced. After this pleasant experience with this Musa, I often wondered why I had been so impressionable to believe Bellfaith's tales of the terrible Musa people. It was the only time I ever felt afraid in Itokama.

Another spirit is the "asi" which has no ancestral connections. This spirit is impossible to see or to detect except by certain specialists known as " asi giama". The asi appears either in the form of a man or as a flying fox, also known as a fruit bat. It is said to have extraordinary ability to hear what is happening in a village and it is usually the instigator of evil acts. An asi can inflict pain by injecting tiny spears into the body while a person is asleep, which may cause the flesh to rot. The only way to make peace with an asi is to provide an offering of fruits, especially bananas, either in the garden of the person or hung from his house. We often saw such offerings hanging on village huts, dehydrating and finally rotting in the sun. The asi consumes only the moisture of the offering!

Tropical ulcers are very prevalent in this tropical country. Whenever we nicked our skin, we immediately applied an antibiotic salve and covered it with a bandaid; otherwise the wound would become infected and develop into an ulcer within two or three days. The Barai contributed this malady to the asi spirit!

The "furufuru" spirits have small human-like bodies and tiny, tiny feet and they wear the feathers from a particular bird in their hair. Rarely are they seen, and even then, they will quickly climb a tree and disappear in a cloud Another spirit group, the "kava", have human bodies and very long legs and huge ears. They carry spears and they live in the clefts of rocks in the high mountain area. They are able to make people do inexplicable acts. Only certain people who have a special desire are able to contact a kava.

The many spirits, their magic, and sorcery have dominating influences on the Barai culture. The people hold the spirits responsible for their illnesses, their misfortunes and their suicides. The "bigman" (headman or village leader) of the village of Serapuna was stabbed and mutilated by an assailant. The wounded man returned to his village and killed himself. We were shocked. The people told us that sorcery had been put on their village leader so that he had no control of his life and must die. It so happened that a provincial official, Owen Nganambu, came to our house to visit and asked to stay the night. Knowing he was a fairly educated National, we told him of this tragedy. With raised brows and animated eyes, he solemnly told us that he possessed special powers. He could see and talk with the spirits and could perceive many bad things that would happen. He rambled on giving us many accounts of acts of sorcery. "Are you afraid of the spirits?"

"Oh, no", he replied, "for I am one of the chosen people!"

Several months later Stephen Tago, the Minister of Defence for the national government, came to stay with us while he was campaigning for re-election in the immediate area. Again we related the same account of the suicides of the Serapuna man and Simieon. He, too, confirmed that an evil spell had been placed on these two unfortunate men and so they must obey and end their lives. They no longer had control of their destiny. We were appalled! Surely the Minister of Defense had to have a higher degree of intelligence to hold such a prominent office in the national government. But we were working and living among these people on invitation. We dare not argue the issue or try to change their traditions. Thousands of years of these strange beliefs could not be changed by two Americans, nor did we try.

Another dominating influence in the lives of the Barai people is the "yam cult." The Barai tribe was named after the baro yam, a smaller yam nine to eighteen inches long and with lavender meat. Most other yams are white inside like a potato and some grow to enormous lengths of up to and exceeding thirty-six inches. Some varieties look like a hand with fingers at the bottom end and tapered at the top to resemble an arm. Actually we preferred the taste of the baro yam. Yams are peeled, cut into chunks and cooked in lengths of fresh green bamboo sections which are still full of moisture. The bamboo is laid on hot coals to steam the yam. Sometimes they cut up the yams and cook them in a cooking pot like potatoes. Other times they are cook them between layers of banana leaves in mumu fashion.

The ritual of planting, harvesting and celebrating the good harvest is known as the "yam cult." The Barai tribe considers the yam a source of wealth. It must be planted in a special yam garden with exact rituals. The harvested yams are stored in a yam house, some to be used for food and some saved for seed. By planting time, which occurs in October and November during the dry season, the remaining yams begin to sprout much like potatoes. In September the men of the family clear and prepare the new garden site, often times building a bamboo fence around the perimeter of the garden. They loosen the soil with digging sticks which are long poles sharpened at one end. It is their only garden tool.

Only Barai men plant yams. To prepare the yams for planting the men core out the center of each yam with a bone from the leg of a cassowary bird, sharpened along each side to resemble a dagger. The extracted pulp is cooked or steamed in lengths of bamboo by the women while the men are planting the remaining part of the yams. After the planting is finished, all of the pulp must be eaten by the family, thus pleading for a good crop. There are several other rituals which can be used to assure proper magic to provide a good yam crop. Sometimes a combination of rituals are used. Often, when available, men place some remains, such as a tooth, a bone fragment, a bit of hair or a fingernail of a recently deceased relative inside the hole of one or two hollowed yams.

Another ritual is to make a path down the center of the garden by placing sticks along each side to mark the pathway. At one end a sapling is used to make a small arch by sticking both ends into the ground. Then at one side of the arch, four sticks are placed upright and a yam is planted at the base of each stick. They must plant two varieties. Next an old yam is laid on the ground in front of the planting. Later when the vines begin to dry and harvesting is near, six more arches are made along the path.

Another source of magic is to bury near a yam a long narrow stone found by an ancestor and passed down from generation to generation. More often a "killing stone "is buried by one yam. Killing stones are in various shapes and were originally used by ancestors to hit their enemy in the temple, rendering them unconscious so that the victim could easily be killed and later cooked and eaten. Some killing stones are carved from a bluish grey stone in the shape of a flat disk. Others are carved from a black rock in the form of a ball, which is the size of a baseball; a few are carved from a softer white stone with hobnails carved at equal distance over the entire ball shaped surface. All killing stones have a hole drilled through the center so that a strong stick can be driven through the stone to make a club weapon. These killing stones are reverently regarded as departed ancestors. Once the yam crop is harvested, the stones are carried back to the village and hold a place of honor in the house of the eldest male family member.

An additional ritual for a successful harvest is to plead to the barome spirit of the recent dead. The family makes a platform or table in the yam garden and places offerings of food such as betal nuts, bananas, sugar cane, yams, certain types of leaves, and small animals such as rats, cuscus or a type of possum. Then one family member calls out to a recently dead relative complaining that the garden is not growing well and so he has provided the offering feast so that the departed relative will cause the garden to prosper.

The Barai also believe in magic to make a successful hunt, calling on a barome to guide their spears. And there are men who can make magic and have the expertise to prepare traps to catch game. They are called "trap specialists".

There are "rainmen" who can control the rainfall by magic rituals. To make rain he chops up a worm and a lizard and places them in a small piece of bamboo tied with a vine. He hangs it in a tree by a small pool of water near a stream of water. Later the bamboo parcel is thrown into the water. Shortly it will thunder, which will call the rain clouds from nearby mountains. He has previously instructed his wife to collect a large amount of food and place it inside the house. Also he has told his friends and the village that he is ill and so will be staying in his house. The rain begins and will continue as long as he remains inside. Once he comes out of his hut the rain will stop.

Many Bari people told us that Christopher from Neokananee was a rain specialist. Once there was to be social dance with food, taped and live music provided by the youth bands. All the Barai villages would attend. For some reason Christopher opposed the event and was very angry about it. The evening of the dance there was a heavy rain and so the dance, which was held outdoors, was spoiled. The Barai people blamed Christopher for summoning the downpour.

Sorcery is the negative magic which is the treacherous type of magic, quite opposite from the positive magic of the yam cult rituals, the rainmakers and trap specialists. Sorcery is instigated by the ubaibogi and asi spirits, so the people believe. Sorcery can also be made by man. When a Barai feels he has been wronged by another person, he may seek revenge with an act of sorcery. He must obtain an object used by the person anything which will have his or her "udi" (body odor). The object is put into a small piece of bamboo or hollow bone by using two sticks to pick it up. His hand dare not touch it, otherwise, his udi would also be on the article. Two such containers must be made and each sealed with honey, wrapped in a vine and again covered with honey. One is retained by the sorcerer, who must carry it under his armpit or in his bilum. The second container is placed under the bark of the black palm tree or buried in red soil.

Family structure and practices are the stimulating, dominant force of village life. The family duty comes first. Gardens are the second most important task and after that, whatever is desired. It is the duty of the grown children to care for the aging parents and even grandparents, uncles and aunts. In this culture, age demands respect and care. When the Barai speak of their father or mother, they may actually be referring to the uncle or aunt because family relationship is very unusual. For example: all the brothers of the actual father of a child are also called father and are regarded as father two, father three, etc. In like manner, all the sisters of the actual mother are mother two, mother three, mother four, and so on. Also, the children refer to the offsprings of father two, etc., and mother two, etc., as their brothers or sisters. At first we found it very difficult and extremely confusing to learn just who belonged to whom. Finally we began asking, "Is he your blood brother or is he your cousin brother?"

In-laws are also treated with great reverence. The wife of the son dare not ever walk directly in front of her mother-in-law. She must pass behind her. It is taboo to ever speak aloud the name of an in-law relative. Another rule is that young unmarried couples and husbands and wives are not to show affection in public. To honor this taboo we had been warned during our Peace Corps training period that we Volunteers must never display affection such as holding hands, hugging or kissing, in the presence of Nationals.

Marriages in the past, and for most part today, are pre-arranged by the parents of the bride and groom. However, young men who have had some education are beginning to rebel against this ancient custom and insist on choosing a wife, but it becomes a long, testy, bitter process to convince and eventually gain parental approval. In either method of choosing a wife, courtship is conducted under rigid rules. If a young girl is attracted to a young man, she may publicly present him with an offering of food. Flirtation still is taboo. Later he may pre-arrange to visit her at night. The ritual is that he will scratch on the bamboo siding near where she sleeps in her parents' house. If she wishes his advances, she will give the same signal to him and then he may enter and spend the night with her, petting and whispering. Sex is forbidden until marriage. All the time her parents will pretend to be asleep. Or the young girl may take her blanket and join the young man outside to spend the night elsewhere. If the father does not approve of the young man, he will start a loud verbal protest; the young man will leave and never again approach that girl. We often had young couples spending the night on our porch or under our house. Sometimes the giggling became so loud that we couldn't sleep, so we would call to them to be quiet or please leave.

Once a bride is chosen, the young man must clear and plant a yam garden, which signifies that he will be able to support a wife and, when the yam harvest time is near, he takes the girl to his garden house and consummates the marriage. A very few couples told us that they had also a Christian marriage ceremony in the village church, but no church weddings occurred during our two years with the Barai.

With the advise of the village councilor, the amount of bride price is negotiated by the parents of the bride and groom. Usually it is based on the ability of the bride, especially in towns and cities where the bride may have secretarial, nursing or teaching skills. There bride price might be as high as 10,000 to 14,000 or more kina. The Barai rate is usually 200 to 600 paid in kina, pigs, yams, mats, etc. Often it is not paid until after the birth of the first baby so that the husband knows his wife can produce heirs. If she cannot have children, he may send her back to her parents and demand the bride price be returned to him, if he has already paid her parents. The groom gets donations from extended family and friends to pay the fee. Later he will be asked by other family members to reciprocate for another man's bride price.

The day finally arrives when the young husband will pay his bride price. In the morning the young bride will present her in-laws with gifts of food, pandanus mats, towels, clothing and the betal nuts. Next is the mumu feast and often the marriage is finalized with the payment for the bride.

Childbirth is endured alone. When the woman knows her time is near, she travels into the jungle, close to a stream of water where she can wash the baby and herself before returning to the village with her newborn. She will nurse the child for two to three years. During this time, sex is considered taboo until the weaning. Sister Dorcus at the Itokama Medical Clinic gave many classes on childbirth and birth control to the women of the Barai villages. She encouraged them to come to the clinic to give birth; however, only a very few of the young women delivered there. The majority continued to seek the privacy of the jungle. She also tried to instruct them in oral birth control. Later she told me that they would forget to take the pill for a few days, so then they would take a lot of pills at one time to make up for the days missed. When they became pregnant again they were angry with her.

It is taboo for a woman or girl during their menstrual period to serve food to unmarried men or boys because the males could get a very sore throat and a severe cough; however, they can cure themselves by eating a piece of her fingernail. During this period, the members of her clan dare not work in their gardens because the plants might die. Another taboo is that there can be no pounding, planting seeds, digging and filling holes if a clan member is ill because this could trap the "udi" of the sick person and death would result.

The Barai belief is that death means that the "vaiai" or physical body will rot and the "udi" (body odor) will soon disappear, while the "kavane" or the spirit will join other departed ancestors to become a barome. When there is a death, burial must be within forty-eight hours or the body will begin to smell. Our first experience of their burial rites occurred about three months after our arrival in Itokama.

Christopher from the village of Kuai (not to be confused with the rain specialist in Neokananee) committed suicide because the mother of the girl he wished to take as a wife forbid him to have any association with her daughter. He was shamed, a situation that the Barai people can not overcome, so he drank a tea made from the poisonous derris vine and died near the house of his uncle, Martin from Sirafe #1 village. He was a school teacher and a handsome young man who had come to our house several times to visit. When we heard of his death we walked to Sirafe#1 to pay our respects. We knew nothing about their death rituals.

Most bodies are wrapped in a pandanus mat and buried in a dug grave. Since Christopher was a more prominent Barai, the young men decided he must have a coffin. When we arrived at the village, Douglas asked Bill to help the young men build a coffin. Bill inquired, "Do you want a rectangular coffin or this type?" He drew a rectangle and a shape of a mummy coffin on the sandy ground . The latter was something quite unknown to them so they chose it. They had brought sawed boards and large nails and a handsaw from Itokama. Meanwhile Christopher, covered with a red and white checkered cloth, was lying underneath a house surrounded by mourners who were wailing and chanting. Two women sat at his head waving white cloths to keep away the flies and occasionally they used the material to wipe the oozing blood from his nostrils . As new mourners appeared and bowed before the deceased, the wailing increased in volume and tears, and the mucous from their noses ran freely.

Douglas took Bill's measuring tape and interrupted the mourners as he took the dimensions of the body. Bill used his knee to hold the boards as he sawed because he must build the coffin on the bare ground. Meanwhile he told me to go to our house in Itokama and bring his hammer and smaller nails. It was a twenty minute walk each way. When I returned I saw him working alone while all the young men and many people were grouped about him to watch "old whiteskin" build Christopher's final resting place. The burial was to be at about 6:00 P.M. When Bill saw he would run out of nails, I made another trip to Itokama. This time, when I returned, Douglas was measuring the height of the body, which was rapidly bloating, so that the coffin would be high enough to accommodate the ever growing corpse. The family had moved up the time of burial to 1:00 P.M. I had to make a third trip to Itokama for supplies, but this time a young boy accompanied me to return with the additional material and I stayed home. Bill related to me that as he pounded the last nail, family members lined the coffin with pandanus mats covered with new table cloths and sprinkled the cloths with a can of Johnson baby powder. Selected, honored, men carried the body to the casket where again the body was sprinkled with a can of Johnson baby powder and covered with more tablecloths. Then Bill was asked to nail the lid on the coffin, which was then carried near to Martin's house where Gordon had dug a six feet deep hole. The people threw flowers into the hole and also on top of the coffin. Father Daniel said a few words; then Gordon began shoveling the dirt. Christopher's burial was completed. The Barai conversation for many days was that no Barai had ever had such a fine coffin. Mr. Bill had honored the family!

Many months later, in my tiny office at the back of our house I was working on the monthly inventory figures for Nahara trade store . Suddenly I heard strange sounds like wailing. I walked outside to see what had happened. Alexison, our neighbor, who lived three houses from us had died. The mourners had arrived and the wailing and chanting had begun. This time I recorded the sounds on our tape recorder. The wife of Alexison could not bear to part with his body, so the wailing continued from sun rise to sun down for three days. At sun down village life continued as normal. On the morning of the fourth day George, our neighbor, and other neighbor men assembled to demand of the widow that he be buried immediately because the stench was terrible. He was wrapped in pandanus mats and carried by the men, who had rags tied over their noses, to his final resting place.

At the death of a landowner, land ownership is passed from father to the eldest son, or if there is no son, to the eldest daughter. Land tenure for garden sites is given by the father to all married children for use during their life time or granted to siblings by the inherit. Brides were often bought from other Barai villages, so it was not unusual to have gardens several hours walk from the village where the people resided. Land boundaries are marked by trees, rock and streams because Papua New Guinea has no recorded land boundary survey system. Barai landowners often showed Bill, as they were walking together through the jungle, a certain tree or rock that marked the corner of their property.

We felt honored that the Barai people divulged so many facets of their culture, which enabled us to better understand them. In fact they, too, seemed honored that the two' old whiteskins" were interested and that we never criticized or tried to change their beliefs. When the mission-aries arrived in Barai land, they had insisted that the Barai tribe must abandon their traditional dress and wear western clothing and that each Barai must take a Christian name. So the people obeyed and, as a result, there are many same names such as Simon, James, George, Martin and John; however the people did retain their Barai names which are only used when they are talking with their own people. When

Bill and I spoke to each other about Martin, we would also name his village. Bill would say, "Today Martin from Sirafe #1 village took me to his coffee garden."

The most fascinating part of their culture were the mystic beliefs of the Barai people which we learned during our first six months in Itokama. We never criticized or tried to change their pagan religion; if we had tried to force a new doctrine, they would have stopped talking about their traditions. When fate introduced an anthropologist to the Barai people, we told her about these beliefs.

We decided not to go the airstrip on this Thursday morning to watch the Talair plane arrive because a mailbag had come on the Tuesday morning flight, besides it was raining. Shortly after we heard the plane take off, Peter arrived at our house and told us three "white-skins," a man, woman and a small child, had arrived on the plane. "We don't know what to do with them," he said. "They were told that they would find a "whiteskin" couple here at Itokama."

We walked to the airstrip. Their baggage was piled under the big poinciana tree next to the old Nahara building; the new arrivals standing beside it looked quite forlorn. Bridget Fontaine, the anthropologist, her husband Paul Fontaine and six-year-old Loa would be living in Itokama, uninvited, for the next twenty months. She would be working with the Barai, learning their culture so that she could write the thesis for her doctorate in anthropology at a Quebec University. They were French Canadians. We invited them to our house for coffee while the village leaders decided where the new arrivals could live. Finally the Headmaster of the school at Itokama agreed to allow them to live for a while in the new house built for a teacher.

Once they were settled in their new home, they complained that the house had no furniture so Bill made them two straight chairs and we loaned them a small native built table from our house. We tried to make them welcome. Loa was a brat and had temper tantrums each time her parents and she came to our house. Bridget was a very pretty brunette woman with a very sexy body. It was obvious from the very first that she enjoyed flaunting her body for all to see. Paul was always in the background in an unimposing, quiet role. On our next trip to Popondetta we asked them if they needed any provisions. They ordered food items and a kerosene pressure lantern, which we practically hand held all the trip back to the village lest it get broken. Paul promptly gave it to Loa to carry, for she demanded it. She fell off the poles going across to the airstrip and cracked the globe. They brought the broken globe to our house to ask if we had a spare. We did not have one, so Bill told Paul that he, Bill, could adhere the broken segments with a special heat resistant glue. Paul kneeled down as Bill prepared to glue the damaged globe; Paul put his knee on the globe. Now there were maybe twenty small pieces. Patiently Bill glued the pieces, one by one, until the globe was intact again. It would suffice until Paul could fly to Popondetta and buy a new replacement.

Always the Fontaines had a problem. "Can you help us?" One time Paul came to ask if Bill could repair their small two burner kerosene cooking stove. With one look Bill could see the problem. The stove was far from setting level, so the oil could not flow up hill to the farthest burner. "Just set the stove level, Paul, and it will work," Bill told him.

Bridget made friends with Councilor James. Soon James built a tiny house adjacent to his home for the new arrivals. When they moved they gave their two straight chairs to the village people, because they had decided they must live exactly like the Barai so that they could gain their confidence. Loa often spent the night with Barai children. Soon she had head lice. "What is this in Loa's hair?" Bridget asked us.

"It's head lice," I replied.

"What can we do to get rid of them?" Bridget inquired.

"Didn't you bring along medicated shampoo? If you allow her to sleep with the Barai children, she is sure to get head lice and scabies and maybe bring home bed bugs".

"What is scabies?"

I gave her a packet of Pretty Hair, a shampoo for head lice, from our Peace Corps medical kit. Next they came to show us sores they had developed on their legs. "You have tropical ulcers. Each time you get a scratch, cut or insect bite you must apply an antibiotic and cover the wound with a bandaid. You're living in a tropical country." They had no medication, so we gave them one of our two tubes of antibiotic salve and a supply of bandaids. They had arrived totally unprepared for this kind of environment. We tried to be friendly and helpful.

Bridget hired a young man named Parmius to teach them the Barai language and act as an interrupter. She spent hours talking with the Barai people, recording the conversations, so that Parmius could later translate them into English . Their tiny house was always full of people. Sometimes Paul sat and listened, but often he wandered around the village visiting and chewing betal nut with the men. Bridget spent a lot of time with councilor James and his family. When Bridget flew to Popondetta on several occasions, Paul and Loa stayed in the village and Councilor James accompanied Bridget. We wondered how the Barai people would regard this relationship. Perhaps the people talked about it among themselves, but they never mentioned the subject to either of us. However, when we went to Popondetta, several store owners and their clerks told us that it was a breech of the Papua New Guinea culture for Bridget and councilor to travel together; they warned us that we must watch for serious trouble in Itokama!

Bridget begged councilor to allow her to accompany him on a trip into Musa country, so that she could interview the tribe. It was a two day walking journey each way. They were gone a week. Later she coaxed him to allow her to go with him on a hunting trip, which would require three or four days away from Itokama. The Barai women are never allowed to go with their husbands on a hunt, because it is taboo. Paul remained in the village looking after Loa. Councilor was spending more and more time alone with Bridget.

About five months after the Fontaines arrived, the councilor's wife, Hilda, took their two-year-old son, who was covered with infected scabies bites, to the medical clinic for treatment. She returned home quicker than usual and found Bridget and councilor James busily engaged in sexual intercourse in her house. Hilda punched councilor in his jaw and ordered Bridget out of her house. Hilda was a sister of Simon Savieko and councilor was the eldest brother of William Suremo. Simon came to our house to tell us about the happening. He told us that Hilda would probably have cut off Bridget's head had she been a National woman, which would have been a legal act, but she refrained because Bridget was a white woman foreigner. The Barai people were visibly upset; the incident was the main topic of village conversation. The next day Simon and William went to the house of Bridget and Paul and ordered them to leave on the next Talair flight on Thursday, the following day. They firmly refused to go. At the airstrip the next day Paul asked me if we had heard about Bridget and councilor. I said, "Yes, and it is an insult to every Barai woman and to me as a white woman. She is no longer welcome in our house. The best thing for you to do is to pack and take her back to Canada!"

"Oh, no," he replied, "The Barai people really enjoy this. It is excitement for them - entertainment! Bridget is a very talented anthropologist!"

"She may be. Did she have to learn for her studies what it was like to have sex with a Barai man? If you were a good husband, you'd take her home before she causes these people more pain!" Paul angrily walked away. The following day Simon and William forced the Fontaine family to leave Barai land and drove them, with their possessions, in the Nahara truck to the Lamington Hotel in Popondetta. Councilor James begged to go along with them, but Simon and William refused. James ran after the truck as it left Itokama. The villagers were jeering and laughing at their foolish councilor. Bridget told the hotel manager and his wife, our very close friends, that they had left Itokama because the men had molested Loa!

For several days, I was treated coolly by the Barai people. I understood their concern; they were suspicious that I might do the same act. After I sought Hilda and offered my apology and sympathy for the crime committed against her, the people treated me kindly again. However, councilor James had lost face with the Barai tribe; his words were no longer the law. Suddenly there was an increase in petty crimes. There were a number of serious fights between members of the soccer teams; several men beat their wives; councilor's neighbor, Nixon who was married, raped a young woman in Kokoro village. She was the younger sister of Victoria Jada who was a neighbor of Nixon. Village harmony had declined.

Soon a new airstrip opened in Musa territory, so the Fontaines went to live with the Musa tribe. Since Musa people frequently journeyed to Itokama, we heard from time to time bits of discontentment over these white-skins. Later Bridget and Paul told the Musa people that they were going to Port Moresby for a few days rest and would be glad to take Musa artifacts and crafts from the villages to sell to artifacts shops in the national capitol. When they returned, they gave no money to Musa people. Soon the Musa told Paul, Bridget and Loa to leave, so for the second time they were ordered out of a tribal area. They returned to Popondetta.

About two weeks later they got a ride with a provincial official who was driving to Itokama on business. The Fontaines had returned to Barai territory uninvited; they moved into the tiny house next to councilor James. People flocked to our porch, especially the women, to ask us why they had returned. We had no answers, but we did sympathize with the fears of the Barai people. Two days later Paul flew to Port Moresby to beg to get possession of their passports which had been held by the Papua New Guinea government when they arrived without a work permit or visa. As soon as Paul left, councilor James moved in with Bridget. A few nights later Hilda and William Suremeo's wife, Wende, broke down the bolted door of the Fontaine house and forced councilor to leave Bridget. The following morning the Talair plane arrived with Paul on board. As he was getting off the plane, a large procession of village people carrying Bridget's and Paul's luggage escorted Bridget and Loa to the plane. Councilor begged to accompany her. Bridget told him to stay with his family, because she didn't want him. He insisted that he was going with her and followed her to the plane. Simon and William restrained him until the plane took off. Councilor James was in a terrible rage. He returned to his house, beat Hilda and his children and threw his family out of their home. Then he threw out the few cooking pots, dishes and clothes and threatened to burn the house. Hilda's hand crank sewing machine lay in pieces outside the door. She and the children sought shelter with Simon and other family members. The village people were terribly upset and right-fully so. Bridget had shouted at Hilda that all white women had lovers. Again the women watched me, but I assured them that it was a lie, an excuse for her actions. They seemed to understand. I was their "old white-skin friend," My behavior and work over the many months we had lived among the Barai proved that the reason for my presence was to help the Barai people.

CHAPTER 9

*"The art of dancing stands at the source of all the arts
that express themselves first in the human person." -
Havelock Ellis*

The "Sing Sing" is the country's ceremonial dance; it is the symphony,
the ballet, the rock concert, the rodeo of Papua New Guinea. It is the
Nationals' unique musical art expressed in many styles of dancing and
chanting throughout the provinces of the country. The dance is
performed at all major celebrations such as wedding feasts, the second
birthday feasts for the first born child and religious celebrations. A Sing
Sing is the authentic observance, heart and spontaneous aspect of the
people. It represents their cultural oneness. In 1987 the Barai people
held a three day extravaganza called a Yam Festival in Itokama. It was
a thanksgiving celebration for the good yam crop, a part of the yam
cult. We were told by some of the villagers that this yam festival might
be the last celebration for the Barai, because the Christians frown on
this type of primitive yam ritual. How sad!

Preparations for the yam feast took over three weeks. First the women
and young girls must dig the yam crop and carry it to Itokama. Often
the gardens were several kilometers from the village so that the
females were able to carry only two loads of yams each day. They
carried the yams in huge bilums and the larger yams were carried on
their heads. While their women were delivering the yams, the men and
boys began erecting temporary sleeping shelters for the wantoks and
visitors who would come to Itokama during the festival days. The
shelters were made of native poles covered with palm fronds and
banana leaves. Many shelters were placed near to, or adjacent to, the
village houses and a large number of additional shelters were built at
the north end of the soccer field in front of the grade school. Suddenly
Itokama looked like a congested village.

Once the yams were harvested , the men started to paint the larger
yams with geometric designs using orange, yellow and white clay. Next

they tied these giant yams between two poles and stood the poles upright in front of their village huts. Other decorated yams were laid in rows, several yams high, to resemble corded wood in front of the villages houses. Still other yams were placed upright in tiers to form small pyramids. The display of yams signified that the husband was a good provider. Finally each family placed poles in front of their dwellings decorated with betal nuts, green coconuts for drinking water, cooking bananas and the sweet bananas for the enjoyment of their guests.

A man blowing on a conch shell signaled that the event was about to begin. The ceremony was opened by the three most prominent men from Neokananee who were dressed in their finest tribal attire. Their bodies were covered with tatoos. They wore painted tapa loincloths, strands of beads and shells draped about their bare torsos, arm bands of woven cane and bones such as pig tusks inserted through their perforated ear lobs and nose septums. Their ankles were adorned with bands of grass resembling tiny grass skirts. On their heads they wore a crown of red and yellow parrot feathers banded with cuscus fur. Each carried a eight foot spear made of black palm, the hunting weapon of the Barai men. They looked like three savage warriors. "Let the yam festival begin!" they proclaimed in the Barai language.

The first day was devoted to paying bride prices and to celebrate the second birthdays of first born children. A bride price ritual begins with the bride, dressed in a tapa cloth laplap and adored with beads and shells over her bare breasts, giving to her in-laws gifts of clothing, pandanus mats, foods and cooking pots. After a mumu feast the bridegroom may pay his bride price to her parents or he may wait until his first child is born. At the ceremony to celebrate the second birthday of the first born child the parents and child must dress in traditional tapa cloth, beads and shells. The relatives present the parents and child with gifts of food and clothing. Finally the child's hair must be shaved off by a grandfather or uncle to conclude the ritual. The parents of the child will provide a feast for the relatives.

The next morning a veil of smoke hung low over Itokama because each family had a cooking fire in front of their house to prepare breakfast for their guests. A typical Barai breakfast consists of roasted cooking bananas or roasted ear corn which is so mature that it can be shelled

The women carry yams from their gardens to Itokama

Itokama village decorated with yams

Three prominent men from Neokananee opened the Yam Festival.
L to R Jacob Pangere, Christopher (the rainmaker)
Alfonso (step-father of Wende)

Natius (wife of George) and daughter Dyzanna.
Celebrating the second birthday of firstborn.

Simon Savieko in traditional dress.

Gordon with kundu drum and Keapus dressed for Sing Sing

Sing Sing dancers from Neokananee preform at Yam Festival

by hand and eaten. Sometimes they make a type of scone from self-rising flour and water cooked in a skillet using canned beef drippings as oil.

The second day was for visiting with wantoks and friends from other villages who had come to Itokama for the festivities. Several of the visitor groups had arrived with gifts of pigs which had been carried from their village. The front feet of each pig had been tied together with a vine and the hind feet had been tied with a vine and then a pole was inserted under the tied feet and carried by two men to Itokama. This was the day to kill a pig and make a big mumu; it was also a day of feasting. At sundown the dancing began.

The traditional Sing Sing would continue from sundown to sunup. There were dancing groups from Neokananee, Kuai and Tama villages and a dancing group from Jaraie village belonging to the Musa tribe which was a two day walk over a rugged jungle trail. For two weeks before the celebrations those villages sending dancers practiced dancing each evening. The choreographer, who was the bigman or village leader, finally selected the best dancers to preform at the yam festival. It was a great honor to be chosen. The dancers, predominating men , and a few women danced to the rhythm of the" kunda" drum all night long. The rhythm was BOOM boom, BOOM boom, BOOM boom, BOOM boom. The men wore huge, colorful headdresses, eighteen to thirty inches tall, made from the feathers of exotic birds such as bird of paradise, cockatoo, parrot, hornbill and cassowary. Cuscus fur was used for the headbands. The women wore small headdresses of parrot feathers banded with tiny masa shells. All the dancers wore either tapa cloth laplaps, tapa loin-cloths or grass skirts. Their bare, oiled torsos were decorated with strands of beads made of Job's tears and other seeds from the jungle, necklaces of shells and pig tusks and green vines. Arm bands woven from cane and grasses held dried birds and grasses. One young man draped strands of blue christmas tinsel about his chest - a modern version of bilas. Some dancers wore bones or feathers in their ear lobs and nose. Most of the men carried a kundu drum which is a hollowed piece of wood about thirty-six to forty inches long shaped on the outside to resemble an hour glass with a handle carved in the smallest part. The drum head is either a lizard or cuscus skin. Some of the women carried a cluster of rattles made with a special nut or dried coconut husks and some women carried fronds of greenery.

The four dancing groups, each comprised of from twenty to fifty people formed in rows of four or five abreast, were spaced the length of the village. The men led the dancing group forward with the women following in the rear. After the dancers had traveled about the length of the group, the rows reversed and counter danced back to the starting place. This was repeated again and again. The men took hop-like steps in rhythm to the kundu drums, swaying from the waist which activated their beautiful feathered headdresses to move and flutter like birds. Small prancing steps were taken by the women as they held their bodies erectly. As all moved in rhythm the dancers chanted in a sing song during some dances and in other dances they yelled wildly and sang. The dances depicted a hunting trip or invoked the spirits or related a story of ancestors. Bonfires and lanterns illuminated the dancers. Watching their moving forms and the waving headdresses in the dim light produced a mesmerizing effect. The throng of spectators, swaying with the dancer's movements, clapped and cheered. One small group of eight men from Serapuna sat on the ground in a circle around a small fire and beat on short lengths of dry bamboo as they chanted. Bill and I spent the night walking through the village to watch each performing group, going to our house for coffee and then returning to watch the Sing Sing and talk with the spectators. Each time we took flash photos of the dancers the crowd cheered.

The all night pageantry taught us how attuned these people were to their ancestral teachings. How reluctant they were to adapt to a more civilized culture! Bill and I admired them for their oneness and their deep seated beliefs.

On the third day of the festival, teams of men and boys played marbles, competing for the honor of a championship in the men and boys divisions. The young people played "white" which is a form of tag and the women clustered in groups to visit and to prepared the evening mumus. At dark another all night Sing Sing began. We two old "white-skins" watched and mingled with the people during the three days of celebration and we thought how privileged we were to have witnessed this wonderful event. The Barai people observed us as well. They conveyed to us that they appreciated the fact that we accepted their life style and did not try to change them. We were one; the ancient world and the modern world living and working together in harmony.

Later we again were reminded how dedicated the Barai people were to their ancestral background. We were asked by the Headmaster to present the awards and diplomas at the first sixth grade class formal graduation exercise held at the Itokama school. The teachers erected a large sun shelter on the soccer field in front of the school. All the forty-one graduates were dressed in their tribal tapa clothes, head-dresses and bilas. As they walked from their class room to the graduation site, they were preceded by six girls dressed in grass skirts who danced and sang as they led the chanting sixth grade class to the shelter. Since this was an important event, their ancestral customs must be included. Parents and friends gathered around the outside of the shelter to watch the graduation program. These parents, who had no education, had sacrificed to keep their children in school because they must pay 1.50 kina each semester for each child. There was pride on their faces as they watched the graduation ceremony!

The Headmaster opened the program with greetings. Then he announced that Margel Craig would give the graduation address. This was the first time I had heard that I was to be the speaker! What could I say to these students? I began, "Education is the key to your future and the key to the future of Papua New Guinea. You and other educated young people will be the leaders of tomorrow. Some of you may become members of the Provincial Assemblies and of the National Parliament. It will be your generation who will instigate new ideas and development in your villages and your country. You must make progress happen...."

Phillip, the sixth grade teacher, announced the names of the students who were receiving an award for the best sixth grade gardener, the best attitude, the most congenial and highest grade. He handed each certificate to me to present to the recipient. The Headmaster called the name of each graduating student and handed the diploma to Bill to present to them. Many of the students often came to our porch to talk to us or to borrow a book. We were proud of their accomplishments.

All sixth grade students are required by the national government to take an examination prepared by the National Educational Department.

Grade 6 graduation ceremony

Only those students receiving a high grade can apply to be accepted at a high school. There were six graduates who qualified. Sadly there are not enough high schools to accommodate the numbers of applicants, so some students must settle for a vocational school instead. At the conclusion of the program the students attended a mumu prepared by the teachers. Bill and I were invited to a faculty reception at the Headmaster's house after the mumu. It climaxed a wonderful day!

There were a few observances where traditional dress was not used. One occasion was World Food Day. The provincial governments gave 100 kina in cash to each tribe in Papua New Guinea to be used for prize money. The theme was nutrition Each school student made a poster depicting type of good nutrition. The posters were to be judged by classes so that one student in each class would receive 5.00 kina for first place, 2.00 kina for second place and 1.00 kina for third. Each class had a garden and so each of the six classes made a display of their garden produce to compete for the best school garden. Adults also brought fruits and vegetables to compete for the title of the best Barai gardener and the women brought dishes of food to compete for the best traditional cook. There was a first, second and third award given for each contest. Three Provincial officials came from Popondetta to act as judges. Bill and I were also asked to be judges. Simon Savieko, who was in charge of the event would be the sixth judge.

I arrived early at the Mission Station where the competition was to be held to watch the gathering crowd. When all the displays were ready and the judging was to begin, Bill was no where in sight. Simon decided to start without him. I told Simon that I did not feel that I was qualified to judge the cooking because I did not know that much about their traditional methods. He understood but he insisted that I must make the pretense of judging. My vote would not be included; however, he and the other judges were curious which dishes I would select for first, second and third place. First we judged the school posters and garden vegetables. Next we judged the best adult garden displays. Now it was time to judge the dishes of cooked food. The first cook had prepared a dish of greens, kaukau and some seafood in a native clay pot. With my fingers I picked out a clam to taste. It really was delicious. "It is very good!" I told her. All the dishes were displayed on the ground and each cook sat behind her dish of food. The only way I knew to judge the food was to taste a bite of each one. I always made a favorable comment to the exhibitor, sometime asking them how the dish was prepared. The third dish was steamed papaya filled with greens, corn, green beans and coconut milk. It was so good. Margaret beamed when I complimented her and I meant every word. I noticed the other four judges were not sampling the food. A crowd of people followed us as we stopped at each entry. And suddenly I was looking down on a dish of steamed, three inch long grub worms. The thought raced through my mind that if I refused to taste this dish after sampling all the previous dishes this cook would be offended. Simon must have noticed my hesitation and so he picked up a worm, ate it and smacked his lips. "I want one too," and I picked up a grub and ate it. It wasn't bad tasting and so I simply smiled at the woman and said, "That is very tasty. I quite like it!" The cook nodded and laughed. Another unusual dish was native salt made from pulverized charred taro leaves. Most of the dishes were combinations of vegetables such as snake beans, shelled wing beans, corn, yams, kaukau, cooking bananas and coconut. There were twenty-two entries and I must confess I was relieved to taste the last dish. Then a young boy ran to tell us there was a late entry that had just arrived and was waiting for us under the lone tree. When we found her she handed me a four inch fish intact with eyes, gills, scales and entrails and said, "You eat!" I did; starting with the head I bit off chunks and swallowed as quickly as possible. The other four judges were never offered a fish. The judges awarded the dish of steamed papaya and vegetables first place, the native clay pot of greens, kaukau and seafood second place and third place went to a dish of tulip tree leaves cooked in coconut milk. I had chosen the same three entries except I reversed the first and second prize winners. Benson Garui, the Barai who was a member of the Oro Provincial Assembly, announced the winners and handed me the prize money to give to each one as they came forward to accept their award. First place cook received 10.00 kina, second 5.00 kina and third 2.00 kina.

Towards the end of the judging I had spied Bill in the crowd. As we walked through the village on our way home Bill said, "I watched you tasting all those dishes. You are going to get sick."

"And where were you when the judging began? Why were you late?" I inquired.

"I just had too much work to do," he replied with a sly grin and a twinkle in his eye.

There was only one type of celebration where the Barai ignored all ancestral teachings. It was called a "Social", which was a night of dancing to music similar to country western played by the boy house string bands and cassette tapes. It was a new innovation patronized by the younger people. They danced apart taking very basic disco type steps or they formed a straight line doing a walk similar to the Lamberth Walk. Sometimes they danced in pairs, but usually girls danced together and boys danced opposite one another. However, there were frequent shy glances at the opposite sex accompanied with giggles and blushes. The parents came to watch the young people, but they seldom joined the dancers. The Barai youth were slowly beginning to pull away from old traditions.

Frequently young boys would ask me, "How do they dance in America?" Sometimes they would turn on their tape player and I would dance for them. Immediately a crowd would form around me laughing and clapping. Papua New Guinea is slowly adapting more modern ways. Change is inevitable. Hopefully they will never abandon, never forget, their ancient culture of dress and the Sing Sings.

CHAPTER 10

"You will never find time for anything. If you want time, you make it." - Charles Buxton

Shortly after we arrived at Itokama to begin our work with BNEA, Simon showed Bill a drum oven in a roofed enclosure near the community building. The women in most rural villages in Papua New Guinea cook over an open fire because they have no stoves or ovens. The drum oven is not costly to build, and it provides a means for baking bread and scones. The oven is made from a fifty-five gallon steel drum which is laid on its side over a fire pit. It has a rack to hold the baking pans and a door at the one end of the drum. A second drum is split and then suspended about one and one-half inches above the first drum to hold in the heat. It has a chimney to carry away the smoke. The external drum is covered on the outside surface with rocks and mortar or with clay to hold in the heat. The BNEA drum oven was not properly insulated and therefore the interior did not get hot enough to bake the bread or scones. Bill volunteered to cover the outside drum with a coating of clay. Simon assigned several boys to carry clay from the Ajari river about two kilometers east from Itokama. Bill showed the boys how to mix the clay with water to make a thick putty substance and how to work the clay to remove all the tiny stones. Bill covered the exterior of the drum with a thick coating of wet clay. Once the clay covering was dry the oven was ready to use. He also made an enclosed firebox. When he built a fire under the oven to test the heat, the oven reached 400 degrees in eighteen minutes. Bill loves to bake breads; in fact he is an excellent cook. He taught Doreen and some women how to make scones and bread to sell in the BNEA trade store. They pounded the dough as they rolled it out to form it into scones with their dirty hands and fingernails because they seldom washed. Bill admonished them to treat the batter lightly and not to over work the dough. After a few weeks the women tired of this project, so the oven wasn't used. One of the problems was that no one would gather the firewood. Later some of the village women asked Simon if they could use the oven to bake bread and scones which the Barai consider a delicacy for their families. The council decided that they must pay 2.00 kina each time they baked. We thought the women should be allowed to use the oven without paying because they couldn't afford the 2.00 kina. We were correct because the oven was not used; the cost of one baking was too high for the women to pay.

In August of 1986 BNEA held a two day show to celebrate the fifth anniversary of the founding of the organization. Many Oro Provincial dignitaries were invited to attend the event. BNEA members set up booths to demonstrate and to display the works and achievements of its staff and members. These displays included Bible translation, Bible study in the Barai language, mimeographed literature, the sawmill project, the bakery which sold scones, traditional cooking and Barai artifacts. There were also stalls where visitors could test their skills at games. Bill had made and supervised the games of darts, pitch rings, spin a wheel and pitch balls.

One display stole the show, a solar cooker. Peace Corps constantly provides their Volunteers with lists of information available from the U.S.A. Bill wrote to the University of Arizona for literature on solar cooking. It was a fun project for him to do in his spare time because there was no need to improvise for cooking fuels since firewood was abundant in the Barai area. He made a 2 x 3 foot x 10 inch wooden box mounted on four legs. Inside the box was a second wall insulated with wadded toilet paper, which was the only available material; the interior wall was lined with aluminum foil to reflect the heat from the sun shining into the box onto the cooking pot which set in the center. The box was covered by glass; a lid covered with foil could be positioned at different angles to reflect the direct rays of the sun onto the cooking pot, which was painted black so that it would better absorb the heat. We actually used the solar cooker to boil our drinking water. It took two to three hours to boil water or to cook kaukau or other foods, depending on the brightness of the sun. The Barai were mystified. "Where is the fire?" they asked. The Provincial guests were totally fascinated with the concept. There was always a crowd around the cooker.

In the afternoons Sing Sing dancers from Tama, Vuisiriro, Umbuvaro, Serapuna and Neokananee performed to compete for the best dancing group, with awards given for first, second and third place. Boy house string bands also competed for similar awards. Often the guitars in the string bands are not properly tuned. Sometimes the performers replace broken strings with fish line or play with the remaining strings. The songs that they play are usually original tunes composed by members of the band. The young musicians dressed in traditional costumes and so the competition was at least colorful if it was not harmonious.

The ceremony was opened with a speech given by the Deputy Premier of Oro Province, Izikeli Hao'ufa, followed by supportive remarks by the Oro Deputy Secretary, Jacob Kairi. Other notables attending were the Executive Officer Joe Banda, Benson Keghana from the Division of Information and the man who was instrumental in initiating the BNEA project, Benson Toroi, the Non-Formal Education Officer for Oro Province. It was a successful celebration. Many of the Barai wore their traditional clothing. Itokama was engulfed with large crowds of people.

We both hoped that this event might inspire Simon, the Administrator and George, the second in command, plus enthuse the BNEA workers to apply themselves to do better work. Since our arrival in Itokama, we had observed the gradual decline of the BNEA members and council. Many of the workers blamed the slow down on poor leadership and the lack of operational money. We had talked seriously with Simon many times about the BNEA deficit and we had offered him suggestions for generating income into the BNEA fund. However this organization was accustomed to operating on grants; therefore, he could see no need to be self-supporting. When we would converse with him, he seemed enthused with our input, but he never implemented any changes in the operation. We had proposed that the sawmill could make a good profit. To do so it had to keep operating on a regular schedule. Simon blamed the saw mill shut down on the manager, but he told us, "It is against Barai culture to demand another Barai to do a task." The BNEA trade store was another opportunity to make a profit. Watching the way it was currently managed, I knew it was operating at a loss. Many times I had begged Simon to allow me to work with the store manager to make appropriate changes, but Simon ignored my repeated requests. There were times that we became very frustrated simply because we had come to Itokama at the request of Simon to work with the BNEA organization, and yet he had refused to listen to our ideas and to allow us to help them. In contrast, we found it was a pleasure working with the Nahara Coffee Growers. Their manager, William, listened to our suggestions and, for the most part, actually tried to follow our guidelines.

Simon had stopped at our house about two weeks before the BNEA show to talk to Bill about plans for the game booths. He was returning home from his garden. We noticed that he had an infected cut on the instep of his right foot. He said he had cut his foot on bamboo. I dressed the wound and told him to come the next day for a clean dressing. It was ten days before we saw him again. He had been staying in one of his garden houses. Now his foot was so badly swollen that it was painful for him to walk on it. He came to ask Bill to make him a crutch. Bill agreed, providing that Simon would go immediately to the medical station. Simon promised that he would go for treatment.

The next day the father-in-law of Simon brought him a gift of a very large pig to be killed for a mumu feast for the Provincial officials during the BNEA show. The pig was tethered on a long, strong vine fastened to a tree. William Suremo's house and yard was next to Simon's yard. Since all village pigs were allowed to roam at will throughout the village, William's pigs often wandered into Simon's yard. The pigs belonging to William kept fighting with Simon's pig. Enough was enough! Simon killed one of Williams's pigs who came to fight the tethered pig. Killing a pig without a good reason is a serious offence. Councilor James, Williams eldest brother, was the man to judge the crime. He did nothing. Instantly William and Simon became bitter enemies. To make matters worse, Simon's foot became terribly infected because he had failed to return daily to the medical clinic for treatment. Simon thought that the infection was due to sorcery made by William against him. All the Nahara employees boycotted the BNEA celebration.

By the time the second day of the celebration ended, Simon was very ill. Bill looked at his foot and told Simon, in no uncertain terms, that he, Bill, was going to the medical clinic to bring the doctor to lance the wound. Simon was feverish and too ill to protest or to take offense of this breach of culture, a demand. Doctor Luke was doctoring in another village, so Sister Dorcus came to lance the wound. She injected a pain blocker and immediately lanced the foot before the drug could deaden the wound. Simon fainted. It was nearly six weeks before he could walk again without the aid of his crutch. For a while his foot had to be kept elevated and so his wife, Theresa, tied a vine around his ankle and then tied the other end of the vine to a tree branch. Bill and I visited Simon each day to try to cheer him. He begged us to bring him cold water, "gigi doi", so each morning I brought him a bottle of ice water from our refrigerator. During his convalescence we learned that Simon had wished to marry Wende, William's wife. However, the parents of William and Wende negotiated that William would marry Wende. So this past bad feelings caused additional tension between Simon and William. Killing Simon's pig simply added fuel to the situation.

After Simon was able to resume his duties, he asked me to check the BNEA records to make a summary to apply for additional grant monies from the Oro Non-formal Education Association. He also needed a profit statement for the BNEA trade store. When I examined the BNEA books, they did not balance, and there were no records to substantiate the entries. Douglas was absent from the village when Simon gave me permission to checked the trade store books. I discovered that the store had lost 3,000 kina in 1985! Douglas was being held in the Popondetta jail for writing a check with insufficient fund to the Koy store to pay on the long overdue account. The Koys had tried for several weeks to collect the amount of the bogus check. Finally in desperation they had the police arrest Douglas when he came to Popondetta to purchase trade store goods from the Koys.

Douglas spent six days in jail. When he returned to Itokama, he had no shame because he had had a wonderful experience. He told the people that he had watched television, had good food with lots of meat, and he had an indoor toilet and shower! His trade store books showed loans to several Barai who were wantoks of Douglas. These debts would never be repaid under the Barai system. Simon was upset with my findings. He decided to appoint Georgie, who was the youngest brother of Douglas, as the new manager for the BNEA trade store. He asked me to work with the trade store and with Georgie to try to turn the trade store into making a profit. Georgie, who had been one of the brighter students in my bookkeeping class, worked very hard to manage the store. His records were detailed and correct. He opened the store each day and he tried to follow my instructions. Sometimes rats destroyed packages of biscuits and gnawed holes in bags of flour and sugar so Bill made a rodent proof cupboard using a framework of wood covered with window screen to store these items in. The next time I went to the store Georgie had the cupboard filled with tin cans of food. "The rats can't damage tin cans. You must store the sugar, flour and biscuits inside the cupboard," I told him. At the end of the first month the store had a profit of 6 kina. The second month the trade store profit was 28 kina and the end of the third month 60 kina. I was happy that finally the BNEA store was operating in the black. Then Peter Ewert returned to Itokama and promptly told Simon to close the trade store and BNEA bank. I was flabbergasted! "Why close the store when it is starting to make a small profit?" I asked Peter.

"Well," he replied, "These people will never succeed in a business because they aren't devout Christians."

"Church and business are two different topics. Being a good Christian doesn't guarantee that a retail store, a manufacturing company or any other type of business will be a successful venture. It is the management and workers and quality products and service that determine a profitable enterprise. You no doubt know a great deal about the Bible and religion, but you evidently have had little business training to make such a ridiculous statement!" I was absolutely furious. Peter still insisted that Simon close the store and bank and Simon did. Bill and I couldn't help BNEA if they refused to listen to our guidelines. Every department was failing because BNEA had no money to pay the wages for workers of the Bible translators, the printers and the adult literacy programs. This organization which had been established to enhance the lives of the Barai was failing.

The national government pays for the mowing and maintenance of all the sod airstrips in Papua New Guinea. BNEA was appointed to maintain and mow the Itokama runway. They received 1,200 kina a year to pay the workers, to buy the petrol and to buy parts to maintain the mowers. David was in charge of hiring workers and seeing that the airstrip was kept in good condition. At both ends and one side of the runway there was a hand dug ditch trench, five foot deep by five foot wide along the edge to prevent pigs from entering the field. But on the far side that bordered the school grounds, mission station and a strip of jungle there was no trench so sometimes wild pigs wandered out of the jungle onto the airstrip and routed holes in the ground. Often the people, especially the children, threw sticks and debris on the runway as they walked across the airstrip on their way to their distant gardens.

Bill was often summoned by David to come to the airstrip to start the twenty inch lawn mower. The workers had no feeling for compression, so they would take turns at choking the mower while they slowly pulled the starter rope which flooded the motor. Bill would dry the sparkplug and motor and then start it for them. There was a small bamboo shelter at the airstrip where the drum of petrol, the mower and the log book which listed the workers and their hours of labor for each mowing were kept. The average time for one mowing was one hundred-five man hours. Usually there was a crew of five men to mow with only one mower. Each worker was paid 35 toea per hour. They insisted on mowing the field in small sections such as one hundred feet by one hundred feet rather than mowing the full length of the runway. They were not always working; usually one man was mowing while four other men sat on the ground chewed betal nut and storied. The important aspect of their job was that they would each receive 35 toea for each hour that they spent at the mowing site. Working diligently is beyond Barai comprehension; that is their way of life! It was SIL who taught them that they must receive a wage of 35 toea which was considered a minimum wage rate for this rural area. Prior to this new concept of drawing pay, they had willing worked at village projects and expected no compensation because it was for the benefit of the Barai people. The daily lifestyle of the men is to work when, and if, they feel like it or want to work. It is the women that tend to the daily needs of their families. The duties of the men is to story, to tell the children of the myths of their culture which they will be expected to pass onto their children. It will take two to three generations before the Barai will understand the importance of work productivity and advancement. Living with these people it was easy for Bill and me to understand their primitive beliefs and we understood that once these mythological values were abandoned, the Barai people would suffer a loss of their heritage. Is progress worth the change?

In September of 1986 the National Aviation Inspector landed at the Itokama airstrip and immediately ordered all flights canceled to Itokama due to the tall grass. We often saw a plane flying low over the airstrip prior to landing to view the runway conditions such as holes made by routing pigs, debris on the runway and the length of the grass which would part, if it was very long, from the air force generated from the propeller. David had gone to plant his garden; The airstrip had not been mowed for over four weeks. The closed airstrip meant Bill and I were isolated. There would be no incoming or out going mail nor could we fly to Popondetta. We had no telephone or short wave radio. I kept repeating out loud, "Slowly, slowly not to worry," but it did not relieve our apprehensions. Suppose one of our family in the USA became seriously ill; Peace Corps would be unable to contact us. What if one of us became ill? We had no means of contacting Peace Corps to medivac us out of the village for treatment. Thankfully at this time Nahara still had use of the Mainland Holding's 4 wheel drive truck. That was our only means of escape in case we must leave Itokama because of an emergency. It was frightening!

Bill and I sent word by a young boy to David in his garden that the airstrip was closed, and we begged him to return and have the runway mowed. He refused. Two weeks passed. We pleaded with Simon to have David mow the airstrip, but again, he told us he could not demand a Barai. We asked Councilor James to talk to David. He refused, so we told him that we two would mow the airstrip because we were the ones who had most to gain by having the regular Talair service resumed. He forbid us to do it. Finally I visited him again and told him that we respected him very much as a leader and a friend; however, we were going to mow the airstrip whether he approved or not. We hoped he would not be angry with us. It was a strenuous task for two old people to push a 20 inch mower in the hot tropical sun. It took me twenty-two minutes to make a round of the airstrip; Bill could cover the same distance in nineteen minutes. He would mow a round while I rested on the ground. As he approached me I stood up and grabbed the handle of the mower and continued without slowing the mowing a moment. I've never felt quite so old before. Most of the people had left the village to plant their new gardens, but there were several boys who lived in the two boy houses still in the village. Once they saw us mowing at the airstrip, they hid in their boy houses until we returned to our house at the end of the day. They were ashamed to have old "whiteskins" doing this job, yet they chose to hid rather than help us. It took us seventeen and one- half hours of actual mowing time to cut the five and one-half acre airstrip. Headmaster Justin and a teacher, John Lucas, and his wife, Bellfaith, and Sister Dorcus helped us rake up the areas of heavy grass. Once the airstrip was mowed, we realized that we had no way of contacting the National Aviation Inspector to tell him that the Itokama airstrip was mowed and in good condition so that the Talair plane could resume the Tuesday and Thursday morning flight schedule.

The airstrip had been closed for five weeks; the grass would soon need to be mowed again. We had not received mail for over six weeks. And then Dr. Martin Lukes came to the house to tell us that he had received a message on the short wave radio from the Popondetta Hospital. A Peace Corps Volunteer who worked in the laboratory of the hospital had a message for us from the Peace Corps Director. He had sent us two letters to ask if he could bring the Washington, D.C Desk Officer in charge of all the Volunteers in Papua New Guniea to visit us. The Desk Officer wanted to visit Volunteers living in a remote primitive village. Finally, the Director had phoned the Talair office in Port Moresby and learned that the Itokama airstrip was closed. He wanted us to rent a vehicle and drive to the Popondetta Garui Airport on the following Tuesday to fetch them to Itokama. William Suremeo said that we could rent the Nahara truck for 80 kina a trip. Dr. Luke radioed the message to the Volunteer at the hospital who then telephoned the Peace Corps Director in Port Moresby.

Bill and I left the village at 4:00 A.M. Tuesday for the Garui Airport to pick up our guests. Our Director rode in the front seat with Bill, while the Desk Office and I rode in the rear of the truck. We two stood up most of the five hour drive so that we could fully enjoy the beautiful scenery. Both of the men were absolutely fascinated with the lush vegetation and the panoramic, one hundred mile journey. As we passed by the native villages we often stopped to shake hands and exchange greetings. About half way to Itokama Bill asked the Director if he would like to drive. He was eager to have the experience of driving on this narrow rough road. After we passed Tama village we stopped at a large yam garden located on the side of a hill across a deep ravine which belonged to Simon's family and called to Simon to come to the truck to meet our guests from Peace Corps. He promised he would return to Itokama the next day to talk with our Director and the Desk Officer. It was 4:00 P.M. when we reached Itokama.

Bill and I were so delighted to have these Peace Corp leaders visit us. The Desk Officer had brought us two pounds of frozen shrimp, and the

Director gave us a can of maple sugar from Vermont with the instructions that we must save these goodies to eat after they left us. Seafood! Maple syrup for our sourdough pancakes! Their thoughtfulness meant so much to us. We talked until nearly midnight before any of us thought about sleep. The next morning Bill took them on a walk to Neokananee and Kuai villages; then we showed them around Itokama and introduced them to the village people. Finally, we told them about our work with the Barai people, our frustrations with BNEA and our joy of working with Nahara Coffee Growers. When we told our Director that we had mowed the airstrip with a twenty inch mower, he complimented us for attempting to keep the airport open, but he said, "You two were not sent to Itokama to mow. You were sent here to transfer skills. I forbid you to mow the air field again."

"But we can't stay in Itokama if the airstrip remains closed." I replied. "We would be isolated with no way to communicate with the Peace Corps office, with no way to send and receive mail. What if one of our children became seriously ill or had a terrible accident or one of us needed medical treatment? Would either of you men want to be in a place with no means of contact with the outside world?" I asked.

"No I wouldn't. Don't worry. I'll talk with Simon today." the Director replied. But Simon never returned from his garden to Itokama to talk with the two Peace Corps officials. They were very disappointed and upset that Simon chose to ignore their visit. It was two weeks later before he returned to the village

They had to return to Port Moresby the next day. That evening the Director told us that he would transfer us from Itokama to work with another tribe if the airport did not remain open. He promised to notify the National Airport Inspector that the grass had been cut. He would also request that the Peace Corps office be notified if the airport was closed again. The next morning we drove them to Garui Airport for their flight to Port Moresby. We were so grateful for their visit and support!

Two weeks later a well dressed National knocked at our door. "I'm the new Assistant Peace Corps Director. I came at the request of the Peace Corps Director to talk with Simon. Is he in the village?"

"Yes, he returned yesterday. Please come inside." I replied. He was a delightful friendly man. Barton had arrived on the first resumed Talair flight to Itokama. The plane also had brought a mail bag. It was a wonderful day. The three of us spent the rest of the day and night talking about our work with the Barai. We showed him the village and took him to Simon's house to make an appointment for he and Simon to meet the next morning to talk at the BNEA building. This time Simon appeared on time. Later Barton told us that he had opened the conversation with, "I came to take Bill and Margel out of Itokama because you are not using their talents. You are not working with them."

"You can't take them. We need them here!" Simon replied.

"Then use them! And you must provide them with a short wave radio so that they can have contact with the Peace Corps office. You must keep the airstrip mowed and open for Talair. If you fail to do any of these things, we will take them elsewhere to people who will appreciate and work with them. These are the rules."

Simon said that he would have the BNEA short wave radio, which he kept locked at all times and was never used, moved to our house. He would keep the airstrip mowed and he would work with us. Later in the afternoon a strange truck drove into the village and Barton arranged to ride back to Popondetta with the driver. We wished he could have stayed longer. Such an intelligent National.

The Anglican church had been saving a portion of the meager weekly collections to put into a separate fund to build a new house for Father Daniel. The Anglican Diocese at Popondetta had also given a contribution towards the project. Their present bush house was beyond repair. Father wanted to use sawed timber for the framework of the new house. Bill drew the plans and figured the cost of the timber and roofing tins; then he insisted that Mother Grace must also approve the house plan because the woman is always ignored. Father thought it was not necessary but, because he didn't want to offend Bill, he agreed. There was enough money in the fund to buy the timber from BNEA sawmill and the roofing tins from the Price Rite Hardware store in Popondetta. Father Daniel asked the BNEA council to supply the workers to build the house. They flatly refused to work without pay to build a new parsonage. Members of the church also refused to work without pay. Every Sunday morning at the close of his sermon, Father Daniel admonished his congregation for refusing to help build a new house for his family. Finally the Neokananee, Itokama and Kuai villages agreed to collect and weave the bamboo siding providing Father would put up the framework, plank flooring and tin roof. Bill agreed to help Father. By himself Father collected the poles to hold the frame and flooring. Day after day Bill and Father worked on the new structure while a crowd of people sat on the ground watching. When it was time to add the siding the village women gathered and split the lengths of green bamboo; then the men wove the sides and put them into place. Later Bill made shelves in Father Daniel's new study to hold his books. At the close of the Easter service the congregation gathered around the new parsonage for the dedication ceremony. The people were so proud of this new home for their pastor!

CHAPTER 11

"Many receive advice, a few profit by it."
- Publilius Syrus

Once Nahara trade store moved into their new building, it became the principal store for all the Barai villages. Monthly profits gradually increased. It was the social gathering place, because the porch, which extended across the entire front of the building, was always filled with people. To enter the store one had to step over bodies. William returned one day, from a trip to Popondetta with a new Yamaha generator and freezer. Bill installed the new generator and taught William and Edwin how to operate it. Sometimes they forgot to refuel it with petrol. They had to learn to keep the deep freeze cold. The generator must run during the day from morning until about six o'clock in the evening so that the contents of the freezer would not defrost; but for the first couple of months they kept turning off the generator to save petrol until such time as the contents of the freezer completely thawed. Bill warned them again and again about food spoilage. Finally we gave them our only thermometer, with two marks on it, the high and the low, where the temperature must be maintained. Bill continued to check the temperature for many months. He taught William and Edwin when to, and how to, change the oil in the generator. This project was so new to their culture.

The freezer was stocked with whole chickens in various sizes, packages of chicken legs, thighs and breasts and sheep tongue and lamb flaps (belly flesh). Each day they cooled pepsi, orange pop which the people called "loiwara", and small cartons of strawberry and chocolate flavored long life milk in the top baskets of the freezer. The people would buy a bottle of pepsi or orange for 90 toea and pass it from family member to family member, each taking a small sip. Orange pop was their favorite. The store now stocked dried onions, a large variety of canned meats such as fish, curried chicken, goose and duck imported from China, luncheon pork and corn beef from Australia, a selection of hard biscuits (crackers), sweet biscuits (cookies), bed sheets, laplaps, shorts, knit tops, blouses, under garments, table cloths, nappies (their word for diapers), baby blankets, pillows, mirrors, writing paper, pens and pencils, envelopes, a variety of soaps, cooking pots, granite plates, cups and forks, spoons and knives. They also added used clothing shipped in bales from Australia and they stocked nails occasionally.

I'd worked only with the Nahara trade store, but never with the coffee division. At the close of the 1986 coffee season, which ran from April through August, I asked William if he would like for me to check the profits for the coffee sales. "Oh yes. I've wanted to ask you to help us with coffee, but you are so old. I don't want you to work so hard!" Again my grey hair was a problem.

"If I were home in the U.S.A., I'd be working eight to ten hours a day. I like to be busy.

Use me!" He gave me his records of coffee purchased from the farmers, the receipts of coffee delivered to the Mainland Holdings agent in Popondetta and the invoices paid by the Mainland Coffee Mills in Lae after the Nahara coffee reached Lae by sea freight. When I totaled the figures of kilos of coffee purchased and the total kilos delivered to the agent at Mainland Holdings in Popondetta, Nahara had a shrinkage of 660 kilos. I added the kilos shipped to Lae from their agent office in Popondetta and I found that Nahara had not been paid for 9,600 kilos! This season they had been paid on the average of 1.00 kina per kilo, which meant a loss of 9,600 kina less sea freight costs. Immediately I took the figures to William. He seemed unconcerned. A week later I talked to him again about the payment shortage and again he said nothing. Perhaps he feared that he would be blamed for the error by the Nahara Directors because the Barai people could not overcome or live with shame. I couldn't sleep at night for thinking about this mistake. Again, I went to talk with William. I presented my finding for the third time. "What does Mainland Coffee Mills at Lae charge you for the use of their truck each year?" He didn't know, except Nahara must pay for new tires and all repairs and sell all coffee to them. "Did you sign an agreement with them? Also do they charge you interest for the cash money they provide you to buy coffee from the local farmers?"

He answered, "No".

We had seen other evidence of expiates taking advantage of the Nationals. I was furious. "Please, William, let's fly to Popondetta and talk with Mr. Taboda, the Westpac Bank Manager. I know how to resolve this matter in my country, but I don't know the course to pursue in your country. Besides we can present last month's trade store profit statement to him. We'll ask him for a loan at the same time, so that Nahara will no longer be controlled by Mainland to sell all the coffee to them. You will then be free to sell to the highest market. WIlliam elected to drive the truck to Popondetta the following day so that we could bring back an order of merchandise for the store, thus accomplishing two tasks.

Mr. Taboda, a most intelligent National, received us graciously. He was pleased with the latest monthly profit statement for the trade store, which was 708 kina. I presented my findings and showed him the original invoices received from Lae; each one was covered with correction fluid. Nahara had a total net profit of only 680 kina for the current year's coffee season, but 9,600 kilo of coffee beans were not acknowledged received or paid for to date. I told him that I had noted on all invoices of previous years that they, too, were covered with correction fluid, which led me to believe that once the correct invoice figures were typed, someone decreed that these invoices must be changed so that all the money due would not have to be paid to Nahara. He agreed with my thoughts. I further told him that Bill and I came to this country to work in behalf of the Nationals, and we deplored expiates taking advantage of the people. He agreed and rose to shake my hand.

"In my country I would know what to do, but I need guidance from you, because you best know what must be done to correct this crime against Nahara Coffee Growers."

"I would advise you to write a letter to Mainland Coffee Mills in Lae. Ask them for a verification list of paid invoices. Don't tell them your findings of the missing kilos of unpaid beans. If they do not give you an account for the total shipment, hire a "solictator", their word for lawyer".

"What solicitor should we engage in Popondetta?" I inquired.

"None! They will exploit you. Hire our Westpac Bank's solicitor in Port Moresby. They will represent you fairly and tell them I referred you to them. Use Kila and Associates." He gave me their address.

I did all of the talking, for William, as usual was silent, speaking only when asked a direct question. He was such a quiet man. "Thinking toward the approaching coffee buying season, Nahara Coffee Growers are very short on cash, although the trade store has a sufficient bank account. If we force proceedings against Mainland Coffee Mills in Lae, they may decide to take the Nahara truck and refuse to extend cash for the coming coffee harvest. Nahara needs to borrow about 5,000 kina to use as cash to purchase coffee from the farmers. Is a loan possible?" I inquired.

"Let me take this request to the lending board," he replied. "Thank you for the monthly profit statements from the trade store and the financial statement for Nahara Coffee Growers, Ltd, Pty. Now the bank has some information on the financial conditions of this company. Bring me the next month's P & L statement from the trade store, and then we'll talk."

It is difficult to establish credit and secure bank loans in Papua New Guniea. Many Nationals do not take the responsibility of repayment seriously. Banks seldom finance vehicles because the country has no registration or system of recording titles. For example: If the bank tries to collect for back payment, or attempts to repossess the vehicle, the owner can give the truck or car to a wantok. This prevents the bank from forcing a settlement because the wantok has not signed the note and therefore owes no money to the bank.

While we were in Popondetta I called on Pennyfather, the Australian Mainland Holdings manager, to substantiate the total kilos of coffee delivered by Nahara to the Popondetta buying station for shipment. His figures of Nahara coffee delivered for shipment to Mainland Coffee Mills in Lae agreed with the Nahara's shipping slips.

When we returned to Itokama I immediately wrote to the Mainland Coffee Mills, a coffee processing firm for export, and advised them that I was a Peace Corps Volunteer working with Nahara Coffee Growers of Itokama, teaching them how to keep better records. "Please send me a list of paid invoices for the current year," I requested. Soon they replied with the summary, which included one additional invoice for 1,800 kilos of received coffee. The sum due on the invoice was totally off set by charges for sea freight. Still unaccounted were 7,800 kilo of Nahara coffee beans!

We would be traveling to Port Moresby in two weeks for the Peace Corps Mid-term Conference and to take physicals and we would have free time to talk with the Kila firm. William called a meeting of the six Nahara Directors to advise them of my findings and our conversation with the bank manager. The directors, Joseph of Itokama, Steven of Kuai, John Michael of Neokananee, Simieon of Kokoro, Serwin of Serapuna and Frank from Umbuvara village, voted for us to engage the Kila Associates to implement collection. It is very doubtful if any of the six actually understood the paperwork, time and cost involved to negotiate a settlement; however, any talk of the possibility of receiving additional monies delighted them.

Kila and Associates assigned us an impressive young lawyer, who was eager to represent Nahara Coffee Growers providing they would send a 500 kina retainer fee. He would attempt to negotiate the settlement with Mainland Coffee Mill by letters, thus avoiding the additional cost of travel to Lae. He made copies of all the invoices and delivery slips and he agreed that the corrections on each invoice looked suspicious. When we returned to Itokama, we told William that Nahara must send a check for 500 kina to start the proceedings for settlement. He immediately called a meeting of the directors. This time he asked that we be present to tell them first hand of our talk with Kila Associates. The directors debated for many hours. An expenditure of 500 kina seemed to them an enormous amount of money. We understood their concern, but we did tell them that no law firm - solicitor - would represent them without a retainer fee, a down payment. We also advised them that the settlement could take many months to resolve. Finally, they authorized William to send the retainer fee check signed by William and co-signed by Joseph who was chairman of the Nahara Directors.

About two months later, William drove the Nahara truck to Popondetta to pick up an order of trade store merchandise. Pennyfather, the Mainland Holdings manager, saw William and demanded the keys to the Nahara truck - NOW! His company was angry that Nahara had filed suit against them. William never protested, he simply handed Pennyfather the keys to the truck and returned without the store goods on the next Talair flight to Itokama. He was a defeated man when he arrived. Pennyfather had talked very harsh threatening William that he, Pennyfather, would see that no Popondetta bank would give Nahara a loan to buy coffee. When the village people learned that the truck had been taken from Nahara, the men and women began to cry. Only Nahara and Benson Garui, the Oro Provincial Assembly member living in Tama village, had vehicles. The sorrow continued for many weeks. Seeing their grief made me question if it had been wise for me to confront the problem of the missing coffee. Money had small value to the Barai people. They could feed their families on yams, kaukau, pumpkins and greens, supplemented on occasion with wild meat. They had their own unique priorities - family, gardens and time to story! I tried to cheer William by telling him this was challenge like "white-skins" face in their culture. He was so overcome with failure to his people! He felt it was the end of Nahara. How could they drive to the Barai villages to buy coffee? And they had no means of transporting it to Popondetta!

"William, we will show you a way! We will fly to Popondetta on the Tuesday morning flight, rent a truck from Oro Motors, return to Itokama with a load of store supplies that evening and drive to Popondetta with a load of coffee very early on Wednesday morning so that the coffee can be sold before closing time and then fly back to Itokama on the Thursday morning flight. You have told us that truck tires only last for 6,000 kilometers over the rugged road to Popondetta. This expenditure is costly to Nahara. Truck rental may not be anymore expensive than truck repairs and petrol." I added "Sometimes problems are opportunities in work clothes. Sometimes problems teach us to operate more efficiently. One day you may decide that this unfortunate happening has, in fact, sharpened your business ability and increased profits for Nahara Coffee Division." Bill and I were trying to increase William's confidence; at the same time we were learning about the many hours of labor involved in harvesting and marketing coffee.

First the ripened reddish coffee "cherries", mostly picked by women and children, must be run through a coffee pulper to remove the outside skin. A small stream of water must be poured with the cherries into the pulper, which means that often many buckets of water must be carried from a river; sometimes it is several kilometers away from the coffee garden. Next the coffee beans are put into two to three inch diameter by three foot sections of hollow lengths of bamboo, plugged with a banana leaf, for at least 72 hour. After this process the women carry the coffee beans to a stream and wash off the fermented slime and carry the beans back to their village and dry them on pandanus mats in the sun for a period of 6 to 7 days. Each morning the beans are spread out to dry and each late afternoon the beans must be re-sacked and carried inside their houses because of the afternoon rains. It is a long, tedious process. Their only method of testing the dryness is to bite a coffee bean. If it is hard, the coffee is ready to sell. After Nahara purchases the sacks of coffee beans, now called "green coffee", they are delivered to a coffee agent in Popondetta who will ship the beans to a coffee processing company. There a thin parchment-like skin will be removed and as "parchment coffee beans" they will be exported to coffee companies, who will roast the beans and sell them as whole beans or ground coffee. So many amenities which we take for granted are the results of long, involved hours of labor. We had learned to appreciate our morning coffee! Next we must help Nahara Coffee Division overcome their financial difficulties by persuading the Westpac Bank to give Nahara a loan.

In early May, William and I flew to Popondetta with the April profit statement from the Nahara trade store with a profit of 738 kina, an increase of 30 kina over March. Mr. Taboda, the Westpac bank Manager, was pleased with the profit. He agreed to give Nahara Coffee Division a 5,000 kina loan for thirty days, to be paid in full one month later, with the possibility of a renewal. Each month Nahara must repay the 5,000 kina loan. If they could show a suitable profit, Westpac would give Nahara another 30 day loan. Each month they must give him the total kilos and kina figure for coffee purchased, the total kilos and kinas of coffee sold and the kilos and kina value of coffee in storage. I felt it was a wise arrangement whereby Nahara must prove credibility each month.

We left the bank and walked directly to Oro Motors to rent a Toyota 4 wheel drive truck for 50 kina per day plus 18 toea per kilometer, load it with merchandise for the trade store and head for Itokama and return and sell a load of coffee within the twenty-four hour period. The rental fee would be approximately 77 kina. When we arrived at Oro Motors they said that they did not have a rental. William was defeated again, but "old white-skin" was accustomed to making things happen, so I pleaded with them and in the end they found a rental for us because I told them Nahara would be renting one of their vehicles many times during the current coffee season.

Enroute home with a load of supplies and two passengers riding on top of the load, William stopped at Emboga village along Oro Bay to buy some betal nuts. By this time it was after 7:00 P.M. and it was dark. After we turned west at Oro Bay and traveled about 30 kilometers on the Pongami-Afore highway, William veered the truck off the left-hand side of the road into high kuni grass. I shouted, "Stop, William!" He did and he was visibly shaken. "Not to worry, William. We are not in danger. You must put the truck in reverse and back onto the road again." It was the first time he had ever driven any other vehicle except the truck provided by Mainland Coffee Mills. I had noticed he was very tense from the moment we left Popondetta. Also he had been chewing betal nut which eventually clouds the brain. He climbed out of the rental truck and paced the road for several minutes; then he got back into the truck and backed it onto the road, and we proceeded toward Itokama. The terrain was rugged with steep mountain passes, hills and valleys to negotiate. Sometimes the truck motor would die trying to travel up a steep hill. Bill and I had often commented how William and Victor, the only other Nahara driver, failed to feel or hear the pull of the motor and know that it was time to shift into a lower gear. They would continue in too high a gear until the motor coughed and groaned and finally stopped. Seldom did the emergency brake still function on a Papua New Guinea vehicle; usually the brake was ruined. Then one or two of the passengers riding in the rear of the truck would get off the truck and search for two big rocks to block the rear wheels until the driver could start the truck, put it into low gear and start forward again. This happened many times on our night journey. It was midnight before we reach Itokama. Bill was relieved that I was home safely. The next morning William left about 7:00 A.M. loaded with sixteen bags of coffee. He would sell the coffee, return the truck to Oro Motors, pay the truck rental fee, bank the money and fly back to Itokama on Thursday morning . This plan was repeated each time the trade store needed more store goods. In the meantime many kilos of coffee beans were purchased from the farmers and stored in the old Nahara coffee storage.

One time William kept the rental truck at Itokama for six days. He drove to the out lying villages to buy coffee and he hauled loads of people to and from their distant gardens. Having the possession of a vehicle made him an important man. Bill and I talked about the enormous rental fee that Nahara would have to pay. It would be a learning experience for William! In the past the trade store had absorbed the one day rental fee as freight cost on purchased store goods. The freight was added to the cost of the merchandise before mark-up. This time the coffee division would have to be charged for the five additional days of rental fees. William was shocked when he returned the truck to Oro Motors and was charged 300 kina plus 72 kina for mileage. "You must figure costs and plan ahead," I told him. "Do you understand that the sixteen bags of coffee you delivered to Popondetta lost lots of money because of the truck rental fee?" The former Nahara truck could haul twenty to twenty-five bags of coffee which weighed forty kilos each or eighty-eight pounds. The rental trucks were smaller and could only carry twelve to sixteen bags of coffee depending how many passengers rode to town and the road condition due to recent rainfall. William had never considered the difference in freight cost for the smaller truck.

The last week of July William took the Thursday morning plane to Popondetta to rent a truck, bring a load of merchandise for the trade store and return to Popondetta early Friday morning with a load of coffee. Again he planned to use the truck over the weekend to travel from Itokama to Afore to buy coffee at the villages, returning to Popondetta on Monday with a second load of coffee When he failed to reach Itokama Friday evening, we were worried that he had mechanical problems. He finally arrived late Saturday and immediately contacted Bill and told him a bizarre story.

After William sold the coffee on Friday, he went to Westpac Bank to cash the check. He was talking with some friends outside of the bank when Mr. Taboda and three police approached him. "William get inside now. There has been a killing. You are in danger! A member of the Provincial Assembly from the Afore District knifed and killed an Assembly member from the Yumi District, after the Yumi representative started the fight. It was an on going feud between the two men. No National from Afore District is safe in Popondetta. Joseph, the Afore representative, has been taken to jail for protection. If you are found, you could be killed. You must leave town at once!"

William jumped into the rental truck and started for Itokama without cashing the check or buying a load of store goods. He stopped at Emboga. Friends in the village insisted that it would be dangerous for him to drive at night, because he would be unable to spot any Yumi traveling the Pangami-Afore highway. He could be forced off the road and attacked so he stayed the night and resumed the drive late Saturday morning. "Bill, would you take the truck to Popondetta on Monday? You are a "white-skin" and so you will not be in danger. Only Nationals in Afore District will be harmed. There will be a serious "payback".

We understood the term" payback". It means an eye for an eye, a tooth for a tooth. It is a common practice in all of Papua New Guinea. If you kill my pig, I can kill your pig, I can rape your wife or I can kill a member of your clan. The methods of payback are different in each area. In Oro Province paybacks can take a very long time as in ancient days, for Oro is a very backward province. They are not instantaneous as in the Highland where the payback would be resolved within a few days or weeks.

We left Itokama at 4:00 A.M. on Monday and arrived in Popondetta at 8:45, the best driving time we ever made. As we drove down the main street enroute to the DPI coffee buying station, we saw what appeared to be a big parade marching toward us, so we turned right at the next street and watched the procession pass. It was a large group of about three hundred men walking in orderly fashion. Their faces were painted with red, yellow, white and black colored clay. They carried bush knives, axes and spears and their bodies were draped with green vines. Their faces were full of anger. After they passed we drove to the DPI coffee buying station and sold the coffee, then Bill drove me to the shopping area. The post office was closed. The Westpac Bank was closed. I walked to Steamships to check prices on canned goods we wanted to buy to take to our house which were not stocked at the Nahara store. We always checked prices in all the retail stores before we made a purchase because they could vary as much as 50 toea per item. I noticed that a lot of young men were standing in the doorway of Steamships. They looked like some of the marchers. Suddenly they ran inside, shouting obscenities and brushed off the items on the check out counters. They grabbed cartons of cigarettes and items of clothing. Patrons were screaming; there was utter chaos. The store manager, an Australian, appeared and ordered them to leave. He locked the doors behind them as they fled. "Paul, what is happening?" I inquired.

It is the beginning of the payback. The Yumi tribe have threatened to rob all the stores to avenge the killing," he replied.

"Can I go outside? I have many errands to do for our people," I asked.

"Margel, this is serious and dangerous. Stay inside!"

Twenty minutes later he opened the doors to the store and I went on my way. Poponda store was closed, and Wing Hay store was closed. I went to the loading docks of Wing Hay. Nahara bought at wholesale most of their supplies from this wholesale-retail company. Andrew Seto, the manager, saw me and immediately asked what I was doing. "I came to place a large order for Nahara and your store is closed, and so is the Westpac Bank and the Post Office. What is happening?"

Andrew immediately unlocked the gate and ordered me inside. "Where is Bill? Don't you know that a payback is in progress in this town? Tell me now where is Bill. I must contact him!"

"He went to Ella Motors and Carnell Carriers."

"I'll call him. It is dangerous for you people to be on the streets of Popondetta. This is a payback. Do you know nothing of the term payback? These Yumi people will stop at nothing. They mean revenge. They have sent runners to Wing Hay, Koy, Poponda and Steamships wholesale-retail stores that they intend to enter and destroy each one. Poponda is the next target, then this store and next Koys and finally Steamships. Earlier this morning they broke into the bar at the golf course and drank all the liquor and beer. Most of them are drunken. Anything can happen!" Andrew took me inside the store. The clerks were running from window to window to watch what was happening.

Their faces were full of fear. Word arrived that the Poponda store had been gutted and ransacked and that Wing Hay would be the next target. I felt like I was watching a horror movie. This was not real! Andrew took me to a window overlooking the park area across the street from the Wing Hay store. A mob had assembled there with bush knives, axes and loot from the Poponda store. They were regrouping to attack. Soon Bill arrived in the rental truck. Andrew urged us to get out of town. Instead, we drove the back route to the Lamington Hotel. The manager, Mike Serefin, met us as we entered the lobby. "What are you two doing in Popondetta? How did you come?"

"We have a rental truck."

"Where is it parked?"

"In front of the hotel."

"Bill, drive it into the fenced area behind the hotel. NOW! I'll unlock the gate."

We watched from the hotel lobby as the mob advanced on the Steamships store. By now scores of police had arrived, shots were fired and the police fired tear gas into the crowd. The mob immediately retreated to the soccer field across the road from store. Soon two helicopters from Port Moresby landed in the soccer field with reinforcements of police. Finally the mob dispersed and all was quiet. The Steamships store was never looted, nor were the Wing Hay or Koy stores. Five men walked into the Lamington Hotel. They told us that their truck had been taken by men at a road block on the highway from Oro Bay to Popondetta. They heard some one call to the men that stopped them not to hurt - just take their truck and scare them. The five men had walked nearly fifteen kilometers to the hotel. We spent the night at the Lamington, loaded the order of store goods at Wing Hay and left the next forenoon for Itokama. At Banderia police stopped our truck and requested that we take a family to their village of Korua. We did. Finally we were beginning to fathom the grave situation of a payback.

When we arrived in Itokama the people greeted us laughing and crying. William told us that the Barai people had been very angry with him for sending us to Popondetta. They feared for our safety. In fact, when the people heard our truck approaching, several men and boys had ran nearly a kilometer to greet us. We assured the people that William had not forced us to go to Popondetta. We had gone because we wanted to help and we had never been in danger. The Yumi's anger was directed at the Nationals living in Afore District, not at "old white-skins." We both noticed a tremendous appreciation and respect from the people which continued to increase during the remaining months we lived among the Barai. They knew we loved them and they showed their love and respect to us in many ways. We never returned from a trip to Popondetta or anywhere, without a flock of people to welcome our return with handshakes, laughter and tears of joy.

When we returned to Popondetta on the following Tuesday, all businesses were closed for half a day for the funeral of the killed Assembly member. The funeral had been postponed three times. The funeral procession of many trucks filled with mourners traveled the main streets several times. The coffin was carried on a truck decorated with flowers. It was a peaceful event. Frankly I was not impressed. My feelings were that this jerk had attacked Joseph the third time. Joseph knew the customs of his people. If he choose to kill the man from the Yumi tribe, then let him alone suffer the consequences. Take him out of jail and tie him to a tree and shout," "Hey Yumi tribe come get him!" That was my solution! The Yumi tribe had sent word to the people of Afore District that to settle the payback they must pay 25,000 kina and provide 100 pigs and 25 ceremonial headdresses, which are regarded as more valuable than pigs. So many innocent people must suffer because of two men's stupidity. I am still angry over this crime.

Bill took another load of coffee to Popondetta the next morning, turned in the truck and returned to Itokama on the Thursday morning flight. He had hired a much larger truck from Carnell Carriers, who also provided a driver, to come to Itokama on the following Monday morning. Bill called on DPI, Mainland Holdings, and Rob Traders to find out which coffee processors offered the best price. When he told them he would bring eighty to ninety bags of coffee per load, they were extremely interested in negotiating a top price. Bill told them he must have cash on delivery and replacement coffee bags. DPI was the highest bidder offering to pay 1.60 kina per kilo for top grade coffee. Nahara was paying the farmers .90 toea to 1.40 kina for beans. It is interesting that prices quoted on the world coffee market are quoted in pounds, not in kilos (2.2 lbs).

The Barai people were jubilant when the big Carnell Carrier truck and driver David arrived at Itokama on Monday morning. They understood that two "old white-skins" were introducing a faster method of transporting their coffee to Popondetta. As we left Itokama at 1:00 PM with eighty-six bags of coffee, the people were cheering and waving and several young men ran after the truck. We reached the big river. The road goes down to the river and on the other side we must travel up a very steep hill. The truck stalled about five foot from the top of the hill. Four times David backed the truck into the river and four times he failed to make the summit. "David this truck has more power in reverse that it has in low gear. Back the truck across the river and turn it around and then back across the river and up the hill," Bill told the driver. Bill and I got out of the truck. David backed across the river to the west side and turned around. As he attempted to back across the river again, he drove the truck off the stone bedded roadway and the truck was stuck in the soft river bed. If you have truck or engine problems when you drive the Pongami-Afore highway, the driver and passengers must solve the problem because there are no service stations, no wrecker service available. Few vehicles travel this road and, should they pass by a stranded vehicle, they'd simply wave and drive on. Nationals walking along the road were far more likely to lend a helping hand. The only way to free the truck was to jack up the rear wheels and gather big stones to put under them to gain footage, drive forward and repeat the process until the truck reached solid ground. Two and one-half hours later David backed the truck across the river and made it to the top of the hill on the east side. We were three very relieved and jubilant people! But there were two more rivers with very long, steep hills ahead of us. David was able to get to the top of the next hill; the third hill, he could not. This time there was ample space on the east side of the river to turn around the truck. Since the truck had no rear view mirrors and the hill we must traverse was a winding roadway, Bill got out of the truck to guide David up the crooked incline. Once David had turned the truck around to start backing up the hill Bill shouted,"David, stop! Shut off the motor now!" Then he told David the right rear dual wheel was missing. We had been traveling along the right side of a mountain. There was no point in looking for the missing wheel because it would have ended up at the bottom in jungle growth. David pulled the truck into the turn-around. He untarped the load of coffee to get the spare wheel. When he looked for the tire tools, there were none. Now the outside lug bolts were lost with the wheel. He had no wrench and no extra lug bolts to fasten the spare wheel. Bill always carried a pair of pliers, so they were able to remove every other lug bolt from the left rear wheel and put on the right rear wheel, but there was no wrench to tighten the wheel securely. We backed to the top of the winding hill and turned around and proceeded for Popondetta. It was 5:15 PM. We had intended to reach Popondetta by 6:30 or 7:00 PM and we were west of Afore which is about one and one-half hours east of Itokama. Every four kilometers David stopped the truck and the men tightened the lug bolts again.

We had Australian friends, Les and Nellie Hartwig, 19 Km. east of Afore. Bill suggested we drive off the highway and go to their plantation because Les had a lot of tools. This took another half hour. When we arrived the Hartwigs had gone to the Highlands to hire more laborers and so Amos, their National caretaker, gave Bill permission to look for tire tools. He could not find them. Now it was 9:00 PM. We left for Popondetta. As before, every four kilometers David stopped the truck and the men tightened the lug bolts. I could imagine spending the night along the road. We were carrying about 8,000 kina in cash from trade store sales and 5,000 kina in deposits for the Nahara Westpac Agent Bank. Rascals, the name given for thieves, are prevalent in Papua New Guinea. They often erect barricades across highways so that they can rob the passengers. Although Bill and I had established good rapport with the villages along the Pongami-Afore highway, there was always the possibility that we would be robbed. It was an uneasy trip; we felt vulnerable.

When we came to Oro Bay David stopped the truck and said, "I'm taking off the right rear dual wheel. We are only fifty kilometers from Popondetta and on a more traveled road. If the right rear tire blows from the weight, we will be able to get help, a ride to Popondetta." It was 4:30 AM when we approached Popondetta. The coffee companies would not open until 8:00 AM. What would Bill and I do in the meantime? I suggested that the driver drop us at the Lamington Hotel. He could come for Bill in the morning.

When Bill and I knocked on the lobby door of the Lamington, the security guard opened the door with a drawn pistol. He was expecting rascals at that late hour. He recognized us. We explained our long journey from Itokama and asked him if we could rest in the lobby until 6:00 AM so that we could have breakfast. We had had no water or food since noon. He told us that our friends, the hotel managers, were on vacation in the United States. Before he could allow us to enter he must awaken the acting manager. Fifteen minutes later a National man opened the door and told us to come inside. "You can't wait in the lobby. I'll put you in room #10." We protested that we could not afford to pay 62 kina for two and one-half hours. "Will you be staying tonight at the hotel?" he inquired.

"I will stay, but Bill will return to Itokama for another load of coffee," I replied.

"There will be no charge for the rest of tonight. You two are old and must shower and have some rest before breakfast." He took us to our room. This was another example of the respect the Papua New Guinean people gave to elders.

In the morning while Bill and David delivered the coffee I arranged and paid for two shipments of store goods, one to be loaded immediately and the second one to be loaded the next day. The two men got back to Popondetta with a second load of coffee at 2:00 AM and delivered another load of store merchandise to Itokama This time I accompanied them and then Bill and David returned to Popondetta with the third load of coffee. Bill and David had not slept for seventy-five hours.

For remainder of the coffee season, when Bill would arrive in Popondetta with a load of coffee, various coffee company personnel would stop Bill begging him to sell them the next load of coffee. Bill passed this information to William. "See, William, you can ask for the top price. You are the manager of Nahara. You are important. You must not sell to any coffee processor until you ask them what they pay for coffee. Always shop for the best market!"

The impact of the payback meant that the Nahara trade store was now the major shopping place in the Afore District. People walked more than thirty kilometers to buy rice and tin fish and supplies. The items were carried back to the villages by women and children. For example: a twelve year old girl would carry a forty-four pound bale of rice on her head for many kilometers. The man would walk ahead carrying his bush knife! The small village trade stores must now replenish their inventory stock at the Nahara store, simply because Bill and I were the only people in the entire area, except for an Australian couple, the Hartwigs, who owned the cocoa plantation east of Afore, who could travel to Popondetta without the fear of being killed. Nahara trade store bought wholesale in large quantities, such as 500 bales of rice (each bale contained 20 packages weighing 1 kilo each or 2.2 lbs), 200 cartons of tin fish, etc. We had to calculate the weight so we knew how much we could haul on the big truck. The store's monthly gross sales increased from 9,000 kina in July to 12,000 kina in August and to 13,900 kina in the month of September. Net profit for September was 3,600 kina.

People carried bags of coffee for many, many kilometers to sell at Nahara Coffee Growers. The Musa tribe had a new sod airstrip at their head village, but now they dare not accompany their shipment of coffee to Popondetta by plane, so they carried bags of coffee on their heads for two days on a jungle trail to sell to Nahara Coffee Growers.

We had scheduled our second year vacation of two weeks to take a trip down the mighty Sepik River in the northern part of Papua New Guinea. Our reservations were confirmed and we had purchased our airplane tickets. Now we were badly needed by the Barai, so we explained the problem to Air Nuginui Airline and they refunded our money. We felt that we must remain in Itokama so that we could help the Bari people.

Bill trucked coffee to Popondetta at least twice a week: I went with him on the average of once a week to purchase trade store supplies and to do the banking for the trade store, coffee sales and agent bank. The coffee crop was very large this year. The people were depositing their coffee earnings to put into an interest bearing savings account at Nahara's Agent Bank for Westpac Bank of Popondetta. I was training William and Titus, Edwin's younger brother, how to do the paper work. The Nahara trade store was open from 8:00 AM until 5:00 PM five days a week. In July, 1987 William asked me to run the store on

Saturday mornings from 8:00 to 12:00 PM and on Sundays from 1:00 PM to 3:30 PM. He had decided that I had the capacity to work seven days a week. On Saturdays he went to his garden and he usually rested on Sundays. Suddenly I was the weekend store keeper and I had to keep the shelves stocked with goods.

I learned how the people shopped. A person would buy a kilo of rice which cost 1.00 kina and give me 10.00 kina. I would make change giving him or her 9.00 kina. Then they would buy a can of tinned fish for 1.00 kina and I would make change again. Next they might buy a cake of soap for .40 toea and I made change for the third time. Each time the person would examine the returned change and then make another purchase. Usually they spent the entire 10.00 kina before they left the trade store. Sometimes the customers could not speak English. If they were Barai people I could usually understand them but often there were people from other tribes who had come to Itokama to shop because of the payback, and so they would point to different items on the shelves. Somehow we managed to communicate!

The payback was still a problem. Towards the end of the coffee season when Bill and the truck driver hauled coffee and returned with store merchandise, they often had to pull off the highway and drive through a village because the people were so afraid that the Yumi people might travel the road, so the villagers would dig a trench across the road or make a barricade of brush. "Bill would call out to the people, "It's old white-skin from Itokama. Not to worry!" And slowly the people would come to the truck to shake his hand. Their fears were very real. Then in September the Yumi tribe sent letters to all of the wholesale-retail stores in Popondetta and instructed them not to sell or deliver merchandise to trade stores within the Afore District.

The manager of Wing Hay had brought three loads of store good to Itokama after the coffee season ended. He finally told us that he was afraid to make another trip because of the threat of reprisal from the Yumi tribe. The Talair plane didn't come regularly anymore unless to deliver the mail bag, because no one could travel to Popondetta except Bill and I. When we wanted to fly to Popondetta we called the airline on our short wave radio- telephone so that the plane would be certain to arrive. We traveled to Port Moresby in early October to attend our Peace Corps Close of Service Conference and we visited the business office for Steamship stores and explained the payback problem. We gave them copies of the monthly profit statements, a letter of recommendation from the Westpac Bank in Popondetta and arranged for Nahara to be able to order up to 3,500 kina of merchandise on credit by mail from the store in Port Moresby. Then we went to the Talair business office at Jackson Airport in Port Moresby and begged them to start a weekly service to Itokama. They never established a weekly schedule, but they would bring a large cargo plane loaded with store goods shipped by Steamship Company in Port Moresby to Itokama or they would come if we called them by radio -telephone that there was a load of fifteen to twenty-three people who wished to fly to Port Moresby. William sent word to all the villages in Afore District that air passage to Port Moresby was available if they would book in advance. Bill and I felt responsible to make every effort to establish a way to purchase store merchandise and airline service to Port Moresby before we completed our two years of Peace Corps assignment.

CHAPTER 12

"Those who bring sunshine to the lives of others cannot keep it from themselves." - Sir James Matthew Barrie

The opinion of the Barai when we first arrived in Itokama that Bill and I were too old to work soon faded from their minds. They learned by watching our daily activities that we were energetic and capable of working long hours. We appreciated our jobs with BNEA and we especially enjoyed working with the Nahara personnel because they listened to our suggestions and made an effort to accept some new ideas. It was also important to us to find ways of helping individuals. Bill had initiated our willingness to aid the Barai people by making new handles for bush knives and he provided a metal file for the people to use to sharpen their knives. Nearly every morning and evening someone knocked at our kitchen door to ask to borrow the file. That was the beginning of our many hours of labor of love to the people.

Doctor Martin Lukes brought two lawn chairs to our house for Bill to repair the broken plastic webbing. Later Bill repaired his sphymomanometer, an instrument for measuring blood pressure. The word soon spread that the old "white-skins" wanted to help the people.

Rose, the wife of a teacher, asked me if I could make her a pattern for a simple dress so that she could sew some new dresses for herself. I scotch taped sheets of newspaper together and taking her measurements cut out a pattern for her. Then she asked me if I would teach her to make bread. She had heard that I had taught Mavis and Bellfaith to bake. Yeast was unknown to the villagers and it was unavailable in the village trade stores. It was important for me to choose a recipe which they would be able to make for their families. I chose a quick bread recipe called Kaukau Bread:

1 cup warm mashed kaukau (a type of sweet potato)
1 cup sugar
3/4 cup milk

2 cups flour
4 teaspoons baking powder
*optional, 1 teaspoon cinnamon, 1/2 teaspoon nutmeg, 1 cup dried fruit
or nuts

(These ingredients could be omitted and still the quick bread was very
good.)

Sometimes I taught the women to make Banana Bread:

1 cup sugar
3 tablespoons oil
1/2 cup milk
1-1/4 cup mashed ripe bananas
1 teaspoon salt
2-1/2 cups flour
3-1/2 teaspoons baking powder

I always gave them a plastic cup marked with a magic marker to show
1/2, 1/3. 1/4 cups because they had no conception of fractions.

Soon Wende asked me to teach her to make bread and then Sister
Grace asked to learn. The women were always so proud to carry home
their loaves of bread to share with their families. Of course we
furnished all the ingredients. Bill saw the need to make each of them
a bread pan so that they could bake bread at their homes. He knew
that the bundles of corrugated roofing tins were shipped from China
with a sheet of light gauge galvanized metal on each side which were
discarded when the bundles reached their destination. The next time
Bill went to Popondetta he asked at the hardware store if he could buy
some of the packing sheets. When the proprietor learned that Bill
intended use them to form bread pans for the village women, he said,
"Take as many sheets as you want. I give them to you." Bill cut a block
of wood and fashioned it to the size and shape of the inside of a bread
pan. Then he cut a piece of the sheet metal and carefully bent it over
the bottom and sides of the wooden form. Next he folded the ends and
locked the ends with a small overlap fold. He gave a pan to each of the
women who had learned to make bread.

We often served coffee and cookies to visitors. Soon a few women inquired if I would show them how to make cookies which they called sweet biscuits. The women had never heard of vanilla or spices such as cinnamon, allspice and cloves. The only seasonings they used in cooking were salt and curry powder. Since peanut butter was often sold at the Nahara trade store, I taught them to make peanut butter cookies. When a recipe called for an egg, I used a substitute of 1 tablespoon vinegar in 1/4 cup milk.

One day Doctor asked me to teach his wife, Sister Dorcus, to cook a chicken like the Americans. He had eaten American fried chicken in a restaurant in Port Moresby. The Nationals boil chicken or cook it mumu stye. His son, Kingsley, was going to be eleven years old (Few Nationals know their actual age or birth date.) Doctor wanted to have a special birthday meal for him. We were invited to the dinner on Saturday evening. He would furnish the chicken if I would come to their house and show Sister Dorcus how to prepare it. I would have to cook over an open fire.

"Could we have the dinner at our house?" I asked. "I'll cook a typical American meal and I'll bake a birthday cake for Kingsley. Sister could come early so I can show her how to fry the chicken." He was delighted with my suggestion.

Kingsley brought his friend, Michael, to the birthday dinner. I had made a jello fruit salad and baked a chocolate cake with peanut butter icing. With my supervision Sister fried the chicken while I made mashed potatoes and a green bean casserole with mushroom soup and onions. Finally I showed Sister how to make the gravy. The table was set with a yellow gingham cloth, china dinner plates, cloth napkins and knives, forks and spoons. When we were all seated at the dinner table Doctor blessed the food. Bill passed the mashed potatoes first to Doctor because it is the custom that the men are always offered food before the women. He filled his plate with about a third of the potatoes and put a spoonful on little Iloi's plate. Kingsley and Michael refused to take any until Doctor demanded that they must taste English potatoes. They refused the gravy and when the green beans were passed to them they made a face. Each took a piece of chicken. Sister and Iloi seemed to enjoy this new experience, but the two older boys picked at their food. Doctor took two more servings of each dish.

When I cleared the table and served the cake, fruit salad and coffee the boys were quite fascinated with the quivering jello mixture. They tried to eat it with a fork, but the bites would fall onto their plates or on the tablecloth. I suggested that a spoon would be better to use. Then they ate a bite of cake and found it was too sweet to their taste. When the meal was finished Doctor announced that he had eaten so much that now he needed to lie down for a while so he was going to his house. I sent the cake and remaining pieces of chicken with them. The next day Doctor Luke told Bill that when they got home Kingsley ate all of the chicken. Later Bill talked to Michael's father, Phillip, and asked him what were Michael's remarks about our meal? Phillip laughed and said that Michael asked his mother if there was any food to eat. "I don't like white people's food. It was awful!" Michael told his parents.

The Luke family evidently told others about their unusual meal because soon Lelia Koki brought a package of chicken to our house for me to show her how to fry a chicken. Then Wende came with a chicken. She also wanted to learn to make gravy. "If your family doesn't like the gravy, you can feed it to your dogs," I told her. Later I asked her if they ate the gravy.

"We all liked the gravy; little Micah tasted it and he liked it so much that he took the skillet outside the house and ate all the rest of it himself."

Several times we invited Barai families to dine with us. Many were uncomfortable sitting on a chair at a table because they ate their meals sitting on the floor or ground. Also they found our food contained unfamiliar seasonings and our desserts were too sweet. Only men like Simon, William and Doctor, who had become acquainted with Western food by eating in restaurants in Port Moresby and Australia, enjoyed our meals. Their families enjoyed the privilege of being invited to our house to see how we lived but they would eat very small portions of food. Several times we offered candy to the children sitting on our porch; however most of them would make a face and spit the candy on the ground. They preferred a hard biscuit. Several times Bill made some popcorn and gave to the children. They loved it! Eventually the Nahara trade store sold two cups of popped corn for 10 toea.

Our endeavor to help individuals did not interfere with our work with the two organizations because we helped the people early in the mornings and during periods that we were not needed by BNEA and Nahara. We were always up by 4:00 or 5:00 A.M. because we retired rather early each evening due to the fact that hordes of flying insects entered our house through the woven bamboo siding by 7:00 P.M. We ate our dinner by 6:30, otherwise our plates of food would be covered with bugs. One night we decided to light a candle rather than to use the kerosene lantern to see if less insects would enter the house with a dimmer light. Insects whirled around the candle; suddenly it fell over and extinguished leaving us in darkness. When we turned on a flashlight, we saw that the top of the candle was encrusted with cremated bugs.

After our early morning coffee Bill would work on some repair for a Barai. The word soon spread to the Barai villages that Bill could fix anything. Often someone would bring a kerosene pressure lantern for him to repair. Many times the mantle was ruined or it needed a new generator. The Nahara store stocked various sizes of mantles and generators. Sometimes the problem was a plugged fuel line due to dirty kerosene. He would clean out the line with a fine wire taken from a wire brush. Women would bring cooking pots with a knife slit in the bottom to our house for Bill to fix. He had found a heat resistant putty in a hardware store in Popondetta to seal the slit. A few women owned hand crank sewing machines and since they allowed their children to play with the machines often they were out of adjustment or were broken. So the women brought their sewing machines to Bill to fix. Anna Grace in Itokama had the only treadle sewing machine, so Bill had to go to her house to repair it. First he had to get permission from her husband to enter her house.

Headmaster Justin brought his guitar to the house. "Bill can you help me?" he inquired. The bottom had separated from the sides due to the humidity and abuse and a riser was loose. Bill reglued and tied the bottom to the body of the guitar to dry. He had no clamps. Then Lelia brought a ukulele which belonged to her son Eddie for Bill to fix. All the strings and the four pegs were missing. "Can you repair this thing?"

"Let me try," he replied. In his spare moments Bill patiently whittled and fashioned four new wooden pegs to tighten the strings. When we traveled to Port Moresby to attend our mid-term conference, we purchased a set of strings. Three days after Bill presented the repaired ukulele to Eddie we saw an older boy carrying the uke. All four strings and two pegs were missing! He also rebuilt several water/diving masks that leaked around the glass or else the rubber had rotted and he had to replace that portion using pieces of a tire inner tube.

"My soccer shoes are coming apart at the soles," Gordon complained. That was the beginning of Bill's shoe repair service because many of the members of the soccer teams had similar problems. Bill hand punched holes with a homemade awl and sewed the sole to the shoe with fish line. He repaired many pairs of shoes for the players.

Douglas brought a battery powered amplifier belonging to his boy house to Bill. "It doesn't work anymore," he said. Bill found a broken wire and he quickly spliced it. Another boy house string band wanted a second speaker for their amplifier so that they could place a speaker at each side of the band which was to play for a disco dance that night in Neokananee. They brought parts of a discarded speaker and Bill rewired and made them a new one. The next day they brought the two speakers to Bill to repair. The wires had been exposed and the band members had caught their feet in the wires. Later there were other requests for repairs to the sound equipment owned by the boy houses. Bill was gaining the reputation that old "white-skin" could repair everything.

The only Barai person to own a bicycle was Simon. He inquired, "Can you fix my bike?" The left pedal assembly was missing and the front wheel bearings needed to be replaced. Probably the drive sprockets had never been oiled and the wheel spokes were loose. We wrote to a Peace Corps Volunteer working in Lae to see if he could find the needed parts. He replied that he was unable to find them. Many months later we found a pedal assembly and bearings in Lae at a sporting goods shop. Bill completed the bicycle repairs and rode the bike to Simon's house.

The lawn mower owned by the school needed repair. John Lucas, the teacher in charge of mowing the school grounds, brought it to our house. Bill tore it apart in our living area and for several weeks one corner of the room was covered with nuts, bolts and disassembled mower parts. Bill had no means to grind the valves. He improvised by collecting the emery dust from the corundum grinding wheel of the hand grinder in the BNEA tool shop. Then Bill made a paste of the dust and attempted to hand reface the valves of the motor. Finally he traveled to Popondetta and purchased some needed replacement parts.

Bill learned that there were fifteen girls that had to sit on the floor in class because there were not enough school desks. He told the Headmaster that if the school would furnish the lumber and three older school boys to help him he would make enough desks for the girls. Headmaster assigned three students. He would need to purchase the lumber on credit because the school was short on money until the next appropriation of funds were received from the government. BNEA refused to allow the school to charge the timber, so Bill and I decided we would pay for the material ourselves. The desk and seat were one unit which provided space for three students. Bill enjoyed working with the boys who were so eager and proud to learn some carpentry skills.

The sawmill crew were carrying the blocks for the walkabout sawmill to a new sawing site along the Pongami-Afore highway. Several young men and an old man stopped Bill ask him to repair the old man's shotgun. He wanted him to fix the gun right away. "I don't have any tools with me to work on your gun. Let me take it to my house and I'll try to repair it," Bill told the young men because the old one could speak only Barai. The old chap refused to part with his precious gun. He followed Bill to Martin's house. Martin, who was one of the sawmill crew, persuaded the old man, his tambu from another village, to trust Bill with the gun. It was a single shot, 12 gauge and stamped on the gun barrel were the words, "Made in Spain - 1830." We only saw five guns during the two years we lived in Itokama. All of them were made in Europe in the 1800's. They were regarded as status symbols and they were handed down as legacy. The guns were seldom fired because shells were available only in the towns and government stations. Only one shell could be purchased at a time and to purchase a shell the owner of the gun must present a casing and tell how he had used the shell. During the payback in the Afore-Popondetta area shells were not sold. The men of Afore District hunted with spears. The old man related to Bill that he would come to our house to collect his gun in two days. Bill repaired it, cleaned and oiled the rusty barrel. The word spread that Bill could also repair guns. Soon a member of the

Musa tribe brought a gun to our house for Bill to fix. His name was Moses and he had married a Barai woman who had a garden along the road between Itokama and Sirafe #1. He, too, was at first reluctant to entrust his gun to Bill. It was difficult to repair a gun with small parts such as a spring missing. Later Bill repaired a third gun.

Martin built a new house in his village, Sirafe#1. Since he was one of our special friends, Bill told him that he would be honored to furnish a pair of hinges and hang the timber door. The rest of the house was made of native bush material. Barai doors were attached with tied vine. While he was hanging Martin's door quite a group of people gathered to watch. Bill noticed that one very old, toothless man had a stick cane with an unusual white stone knob. He mentioned it to Martin who replied that the cane head was an ancient "killing stone" which had belonged to the old man's ancestors. Bill told Martin that he would like to buy the stone. At first the old man refused and then he called his four sons and they retreated into the bush to hold a council. When they returned the old man said he would sell it for 5 kina. Bill bought our first killing stone. Later a man from Umbuvara brought us a flat disk shaped killing stone which we bought for 4 kina. Now we had two.

Bill was often requested to doctor pigs in different villages. During our training period, Peace Corps had told him not to treat pigs because, if they should die, he could be held responsible for the death. He often saw pigs who were having difficulty breathing, a sign of pneumonia aggravated by the high humidity and cool nights. He had doctored his own farm animals and so he mentioned to Simon that one of his pigs was very ill. "I might be able to cure him with a shot of penicillin, but if the pig should die I will not be held responsible for its death." Simon urged him to inject the pig and vowed that he would not be angry with Bill should the animal expire. So Bill went to see Doctor Luke and told him that he needed to buy some penicillin. "You can have all you need. The national government provides all medical clinics with free medicines," he replied. He gave Bill two bottles; one was a salt solution and the other contained 10 c.c. of penicillin crystals which were to be combined with the salt solution before injecting. Simon's pig responded immediately because it had never had any type of medication. Other villagers heard about Simon's pig and they also came to Bill to doctor their pigs. Bill walked from village to village to administer penicillin to pigs. He would inject an ill pig and then other villagers would bring a pig to him to receive the same treatment regardless of whether the pig was ill or not. It was a novelty to the people. "Come to my house tomorrow morning at 7:00 A.M," they might tell Bill, but often when he arrived he learned from a neighbor that the owner of the sick pig had already gone to his garden. Bill must make another trip to inject the pig.

As I taught some of the women to bake, Bill was conscious of the fact that they must bake for their families by putting a bread pan inside a big kettle which was placed over a fire and then coals placed on top of the inverted kettle lid to form an oven. We had learned in our training to make drum ovens and to make a stove/oven from a metal drum. He related to Doctor that he could make Sister Dorcus a stove/oven if Doctor would provide a fifty-five gallon steel drum. He exclaimed, "I have a drum. Please make Sister a stove and oven!". The drum was extra heavy and stamped on its side was, WWII!" Using a cold chisel Bill cut the drum into three rings or sections. The center ring was discarded. From one of the end sections he cut and made a small hinged door along the side to insert firewood. He cut the other end section in half, thus forming two half circles and mounted one half circle section on top of the other drum end which would serve as a stove top. When one wanted to bake, one placed the other half circle against the mounted half section to form an oven. A metal stove pipe, with a draft control to govern the fire , vented the smoke outside of the house. While Bill was making the stove he was surrounded by an audience of villagers.

Lelia Koki came to our house after watching him make Sister Dorcus a stove to beg him to make one for her. "I'll be glad to make you a stove," he told her, "if you will furnish a steel drum." Months passed. She came to our house many times and reminded us that she wanted a stove. He husband did not seem anxious to secure a drum for her. They were expensive to buy. Nahara and BNEA had to pay a 25 kina deposit on each drum of petrol and then there was a freight charge which increased the cost of an empty drum. BNEA failed to return them to collect the deposit fee. One day Bill loaded all the empty drums on a Nahara rental truck and took them to Popondetta. He collected the deposit fees for BNEA and then asked the Shell station owner what he charged for drums. Bill told him he wanted to buy some empty drums to make stoves for some of the Barai people. They were light weight drums, but they would last for a while. "If you are want drums to make stoves for the village people, you can take as many as you want. There will be no charge. You are doing this work without pay as a Peace Corps Volunteer. If you are willing to give your time, I will give you the drums," he replied. And so Bill returned with several drums and Lelia finally had her drum stove oven.

Victor Koki built a new bush house for his family. He came to Bill to ask him if he would make Lelia a rodent-proof cupboard like he had built for BNEA? "If you will furnish the window screen and the lumber for the frame, I will gladly make you a cupboard for your wife," Bill answered. Later he also made a rodent-proof cupboard for the Nahara trade store.

One morning as we drank our coffee Bill said," William works at a table made from native bush material. He deserves a desk. If he would buy a sheet of one-half inch plywood I could build him a simple desk with drawers. He seems to appreciate our work with the Nahara Coffee Growers, Ltd, Pty."

"Ask him if he would like you to build him a desk," I replied. William Suremo was excited when Bill volunteered to make him a desk. He ordered the sheet of plywood which cost 36 kina on Bill's next trip to Popondetta. Bill calculated and measured before he began cutting the plywood because there was no room for an error. He made a desk with a center drawer above the kneehole and a small drawer and a deep drawer on the right hand side. Bill stained the plywood desk with a mixture of kerosene and tar and sealed the finish with a coat of clear varnish. He also made William a three tier letter basket stained and finished the same as the desk. The day that Bill and I started to carry the new desk from our house to the Nahara building, we were joined by a host of people. They were so excited that William had a new desk! Some of the men took the desk out of our grasp and insisted on carrying it to the Nahara building.

Since we had shown the people that we were interested in helping them, Simon approached us with two new ideas. First he thought it might be beneficial to make a library in the BNEA Community building for the Barai people. He asked if Bill would make some shelving for books. By the time the shelving was completed, Simon had lost interest in the project; they were never filled with books for the people to use. Next he asked Bill to make six boxes to use to ferment coffee cherries rather than to place the cherries in lengths of bamboo. He wanted to know how much each box would cost so that he could sell them to the people for a handsome profit. Bill made the boxes of lumber, 36 inches by 30 inches by 8 inches, and sealed the cracks with pitch to make the boxes water tight. Simon used his fermentation box once or twice. The other boxes were never used. The people were reluctant to adopt new methods.

There were many other tasks that Bill accomplished such as repairing coffee pulpers which removed the skins of the coffee cherries prior to the fermentation process. The pulpers were usually located in coffee gardens a far distance from a village which meant that Bill must walk many kilometers to adjust the pulpers. Usually one pulper was owned by one clan or by one extended family. They were expensive; a pulper cost about 300 kina for the best model or 225 kina for a cheaper model which had limited adjustments.

In 1987 there was a National and Provincial election. All Provincial incumbents were given 20,000 kina and each National incumbent was allotted 40,000 kina by the government to give to the people to buy votes. The candidate running for an office the first time was at a tremendous disadvantage. William asked me if I would write to the National incumbents, Stephen Tago and Akoi Doi, and to Benson Garui, the Speaker of the Provincial Assembly, to ask each of them for a contribution for the Nahara Coffee Growers. Benson Garui, who was running against Tago for a seat in National Parliament, told William that he was giving coffee pulpers to many Barai families and so he would not be able to contribute money to the Nahara Coffee Growers. The pulpers passed out by Benson were a cheap model which lacked adjustment features. Soon Bill was hurrying from Barai coffee garden to Barai garden trying to regulate the machines. Bill walked many, many kilometers through jungle area to service the pulpers.

Stephen Tago was running for re-election to National Parliament and he held the office of National Minister of Defense. He was a member of the Yumi tribe. Akoi Doi, a Musa, was also running for re-election to another seat in National Parliament. Both came to Itokama to give speeches hoping to gain votes from the Barai people. Akoi Doi came first to Itokama. Standing in front of the Nahara building, Doi, an eloquent speaker, talked to the Barai people and then he presented William, as the manager of the Nahara Coffee Growers, a check for 2,000 kina. I personally thanked Doi on behalf of Nahara and I assured him his contribution would be spent wisely. A few days later Stephen Tago and his staff came to Itokama. Tago asked Bill if he could sleep at our house. "You are most welcome," Bill answered. His staff found lodging in Barai homes, but they came to our house for breakfast and dinner. Tago had a flamboyant personality. This was the second time he had stayed with us. He told us about the peoples of Oro Province which he represented. We learned from him; his staff were courteous and friendly. The first morning we invited Simon representing BNEA, William representing Nahara and Councilor James as Headman of Itokama to join our guests for breakfast. We advised them that since we were Peace Corps Volunteers we could not influence or participate in any political decisions, yet they were welcome to express themselves in our home. Bill made sourdough pancakes served with maple syrup, pork luncheon meat, tomato juice and coffee. Simon was too busy to attend, but William and Councilor James had a great visit with our guests. When our visitors departed to go to the Nahara grounds for Stephen Tago's address, Mr. Tago told Bill and me to wait at our house until he sent his car and driver to transport us to the political address site. After Tago's address he presented a check for 2,000 kina to the Nahara Coffee Growers. "Your generous donation is greatly appreciated by the 831 leaseholders. The money will probably be put into a savings account to eventually be applied toward the purchase of a truck," I told Tago after the meeting.

There are over eleven different political parties in Papua New Guinea. Parties must join together to form a coalition in order to form a government. We enjoyed watching the election process unfold in Itokama. It was at least a week or more after the election before the returns became official. Benson Garui defeated Tago. Akoi Doi retained his Parliament seat. Later he was appointed the Speaker of the House of Parliament and still later he became the Deputy Prime Minister of Papua New Guinea.

The village of Neokananee provided our next excitement. The village purchased an old truck from a man in Popondetta. "Bill, our village has bought a truck. Can you teach me to drive it?" James Pangare of

Neokananee inquired. The only Barai men who knew how to drive a vehicle were William Suremo and Victor Koki from Itokama and Benson Garui from Tama.

"Sure. I'll be glad to teach you to drive providing the truck is safe," Bill replied.

"We need to take the Neokananee soccer team to the Korua soccer field tomorrow for a match. Will you drive the truck for us and show me how to drive it?" James asked. Korua was the next village east of the Big river and belonged to another tribe.

"Neokananee bought a truck? How did you raise the money to buy it?" Bill inquired.

"Well, Brian had about 700 kina left from the government grant for the O'kari nut project and so he gave that to us. And some of us will give money. It only cost 1,500 kina," James told Bill. "I first saw the truck in Popondetta . The fellow who had it for sale drove it to our village twice. The people in Neokananee got real excited and called a meeting. The village decided to buy it so we could have a way to go to town and to Afore. We gave the owner the 700 kina and he gave us time to collect the other 800 kina from the village families," James continued. Bill and I had seen the same old yellow truck with "For Sale - 400 kina" in the lot in front of Steamships store at Popondetta.

Bill drove the soccer team to Korua on Sunday afternoon, about twenty kilometer east of Itokama. There were twenty nine boys from Neokananee and Itokama in the truck and six other boys ran just ahead of the truck all the way to Korua. Bill could only reach a speed of ten to fifteen kilometers in third gear. It was dark before the truck returned to the village. Bill was exhausted. The front end was loose; the brakes were terrible. "That truck isn't safe," Bill told me. "It is a disaster! James Pangaree wants me to take him and a load of people to Popondetta. I told him that I wouldn't drive that truck any further distance than I would want to walk home. No brakes - loose front steering! Traveling over those mountain passes, who knows what might happen! James has no business learning to drive that wreck of a truck. Somebody will get hurt."

A friend of James who lived at Tama agreed to drive the Neokananee truck and he also instructed James how to shift gears. When they approached the Neokananee trail to the east of our yard the truck must slow down to enter the narrow muddy path full of holes routed by the pigs. Time after time James would kill the motor as he pushed the brake without engaging the clutch. The Barai people laughed. Bill and I felt embarrassed and sorry for James. The ones that laughed at him could not have driven any better. Neokananee village could not afford the cost of the petrol nor could they afford the price of the motor oil. James would beg three liters of petrol from the BNEA airport maintenance to drive to Tama. The tank was never filled and with luck the oil reached the bottom of the oil dip stick. James and his friend from Tama made one trip to Popondetta. The seller saw them and threatened to reclaim the truck because there was still money due. He had to be a real con man! After a few weeks James took a truck load of people to Tama. Halfway there the truck stopped and refused to start again so the truck was abandoned. Gradually the tires and the parts began to disappear. "Not to worry, not to worry." The people still claimed ownership of the truck. This episode was considered by the Barai as one giant step forward for Neokananee village!"

Deserting vehicles along the road is a common practice in Papua New Guinea. We passed old trucks each time we drove to Popondetta. A road maintainer owned by the Highway Department was left on the side of a steep hill where it went out of control. In Afore a Ford tractor sets near the market place with tires and parts missing. These machines belong to people who still claim ownership. It isn't important that the machines don't function; the important fact is the ownership.

CHAPTER 13

"Go where he will the wise man is at home. His hearth the earth, his hall the azure dome." - Ralph Waldo Emerson

The first of October, 1987, our group #9 met in Port Morseby to take our close of service physicals, to arrange for our flights home and to sign the necessary papers to conclude our two years of Peace Corps work. December 10th was set as the departure date to the United States

The Peace Corps Director had previously asked Bill and me to consider extending for one more year. The Papua New Guinea government had requested that Agriculture Extensionist Volunteers be sent to several high schools to help with the agricultural projects such as cattle, pigs, poultry and school gardens. He needed us to monitor this new project. I was reluctant to sign up for the third year. A son-in-law had three major heart attacks in July and August. It made me realize that our families might need us. I wanted to enjoy our children and their families, our grandchildren. "It's time we go home," I told Bill.

"Would you consider staying for an additional three months?" our Director inquired. "We have a new group of Volunteers arriving in November. Six, three men and three women, are classified as Agriculture Extensionists. You would travel to six or seven high schools who have applied for Peace Corps Volunteers to work with their agricultural programs. We need to know what they expect of the Volunteer. Will he or she be required to teach classes? What kind of housing will be provided for them? Do they have livestock and poultry? We will send a questionnaire for you to complete at each school which will provide us with information so that we can assign a Volunteer with the proper skills. You will need to travel the month of November while this new group is taking training at Goroko." We agreed to extend for three months, providing we could spend the balance of October and the month of December at Itokama and finish our work with the Barai. The Director told us to fly to Port Moresby on November 3rd to get our schedule, instructions and plane tickets for our month of travel.

The day we took off from the Itokama sod airstrip to fly to Popondetta and take a second plane on to Port Moresby was a breath taking experience. A new pilot was at the controls of the Islander and the Talair training instructor was there to assist him. Talair hires inexperienced new pilots from Australia and New Zealand who come to Papua New Guinea to gain 1,000 hours of flying time so that they can transfer to better paying jobs. This new pilot was ill groomed and his shaggy hair showed large patches of grey. He taxied to the north end of the field to prepare for take off. As the plane neared the far end of the airstrip a red light on the instrument panel began flashing and the stall horn blared, so he braked the plane and returned to the north end for another attempt. After the third try the plane lifted off skimming just over the tree tops. The instructor turned around and smiled at us, shaking his head. "Sorry to frighten you. This is his first day."

"Not to worry, not to worry," I muttered. The Garui airfield at Popondetta was much larger and it had a tarmac surface. As the pilot made the final approach at Garui, the instructor was giving him counsel "Pull up and make another circle. You are too high and the air speed is too fast!" He finally landed the plane on his third attempt.

Flying with an experienced bush pilot over mountains and jungles, and landing and taking off from rural airstrips requires a bit of inner calmness from the passengers. These pilots have no ILS which stands for Instrument Landing Systems; nor do they have VOR, Very high frequency On Range with omni stations which keeps the pilot always in contact with location. They have ADF, Automatic Direction Finder, tuned into a commercial radio system. It does not direct the plane to an airport, rather it directs the pilot to a city. Most of the pilots use dead reckoning; with a topography sectional map which shows mines, roads, villages, mountains and rivers placed across the pilot's knees and positioned in the direction he is flying ;he flies from check point to check point. He does not know the wind velocity which means he could miss an airstrip by a considerable distance! Jackson International Airport at Port Moresby is the only airport in Papua New Guinea to have an Instrument Landing System.

The pilots, both the expiates and the Nationals, were always friendly and accommodating. We can't praise them enough, especially the men who flew regularly to Itokama. They brought us sacks of paperback books and frozen meat sent to us by the manager of the Lamington Hotel. If we ran out of stamps they would mail our letters at the Popondetta Post Office for us. We always gave them a 2 kina tip because it meant that they might wait in line for over thirty minutes to buy a stamp. The post office was usually filled with lines of people. Sometimes they flew the plane over a different route from Itokama to Garui Airport just to show us new territory. "You haven't seen this area before," they would tell us. One day the pilot changed his course and flew us over Mt. Lamington, an active volcano. Barry from Australia had a difficult time understanding PNG time. Often a passenger leaving from Itokama might ask him to wait as much as twenty minutes while the National collected his baggage and brought his family to board the plane. Several times Barry refused to wait and took off for Garui. Finally so many Barai people complained to Talair that Barry was fired. He was replaced by a pilot, named Richard, from New Zealand who soon made friends with the village people. He often carried cartons of surplus vegetables grown in the school gardens and deliver them to the Popondetta market, collected the money and brought it to the Headmaster on the next flight. He told us that he had informed Talair that he absolutely refused to fly government officials. Twice the officials had spit their red betal nut saliva on the floor and urinated on the back wall of his plane. He had to clean the interior of the plane!

One morning the Talair pilot instructor flew to Itokama in dense fog to take us to Popondetta. We had notified Talair the week before that we needed to leave Itokama on the following Thursday to attend a Peace Corps Conference. That morning we were certain that no plane would dare to attempt to fly over the mountain range to pick us up. We did not bother to take our baggage to the airstrip. About 10:00 A.M. we heard a plane and then we heard it land. The instructor pilot flew us directly east to Oro Bay and then turned back west to the Garui Airport which took forty-five minutes of flying time rather than the usual fifteen minutes. We were the only passengers. "We can't believe that you came for us." He replied, But I knew you needed to leave today."

Sometime when the plane landed at Itokama the pilot simply opened the cockpit window and called, "No mail bag. No passengers?" then he would shut the window and take off. When the plane landed on sod strips the pilot often would first fly low over the field to look for debris, ruts made by pigs and to see the length of the grass before he must determine if he must make a "soft landing." which was often necessary at the Itokama airstrip. I asked another Peace Corps Volunteer who worked in Port Moresby to give me a professional description of the term "soft landing"; he was a licensed pilot. The following three paragraphs are Lee Robertson's explanation and exact words:

> As the pilot approached the landing site he wondered, as always, if the grass would be cut short enough to accommodate an easy landing. He entered a left-hand pattern, not for traffic reasons but for reasons of looking at the field itself. He thought to himself at the time out of habit," GUMPS, which translated to "Gas, Undercarriage, Mixture and Prop on short final." He did not need these things but they came from habit. He turned on the downwind leg and looked at the field. Still too high to really see the length of the grass, he turned onto his base leg and began to descend. He then turned onto his final approach, still looking at the grass strip, and was then finally able to determine he had tall grass. At that time he opted to make a soft field landing.

Soft field landing is a maneuver in which the pilot needs to keep the airplane going as slowly as possible before actually touching down and still maintain flying speed. He neared the point of a normal touchdown and at that point cranked in forty degrees of flaps, the limit, and gently lifted up the nose of the aircraft while at the same time reducing his speed. He now read the air speed indicator and it registered sixty-five knots. More back pressure on the yoke and the nose raised slightly. His intent was to put the main gear down first and at the last possible moment the nose gear would naturally drop due to gravity. In this manner he could minimize the drag effect of the tall grasses below and prevent the possibility of a ground loop. He looked at the airspeed indicator once more and now it read fifty-five knots. The stall horn sounded as he expected but he continued to keep the nose up as he knew that even if a stall occurred he would be at a safe level of altitude to deal with it.

The tall grass hit the wheels of the airplane with a hissing sound; he felt the speed deteriorate even more and he knew he must put the plane on the ground. He pulled back the yoke and the nose went up even more as the main wheels settled onto the ground and through the grass. He rolled out the bulk of the runway; the nose wheel slammed down abruptly and the plane came to a stop within a few feet. He felt good at the time that the soft landing had gone just as he had planned.

We could have many more soft landings as we began our month of travels in Papua New Guinea. Our first assignment from Peace Corps was to fly to Mendi located in the Southern Highlands Province. From there we must find a vehicle to take us to Kagua High School which was at the very least a three hour journey. "You will probably stay at the Headmaster's house," we were told. The details of our trip were sketchy and incomplete, but we had already learned to seek help, rides, accommodations and to make things happen. "Seek and you shall find. Ask and it will be given. Make things happen." This was our motto!

The Highlands area is the highest region of the middle mainland, 65,248 sq. km. with a population of 1,118,800. It is the most densely populated and most productive agricultural region of Papua New Guinea. Coffee is the major cash crop; however you will also find tea and vegetable gardens. Flying over the area you see small plots of farmed ground which signalizes the agricultural development and progress made since the Leahy brothers first penetrated this land to look for gold in 1934. The Highlands is divided into five provinces which are:

Eastern Highlands
Western Highlands
Southern Highlands, 25,988 Km., Pop. 235,600
Chimbu (or Simbu)
Enga

First our plane landed at Tari which is northwest of Mendi. There was a huge gathering of Nationals dressed in their tribal clothing who had come to the airport to greet a chartered plane of tourists. When we landed at the Mendi Airport no one was there to meet us and so we asked at the ticket counter, "Where can we find the Provincial Department of Education Office?"

"It is a way up the street," the man replied. How far is a way up the street we wondered. One time in another foreign country I had asked directions. "It is as far as a dog can run." That told me nothing because I had never ran behind a dog until it could go no farther. Bill and I smiled at each other and started walking. After a while we found the office. The Assistant Deputy Minister of Education was an expiate who took us to his house for lunch. He told us that he would arrange for the Provincial vehicle to drive us that afternoon to the Kagua High School. While we were eating lunch, an English teacher from the school arrived. He was a VSO Volunteer from England. When he learned that we were going to Kagua High School, he gave us the keys to his house which was located on the school grounds. "I came to Mendi to buy groceries, but I am certain you can find enough food to eat. Help yourselves. I'll be back on Sunday afternoon," he said.

The drive to Kagua was a beautiful trip. The countryside is more open so that one can see great distances. It was a new experience for us because in the Barai area we could only view the mountain tops otherwise we simply looked at walls of jungle growth. These lower mountain slopes were covered with grass except for trees which cloaked the summits in contrast to the dense jungle foliage we were accustomed to seeing in Oro Province. The gardens were fenced with sticks which were surrounded by dug trenches to prevent the pigs from entering the farmed areas. The road to Kagua was a coarse gravel surface and wide enough to pass on coming vehicles. Several crews of men along the road were cutting the roadside grass by hand using grass knives. We noticed as we passed villages that the people were shorter and their dress was different. The men wore vines wound about their waists from which grass or leaves were hung to cover their front and backsides which is called" arse grass", while the women wore grass skirts or skirts of undecorated tapa. Many wore Western type clothing. We learned that these men hunt with bow and arrows made of black palm rather than hunting with spears. The Mendi area is the home of the famous Huli wigmen who wear headdresses made of human hair decorated with cuscus fur, feathers and everlasting(straw)flowers.

Widows paint their faces and entire bodies with bluish grey clay and drape many strands of Job tear beads around their necks to show that they are in mourning. Each day of mourning one strand of beads is removed. When the last strand is discarded, which may take as long as nine months, the widow can bathe for the first time since her bereavement period began. In contrast brides paint their bodies black with a tree oil mixed with soot. They must wear this for one month before the marriage can be consummated. The bride will use this month to become acquainted with her new in-laws. Meanwhile her groom can learn ways to overcome any spell cast on him by his bride.

When we arrived at the Kagua school, the Headmaster seemed surprised to see us. He said that he had received no information that we were coming. He was even more surprised when we told him that we were told that we would stay at his house. "Not to worry because one of your teachers, Tim, has given us the key to his house in case it is not convenient for us to lodge with you," Bill commented. His immediate wide smile showed his relief!

Tim's house was made of sawed timber and had three tiny bedrooms, a bath and a kitchen/living area. He had warned us that he had a pet pygmy possum in a cage in the one bedroom which he used as his study. It slept during the day and came out of its cage at night and roamed the house. We shut the door to his study! He had also asked us to feed his pet tree kangaroo which lived in a huge cage that contained a large tree limb at the side of the front porch. That evening we ate cheese and crackers, cold pork and beans, an apple and instant coffee for our dinner. We had fortunately brought a supply of canned food with us and a pair of twin size bed sheets, towels and soap. There was a cot in one bedroom and a cot in the living area. The DC electricity operated from 8:00 A.M. to 10:00 P.M. We slept well that night and had coffee and cookies the next morning for our breakfast.

Headmaster Raphael Noipo told us that he would be gone for the day, so we walked around the school grounds. There were several houses for teachers, and there were at least ten buildings used as classrooms, an old mess hall and kitchen plus a new modern mess hall recently constructed at a cost of 75,000 kina. It was beautiful! Later we walked east on the road past the school grounds and came to a Catholic Mission. First we encountered Father Albert from Pennsylvania. He went to the main house to summon Father Don, who was from Kansas. Both had worked at this Mission for many years. Father Don showed us around the Mission grounds, and then invited us inside for coffee and cookies. He told us that the Mission did the repairs for the Kagua High School in exchange for the use of their pasture land for the Mission's herd of cattle. They also butchered and sold meat to the school. Later Father Don insisted that we must stay for lunch. Gilalamo, a teacher we had met from Kagua High School, had seen us walking toward the Mission, so he came to take us for a drive to the town of Kagua, past the market to where a huge group of people were assembled to ask for compensation for some recent tribal dispute. All the men were armed with bows and arrows, bush knives and axes and their faces were painted. One man wore a three inch wide headband which contained a row of green scarabs. His face was painted black. I offered to buy his headband, but he refused. The group, who must appease the offended tribe, stood along the roadside. They held poles adorned with kina notes trying to show the accusing tribe, who milled along the hill on the opposite side of the road brandishing weapons, their willingness to settle the feud. Then Gilalamo drove us to the tiny village of Sumbuna. He stopped along the way to buy us both an ear of roasted corn to eat on the return journey to the school. It was an interesting day. After we reached Kagua it began to rain.

The next morning we walked to the trade store near Kagua to buy more food. Just as we got back to the school grounds it began raining again, so we spent the day reading. Tim came home about 6:00 PM. It had taken him seven hours to make the trip from Mendi to the school. After dinner we spent the evening talking; rather he talked and we listened. He asked us, "What university degrees do you have?"

"None", we replied.

"You Peace Corps Volunteers are so unqualified. Why are you sent to help these people? It is disgusting!"

"You are paid minimum wages. We work for no pay," we replied. We did not argue that accusing remark because evidently he was quite firm in his conviction, and we were guests in his house. Peace Corps Volunteers often experience this type of criticism from volunteers of other countries. It was a long evening of conversation. He expounded

A tribal dispute near Kagua village

A headband of scarabs.

on his intellectual abilities, his contributions to the people of Papua New Guinea.

The next morning we met with Headmaster Noipo. He took us on a tour of the school grounds and introduced us to some of the teachers Each class had a garden project. In the past years the school had raised cattle, sheep and pigs but this livestock project had been discontinued. The school maintained large coffee gardens, a nursery for starting coffee plants and they raised vegetables for the school cafeteria. Each graduating tenth grade student was given five coffee plants to take to his or her village to encourage the student to plant a small coffee garden. The Headmaster told us he was eager to have Peace Corps Volunteers because they worked without wages. He had requested an agricultural volunteer couple to help with the school gardens, but also he expected them to teach in the school. The new Volunteers would have the house now occupied by Tim who would be leaving at the end of this school year, December 10th. We completed the thirteen page questionnaire for Peace Corps. The Headmaster told us again and again his reason for requesting a Peace Corps Volunteer couple was to secure two teachers who would not require pay. He drove us to Mendi late in the afternoon.

The next day we flew to Karkar Island which is located in the Bismark Sea and is in the Province of Madang. It has an area of 362 sq. Km. with a population of 25,000. In the center of this island is an active volcano which erupted in 1974 and again in 1979. A road around the perimeter of the island can be traveled in about four hours. It has the most productive copra plantations in the world. Except for the volcanic mountain, Karkar is relatively flat. There are good beaches for snorkeling and fishing. Karkar High School is near to Kulili wharf and airport. The school grounds cover a large area. Each student had a tiny garden plot to provide food for lunch. The school cafeteria supplied only two meals a day. The evening meal was usually rice flavored with tinned fish and scones fried in beef drippings. The cold leftovers were served for breakfast.

We stayed with Bob, a volunteer from our Peace Corps group #9 who was a teacher. The first evening someone knocked at his door. Moments later he informed us that one of his students, a thirteen year old girl, had come to ask him to take her tomorrow to the Gaubin

Hospital for treatment for gonorrhea. She was a promising student. He was very upset because this type of problem was a constant occurrence. At Mendi another Peace Corps Volunteer who worked in the Health Department had told Bill that social diseases were a primary problem. He had nine hundred cases each month. Once they were cured, they would later return again for treatment for the same type of infection. Bob arranged for the school driver to take the girl to the hospital and invited us to accompany them. We enjoyed the drive to Gaubin. Enroute we passed Kulkul village, which was preparing for a Sing Sing that evening. On the return trip to the school the driver stopped at Kulkul so that we could watch the dancing. Their costumes were much different from the Barai dress. The dancers wore grass skirts of red leaves and greenery of leaves around their shoulders. They danced to the rhythm of kundu drums and a huge garamut drum, which is a hollowed tree trunk beaten with a stick to give a deep, loud, echoing sound. Their headdresses were made of white feathers. What a colorful event!

The next day we toured the high school and talked with the Headmaster and the agricultural teacher. They told us that they had requested a Peace Corps Volunteer because they worked without a wage; therefore the salary of one teacher could be used to buy supplies and for some needed repairs. The Headmaster was not interested in an agricultural program. There was a piggery with shelter and pens which housed two very skinny pigs fed on the scraps from the mess hall. The school owned a Ford tractor which could not be used because the electrical wiring system was missing. Clearly there was no interest in getting it repaired or pursuing any agricultural program.

We flew the next morning to Madang where we made arrangements to travel by vehicle to Brahman High School located southwest of Madang just west of the Ramu River in beautiful Ramu valley. Sugar cane is raised in this area which is processed at the Ramu Sugar Refinery that supplies all the sugar for Papua New Guinea. Matt, an Australian and the founder of Brahman, picked us up late the next afternoon at the Catholic diocese where we had spent the night. During the three hour trip he told how the school was established. Using his own money and gifts of monies from his immediate family, Matt had built the narrow dirt road to the Brahmam site. At one point on the roadway an incline was so steep that a truck was stationed at that place to pull large trucks

to the top of the hill. Next he had fostered the high school project and
built a tradestore, sawmill and a hostel.

The school, the teachers, the agricultural program, the large trade store
and the sawmill operation were all controlled by Matt. The next
morning he drove us over the school land pointing out the cropland
and pastures, explained his sawmill/timber operation and introduced
us to the clerks in his trade store. He told us that wild cattle were a big
problem in the area. About forty years ago cattle were brought to
Ramu Valley by some Australians; however the Nationals soon tired of
caring for the animals and abandoned them leaving the cattle to roam
the land. Later we were able to tour the school by ourselves. The
Headmaster told us that all school decisions were made by Matt and
so he was very frustrated and unhappy with his position because he had
no authority whatsoever. Other teachers told us the same story. Matt
had established his own dictatorial kingdom! His accomplishments were
impressive; however, he needed to delegate authority to key people in
his sovereignty. He drove us to Madang that evening.

The next morning we flew to New Ireland in the Bismark Sea stopping
first at Manus Island, the largest island of the Admiralty group. When
we landed at the Lorengua's airport the pilot informed us that there
would be a long delay because the plane's communication system was
not working and so he must wait until a replacement plane arrived. He
suggested that we might enjoy visiting the WWII Memorial which was
within walking distance of the airport. Finally we reached Kavieng, the
capital of New Ireland,late that afternoon. Phylistus, a lady who worked
for the Provincial Department of Education, drove us to the Manggai
High School which was about fifty kilometers south of Kavieng on the
Boluminski Highway paved with crushed coral.

New Ireland is a long narrow island, area 9,974 sq. Km. , population
58,000 , with a ribbon of mountains extending through the center for
almost the length of the island which is from six to ten kilometers wide.
Coconut plantations line the highway. Copra, coffee, rubber, fishing and
timber are the major source of income. The island is famous for the
unique art of "shark calling" where certain gifted men, traveling alone,
navigate an outrigger canoe to shark infested waters. The man calls the
shark by shaking a rattle made of dried coconut shells in the water
beside his canoe. When a shark surfaces to investigate the noise, the"

shark caller" spears the fish or slips a vine noose over its head, clubs it to death and lifts it into his canoe. He is regarded as a hero by his tribe because, not only does he perform this dangerous act alone, he provides meat to feed his people.

The fifty kilometer drive to Manggai convinced us that this island was truly a tropical paradise. We saw glimpses of bright blue ocean fringed with white sandy beaches, grassland and palms. At a little village the driver stopped to buy some "laulau" for us to eat. It is the pidgin name for malay apple, a small pear- shaped fruit which is bright pink on the outside and has a crisp white flesh. It was nearly 6:00 P.M. before we arrived at Manggai High School. We were to stay with another Volunteer from group#9, a lady English teacher who would return to the U.S.A. the first part of December.

The next morning Bill and I walked the school grounds. The classroom buildings frame three sides of a U shaped lawn bordered on the fourth side by a low stone fence. Before morning classes begin the students and teachers gather in this open area for the opening ceremony. One of the teachers give a short inspirational talk followed by school announcements. Then the provincial and the national flags are raised to the top of the flagpole while the students sing the provincial and the national anthems.

Gisuwat Siniwin, the agriculture teacher, was eager to show us his facilities. There was a poultry house filled with laying hens which provided eggs for the school cafeteria; the additional eggs were sold locally. A herd of about twenty cattle were raised to supply meat for the school meals and to sell the extra animals for a profit. We walked the many paddocks of pasture. The students were assigned to and taught how to care for the hens and cattle. Previously the agricultural program included pigs, but this project had been dropped, except for five pigs that were kept to eat the scraps from the mess kitchen. He was interested in raising pigs again if a Peace Corps Volunteer was sent to Manggai High School to help him. Then he took us to the four school gardens; each class was responsible for planting and caring for a garden to provide vegetables and fruits for the three daily meals; the extra produce was sold at Kavieng. These students had balanced diets with a variety of foods. Next he took us to his small office to show us the records he kept on each project. We were amazed at his profits, his enthusiasm and energy. The Volunteer teacher had told us that he worked long hours with his students before and after school hours. "They adore Siniwin and work hard for him because he is their friend," she confided.

The entire school was impressive. The library contained hundreds of books supervised by a librarian; a large Home Economic room had bolts of material and a dozen electric sewing machines plus a well equipped kitchen. Students were very friendly and often they stopped us to ask questions about America. Teachers begged to talk with us and show us their program plans. The Headmaster and Siniwin were anxious to have the help of a Peace Corps Volunteer. We certainly intended to recommend that Manggai High School be seriously considered.

The following morning Headmaster Pulman of Medina High School about forty kilometers south of Manggai came to drive us to his school. The school grounds were beautiful! Classrooms were built in a semicircle facing a huge meadow which included a soccer field. Beyond the school buildings an amphitheater had been constructed in the side of a hill. Pulman told us that the only agricultural program was the school gardens and five pigs managed by a woman teacher. The pigs were foraging in a lot with no shelter except for a few trees for shade. A small poultry house made of bush material, which could accommo-date twenty-five laying hens, was empty. "If I could have some help from a Peace Corps Volunteer, I would be very willing to raise some chickens and more pigs. I am so busy with my teaching and overseeing the school gardens. Have you seen our garden project?" she inquired.

The Medina School gardens covered a huge area of about three hectares plus an orchard of guava and mango trees. It was our first time to see lettuce and chinese cabbages growing under shelters made of native poles covered with palm fronds to protect the crops from the hot sun. There were varieties of other vegetables such as kaukau, greens and staked pole beans. The gardens supplied food for the school and the additional fruits and vegetables were sold in Kavieng.

Headmaster took the three of us to his house for cordial and melon and to meet Mrs. Pulman who also taught at the school. Then he drove us around the area and stopped at a bush house. His wife and the other lady teacher went inside and returned with two pandanus bilums for Bill and me. They told us that string bag bilums are not made by the women in New Ireland; they weave bilums of pandanus leaves. About 6:00 P.M. Headmaster and his family drove us the ninety kilometers to the Kavieng Hotel. We promised him we would request that a Peace Corps Volunteer be assigned to Medina High School.

Our visit to New Ireland Province had been a wonderful experience. The people are very friendly and they look different. Many have blond curly hair which we were told is due to diet, a genetic factor or maybe a dye. Most of the women and some men wear laplaps rather than Western clothing. We were surprised to learn that the women own and inherit the land and are the head of their households. Our plane reservations to return to Port Morseby were for 9:00 A.M. the next morning. We checked our luggage and then were told that the plane was still at Rabual, New Britain because of engine failure. The baggage had been pulled outside the tiny terminal building. It began to rain. At 4:10 P.M. a replacement arrived and we boarded the plane. The pilot announced that we would be first landing at Manus Island, then Wewak in East Sepik Province on the northern coast of Papua New Guinea and then at Jackson Airport in Port Moresby.

By the time we finally reached a motel it was too late to eat. Then we discovered that the contents of our luggage were soaked from the afternoon rain. We were two very weary travelers! In the morning the manager of the motel offered to send our sodden clothing to the laundry while we took a PMV to the Peace Corps office to pick up our next travel plans. A day later we boarded a plane to travel to Morehead Station in Western Province to visit another high school.

To reach the Morehead Station school we must land at Daru, the provincial capital , and spend the night before taking the final flight to our destination. Daru is a small town located on a tiny marshy island off the southern coast of the mainland near the entrance to the Fly River which is the major shipping route to OK Tedi Gold Mine located in West Sepik Province. We checked into the Dwyer Hotel overlooking the bay area. Shacks and improvised shelters occupied by Nationals, who had traveled down the Fly River to buy supplies and seek medical treatment, lined the waterfront which was cluttered with their garbage and debris. When the tide went out, it left a sea of mud two hundred to three hundred feet to the water's edge. The stench was nauseating! We saw people wadding in knee-deep mud to their boats which were tipped sideways from the lack of water to keep them afloat. The streets of Daru were unpaved and the passing vehicles kept the air filled with dust. We visited the town market filled with pineapple, bananas, sago and smelly fish; there were no artifacts for sale. Then I tried in vain to buy a pen in the two poorly stocked trade stores. "I'll be glad to go to Morehead Station!" I remarked.

"Will you? Do you think that Morehead will be better than the provincial capital?" Bill inquired.

Nelson, who introduced himself as the Headmaster, and a student met our plane at the dusty Morehead dirt landing field. "We will take you by river to our school. It is about five kilometers," he explained. As we traveled up the wide, muddy river in a small dingy powered by an outboard motor, they pointed to crocodiles and their nests along the bank. A group of boys greeted us speaking in English as we arrived at the landing near the path leading to the school about one-half kilometer in the bush. Near the end of the path we passed a piggery made of native materials and fenced with native poles. Some boys were cooking something in a huge iron kettle suspended over a fire. "We catch fish in the river and cook them for our pigs," they proudly told us.

Then we passed by a long building also made of native materials. "This is our carpentry shop," Nelson told us. Next there was another large building also made of native materials which he said was their classroom.

"Where is the high school?," we inquired.

"Oh we do not have a high school. This a vocational school. Our students learn some basic reading, writing and math, but mostly they are taught how to make furniture, like chairs and small tables. Tomorrow I will show you everything," Nelson explained.

"Peace Corps was under the impression that this was a high school. They received an application to send an agricultural skilled Volunteer."

"I know," he replied. "I heard that the government was requesting Peace Corps to send Volunteers to assistance in high school agriculture programs so I applied for a Volunteer to help at our vocational school. We have thirty-two boys but we have many more applications for next year and we have also received several applications from girls who want to be admitted to the school. This means we must build a dormitory for girls and make another dormitory for the boys. We really need your help. Tomorrow you will learn about my work and you will want to help." Then he took us to his house where we were to stay.

The house made of sawed timber had been built by a young woman anthropologist from Australia who had lived in it for five years. There were three small bedrooms, a living room, kitchen and a room which contained the base of a shower with a drain but no plumbing. Nelson showed us our bedroom which was just large enough to accommodate the two thin foam mattresses covered with worn sheets placed on the floor. Soon a boy brought a pail of river water which he put in the shower room with a small granite bowl. We understood; we were to stand in the shower base, pour water over our body, soap and rinse with more bowls of murky river water. Not to worry! Nelson pointed to the liklik haus.

He introduced us to his wife, Nobi, who like Nelson spoke excellent English. A young woman, perhaps seventeen, he introduced as his daughter. Nelson, Bill and I sat on the porch and visited until dusk and then Nobi announced that the evening meal was ready to serve. The three of us sat at a small table, and Nobi brought plates of fresh fried fish caught in the river, greens and fresh fruit. Bill and I insisted that she eat with us, but she refused. Later Nobi and another woman filled plates and sat on the floor at the far side of the room. The meal had been cooked on a pressure Bunsen burner set on the kitchen floor. They washed the dishes in cold water poured from a bucket into a double stainless steel sink which had no faucets, only a drain.

Bill and Nelson went to bed rather early. Nobi smiled at me and indicated that she would like to talk. We visited for at least two hours. I found her very intelligent and interesting, and we chatted about our two very different cultures. When I finally entered our bedroom and turned on my flashlight, I gasped because there were dozens of huge cockroaches scurrying across the floor, bed and up the walls. "Just shut up and go to bed! You can't kill them all," Bill exclaimed. "They nearly carried me away when I went to the liklik haus." Bill is such a kind, quiet spoken man. He had never before addressed me in such firm tones.

The plane would not return to Morehead Station for three more days. I could not possibly sleep with all the cockroaches which were over two inches long. They were huge! But on the other hand I could not go with out sleep for three nights. One can overcome fears when there is a need. I had been so afraid of spiders when I arrived at Itokama and I had learned to deal with them and the rodents, bugs and lizards that invaded our house. I laid down on the mattress; a cockroach ran across my arm and I turned on my flashlight and watched it run up the wall. For the three nights I slept well and peacefully.

In the morning Nelson took us on a tour of his vocational school. We were impressed with the workmanship of the chairs and tables. The students loved him. Close to the school site was a native village. Nelson introduced us to many of the people who very were friendly as we walked through their settlement. They kept their pigs in caged enclosures and fed them mango fruit, kaukau and vegetable peelings. On the second day the village men and Nelson went on a hunt to kill a deer for our dinner. The Australians had imported deer to Western Province many years ago. Nobi told me that when the men made a big hunt it was the women who walked through the forest to chase out the deer to the edge of the river so that the men could shoot them with arrows. This day they returned with a wallaby and we had some of the meat for our evening meal. It was very good. Earlier I had asked Nelson's daughter, "Who is this other woman that I have observed helping with the meals? Is she your auntie?"

"Oh she is my Mother, my Father's first wife. Her name is Sibura. She cannot speak English but she can speak pidgin," she replied.

Nobi spoke such good English and was evidently well educated so that I could imagine why Nelson found her fascinating and desirable to have as his second wife. I must make an effort to include Siburo in further conversations. The two women worked together preparing the meals and sharing the house work. They washed the laundry in the river and cared for the other five children. "We are going to the well to fetch water for cooking," they announced. "Would you like to go with us? This well is used only by our family. The village people and students get their water from the river." Bill and I were eager to join them. It was a dug well filled with milkish water. Siburo slowly lowered a bucket to fill with water being careful not to disturb the silt at the bottom. There was an audience of students and villagers watching this exciting scene. We understood that the Nelson family were revered by their neighbors. Nelson was so eager to secure a Peace Corps Volunteer. He had told some of the village men the reason we had come to visit the vocational school. He asked me to speak to the village people that night at a meeting outside the church to see if they would be willing to build a native bush house for a Volunteer.

The village men were quite receptive and announced that tomorrow they would start to build. "Wait until Nelson is advised that a Volunteer will be sent to Morehead Vocational School," I replied. "There are not enough Volunteers arriving to fill each request!"

At the end of the meeting Nelson told us that a group of the villagers, including Nelson, Nobi and Sibuna, were going to dance for us. The women wore ankle length grass skirts decorated in greens, reds and tans. They were the most striking grass skirts we had seen. When I expressed our admiration for their attire, Nobi announced that she would give me her skirt when we left for Port Moresby. They danced to kundu drums, but the rhythm and dances were much more lively than we had ever seen. The men danced in front lines doing fast gyrations and jumps while at the back the women swayed and twirled their beautiful grass skirts.

After the dance Nelson, Nobi, Bill and I sat on the porch and talked. We told Nelson that if we had decided to extend our Peace Corps assignment for a year or two more, we would enjoy working at the Morehead Vocational School. Earlier Nelson had indicated that he owned a lot of land in Western Province. After our statement he immediately told us that he would give us land to use for our lifetime if we would come here to live after we finish our Peace Corps duty. We were tempted. The next morning Nelson announced that he would walk to Morehead Station to talk with the O.I.C. of the Non Formal Educational Department and to pick up supplies. He told us that there was a road at the back of the village which ended at a small bridge to cross the river to Morehead Station. The O.I.C. would drive him home. Bill gave Nelson a 10 kina note to buy the groceries. Bill and I spent most of the day roaming through the village and visiting with the people. They took us outside the village to show us their huge yam house where all the people stored their yams. Later some students took us through the adjacent forest, showing us the trees they used for building, edible plants and those used to make dyes. Then we ended at the river and they pointed to their favorite fishing holes. They caught fish by sticking poles with baited lines in the riverbed and periodically they would check to see if there were any fish. The Morehead River emptied into the ocean about fifty kilometers to the south. When the tide was in, the river water flowed to the north and when the tide was out, it reversed the water flow to the south.

It was early evening before Nelson and the O.I.C. arrived. They were both slightly intoxicated. Bill and I suspected Nelson had used the 10 kina to buy beer because he brought no supplies to the house and soon the two men disappeared. When Nobi called us to eat she told us we must eat alone; Nelson would not be eating. The two women were very quiet and there was no visiting after dinner.

The plane was to arrive at Morehead Station the next afternoon. In the morning Nelson told us that he and the two women would take us by boat to town. His eyes were glassy and Nobi looked angrily at him as he staggered down the path to the river. Both women showed their embarrassment. Neither Bill nor I felt comfortable traveling on a river infested with crocodile with a drunken man zigzagging the boat from side to side. When he finally docked the boat, Nelson disclosed that he was taking us to the house of the O.I.C. for refreshments and a short visit. The wife of the O.I.C. served coffee and sweet biscuits. Then she left the room and returned with a large tote bag woven of pandanus leaves and gave it to me. I opened our suitcase and found a clean white muslin blouse and gave it to her and then I gave a blue laplap to Nobi and a brown laplap to Siburo. Nobi exclaimed, "Oh, I forgot to give you my grass skirt. I have been so upset!" When it was time to walk to the airstrip, the O.I.C. and his wife thanked us again and again for honoring them with our visit.

We were glad to board the plane to Daru, but we had enjoyed the experience of Morehead Vocational school. This time the pilot flew a different route stopping first at Bensback Lodge and wildlife park along Bensback River about twenty-five kilometers from the border of Irian Jaya. It is a paradise for photographers because the park contains abundant varieties of birds and animals and fishermen can ply their skills to catch barramundi in the river. The longer flight gave us the opportunity to view the terrain of marshes and lowland savannahs interspersed with ribbons of streams which empty into the sea or connect with the Fly River.

Our month of travel had afforded us the opportunity to talk with people from many different tribes, to observe their traditional dress and customs and to view the landscape. It simply confirmed our opinion that Papua New Guinea is the most beautiful and fascinating country in the world.

CHAPTER 14

"To leave the world a bit better, whether by a healthy child, a garden patch or a redeemed social condition; to know even one life has breathed easier because you have lived. This is to have succeeded" - *Emerson*

Two years in Peace Corps is a short time to make a difference in a third world country. We did not travel to Papua New Guinea to force them to change their culture; we went to help them, but only if they wished to change. We did not go to build a monument to ourselves; we went to teach skills and to build friendships with the Nationals. We were anxious to return to Itokama to see how the people had carried on some of the projects during our month away from the village.

On our return trip to Itokama we had to stop over in Popondetta for three days. This delay gave Bill the opportunity to check with the manager of the Agricultural Bank to see if William Suremo's loan had been approved to build a new house of sawed timber framework and a tin roof.Since William was unable to travel to Popondetta due to the payback situation, he had written a letter to the bank giving Bill Craig his power of attorney to negotiate the loan. It was an unbelievable show of trust by William. The loan for the house had been approved.

Pennyfather, the local agent for Mainland Holdings, saw me walking to the Wing Hay store and asked me to come to his office to talk. He was quite concerned because he had learned that three more coffee cooperatives had filed similar lawsuits against Mainland Holdings for discrepancies in coffee shipments against paid invoices. He was beginning to wonder about the reliability of the company; he was opposed to cheating the Nationals.

When we arrived at Itokama on the following Tuesday morning flight the people greeted us with their usual warm greetings of handshakes, laughter and tears. This would be our final month among the Barai. There was much work to finish before we departed.

Bill immediately checked the Nahara Bakery. At the end of the coffee season he had approached William with a proposal to use the vacant old trade store area in the coffee storage for a bakery to provide fresh bread to sell at the new trade store. Bill built a drum stove oven which could bake twelve loaves at one time and then he taught two women to bake bread. Wende, whom I had taught to bake bread, would be in charge of the bakery. They made bread on Monday, Wednesday and Friday. It was difficult to maintain an ample supply of firewood to heat the oven; the men and boys were reluctant to cut firewood even for a wage. The village people waited outside the bakery to buy the bread for 1.00 kina a loaf and seldom were any loaves left to take to the trade store to sell. Sometimes yeast was not available in the Popondetta stores. We had brought a case of yeast from Port Moresby. The bakery ran out of yeast during our absence so the women had made baking powder biscuits instead of bread. We were thrilled that they had improvised and kept the bakery operating.

Next Bill started working on William's house. In October William had hired the BNEA sawmill to cut timber for his new home. He had purchased a tree and moved the sawmill to a new location in the jungle across from the airport. The house blueprint called for three 6 x 8 ft.bedrooms, a living area, a kitchen and a porch along the east and north side of the house which would be a pleasant place to sit and "story" and enjoy the beautiful views overlooking a coffee garden on the north and a deep ravine to the east. Bill had insisted that Wende must approve the house plans as well as her husband. The timber had been sawed, the footing poles set and the floor joist and flooring laid prior to our month away from the village. When it was time to erect the inside partition framework William decided to make two larger bedrooms instead of the three. Wende was very disturbed because they had two boys and a small baby girl and so they needed two bedrooms for their children but William flatly refused to change his mind. Bill and a crew of four men finished the house except for the bamboo siding which could be added after we left Itokama. He also wired the house for lights to be operated from the trade store's Yamaha generator.

I was so anxious to find out how Nahara had progressed during our absence. First I talked to Titus, who was in charge of the Agent Bank, and I checked his reports of deposits and withdrawals he had made to the Westpac Bank at Popondetta. I complimented him for his good work. The Agent Bank had been quite a challenge for me. For a couple of months I had been in charge while I taught Titus how to do the paperwork. New depositors who did not speak English must complete a special application form giving their name, village, last name of their father and clan name. Many Barai people had adopted Christian names. Some gave their Christian name while other put their Barai name on the applications. When a person applied for a savings account and did not speak English, I would need an interpreter to assist me. Now if that person was an in-law of the applicant, he or she could not repeat the name of the applicant because it was taboo! I would take these applications to the bank in Popondetta and they would issue the depositor book. Later the applicant would come to the Agent Bank to pick up his or her deposit book. It might have been issued to a Christian name or a Barai name. For example: John Michael's passbook (there were two John Michaels from Neokananee) had been issued under Silva Arani. Titus had been eager to be in charge of the new enterprise. He had visited the Westpac Bank and saw that some of the bank tellers wore tee shirts inscribed with WESTPAC BANK. He wanted a shirt to wear during the banking hours. Taboda, the Westpac Bank Manager, sent Titus a shirt. Now Titus felt like a real bank executive and so he had tried very hard to learn all about the new Agent Bank in Itokama. Next I must check the Nahara Coffee Growers books.

William gave me the net profit statement he had made for November. The December store inventory had been taken and he was in the process of pricing the inventory and completing the profit figures. Now I knew that he had learned well and so I praised him for his work! Then he told me he had a problem. Early in the year we had talked with him about the need to pay a small dividend per share for the first time; Nahara Coffee Growers had been organized ten years ago. "If Nahara makes a profit, you should consider paying a small bonus to each shareholder," we told him. While we were away during the month of November he had called a meeting of the Directors and told them that Nahara Coffee Growers had made over 15,000 kina for the year of 1987 plus the 4,000 kina gift from the two political candidates, Tago and Doi. He proposed that they pay a small dividend. So the Directors voted to pay 7,500 kina in dividends. William understood that most of the year's profit must be reserved to finance the 1988 coffee purchases so that it would not be necessary to acquire a bank loan and to save money to purchase a truck. The Directors insisted that half of the year's profit be returned to the shareholders. "Please come and talk with the Directors," William pleaded. We did. However the Directors did not seem to understand money matters but after much talking they finally agreed to pay .40 toea per share, a total amount of 2,895.60 kina. The original shares had sold for 1.00 kina per share.

The day of the shareholder meeting the village was filled with visitors and shareholders. The meeting lasted all day and included electing a Board of Directors; the same Directors were re-elected to serve another year. Some shareholders came expecting to receive as much as 500 kina per share! The mentality of these people is unbelievably child-like in business matters. At the close of the meeting the shareholders came to the window of Williams's office to record their name, verify their number of shares and to receive their dividend paid in cash.

During our absence the Directors of Nahara had voted to have a mumu in our honor on the evening of December 18th at the coffee storage building. That evening the building was soon filled with at least one hundred twenty-five people and a crowd waited outside the door. "This mumu is made by Nahara. Let the people outside make their own feast for Bill and Margel," William announced and he locked the door to the storage. Then he told us that he had killed one of his pigs for the mumu, a definite sign of honor to us. Neither Bill nor I had ever had to taste their wild pig meat; this time we must because otherwise they would feel insulted. It was tough and fat but we indicated our delight at having a pig killed in our honor. I had been taught as a child to never lie but here among these people it seemed permissible on occasion to utter tiny white lies to convey our appreciation to them. We all sat on the floor to eat the feast of pig, kaukau, yams, pumpkin tip greens cooked with chicken, rice and corned beef, corn, beans, pumpkin, papaya and pineapple followed by cups of coffee. The Youth Bands from Itokama played their guitars and sang to us. Then William, standing behind a small table in the center of the room, talked about our influence on the village people and he thanked us for helping and working with Nahara Coffee Growers. Next Dr. Martin Lukes talked and then Simon made a speech. Finally I spoke trying to express to them our thanks for their cooperation, their many acts of kindness and for their friendship. How can one communicate in a few minutes the compassion and love we felt for these Barai people and convey to them the effect they had made on our lives?

"Bill will you come stand beside me?" William asked. "We have some gifts for you." Wende followed Bill to stand beside William. She gave Bill a large woven pandanus mat which she had made. There were diagonal lines of small purple squares on it. She used old discarded carbon paper to make the dye for the purple design; for months I had given her the old carbon paper from the Nahara office. Serwin, a Nahara Director from Tama village, gave Bill a double boar tusk necklace which is held between the teeth to decorate the mouth at a Sing Sing. Frank, a Director who lived in Vuisiriro village, gave Bill a "killing stone" mounted on a pole and decorated with feathers; we understood that he was giving up an ancestor! Our eyes filled with tears. Then Frank gave me a type of folded pandanus mat which can easily be carried in a bilum and a piece of tapa cloth painted with the Barai black and red pattern. John Michaels, a Director from Neokananee, gave me a boar tusk necklace decorated with a bit of tapa cloth and cuscus fur. Steve Imoi, the Director from Kuai village, placed his own traditional headdress on my head which was made of parrot feather banded with tiny nasa shells; I had seen him wearing this headdress many times.

Steve often helped me wait on the customers in the trade store. Bill and I were very touched with these gifts which were items that the givers held very dear; they had parted with gifts far more precious than money, in fact they had parted with their prized possessions. We were so touched, so overwhelmed by their generosity!

Brother James and Sister Daus helped us carry the gifts to our house afterwards. "Stay a while and talk," Bill said. Then Sister Daus handed me four small pandanus mats about the size of place mats. There were tears in her eyes as I hugged her. "Brata Bill em i bilong yu," (Brother Bill it belongs to you) and James handed Bill a "killing stone" mounted on a stick and decorated with cassowary feathers. "Bilong yu nau!" he repeated (It belongs to you now.)

"Brata, mi no ken kisim ston bilong yu. Em i tumbuna bilong yu!" (I can't take this stone from you. It is your ancestor.)

With tears streaming down his handsome black face, Brother James repeated, "Yumi brata; tumbuna olsem." (We are brothers; same ancestor.) and he took the killing stone from Bill's hand, kissed the stone then handed it back to Bill.

I had brought a large tan, lacy woven straw hat with a wide floppy brim from the U.S., but I had never worn it. I tied on a pure silk scarf, red with a yellow design, for a hatband and placed it on Sister Daus's head and I fastened a red necklace from the Philippines around her neck. Bill gave Brother James his hatchet which he had autographed and fastened a necklace of blue beads from the Philippines around his neck. Weeks before I had knitted each of them a bilum. Sister Daus sat in my chair sobbing because we were leaving them. It had been a very emotional evening.

The next day we gave to each of the Nahara Directors and William a bilum that I had knitted in multi colors of yarns; each bilum was of a different pattern. We gave Wende a needlepoint picture that I had made and Bill had framed. We gave necklaces to some of our favorite village children. Bill gave Jeffery, a young school boy, who helped to build the school desks and had recently graduated from the sixth grade, a wooden attache type box that Bill had made and Jeffery had admired. The last few days were filled with reflections and feelings. We were anxious to return to the U.S.A. to be near to our families and friends and yet we felt sadness at leaving our Barai friends. How can one have the better of two worlds? Impossible!

Martin from Sirafe #1 brought his own traditional headdress to give to Bill and he in return gave Martin a wrench for his coffee pulper and fastened a necklace which we had bought in Madang around his neck. I gave him one of my dresses for his wife. Women came to the house to ask if we would have anything to sell when we left them such as bath towels, sheets and cooking pots. Our days were filled with last minute duties. Check the Nahara books, order more trade store goods by radio.

I had spent hours on the porch during the last year making phone calls for Nahara and for the village people. "Bravo 24 Neokananee Village. Come in Port Moresby," I called over the short wave radio asking for the long distance telephone operator. One time it had taken over nine hours to make two phone calls, one to Peace Corps and one to Popondetta for supplies. First I must wait until the radio was free of calls before I could contact the operator, then she would tell me that she was processing other calls ahead of mine and so I must sit on the porch and wait until she called, "Bravo 24 Neokananee; come in please" and then I could place my phone call. Hopefully the number would not be busy because otherwise I had to start the process of making a call over again. One hour in the morning and one hour in the afternoon the radio-telephone service was reserved for the ships at sea to report their locations, cargo information and their docking schedules.

I had to record the cost of each phone call, collect the money and give the record and the money to Simon so that BNEA could pay the phone bill. One day when I placed a phone call the operator told me that BNEA had not paid their phone bill for three months; she did not know how much longer she could handle our phone calls. Each time I turned on the radio our porch filled with people who found the radio communication so entertaining. Sometimes I tried to do needlework on the porch while I was waiting for the telephone operator to reply, but the people would gather so close around me, leaning over my head that I was afraid their headlice would get into my hair.

Bill checked the Nahara generator, changed the oil and filter for the last time. He made a few more bushknife handles, repaired a couple of umbrellas, injected a few more pigs. I gave a few more knitting lessons, treated more tropical ulcer wounds - for the last time? And we both worked with Nahara and BNEA . We both kept thinking, "Is this the last time I can or will do this for my friends?" Each visitor on our porch became more important, more special. We knew that we would miss these contacts so much. It is impossible for me to write words to describe the close bonds we had made with the Barai people in twenty-four months. We were scheduled to leave Itokama on December 29th.

Since the beginning of October we had to cook over an open fire on our porch because the new tank of LP gas had lasted only four days. Evidently the tank had not been properly filled and the Popondetta stores were out of LP gas until the next shipment arrived by sea freight. We hired boys to cut us fire wood and we cooked our meals with an audience of Nationals watching us, laughing and shaking their heads in disbelief at our extravagance with fuel. For us it was another

Farewell gift for Bill. A killing stone from Frank,
a Director of Nahara.

The Martin Luke family give us a farewell mumu.

challenge like learning to wash clothes in a stream during the recent drought; it was one more learning experience. We had learned to cope with the conditions in another culture.

One day Clarance Vato walked from Kokoro village to give me a folded pandanus mat. He was my brightest student in the second two week bookkeeping class that I had taught in July. By this time we had given so many things to special friends. "What could I give to him in return?" Then I remember a grey tee shirt inscribed with "Nashville, ain't nothing like it" which I often wore to class and he had admired it so I gave it to him and said, " Remember your old "white-skin" teacher. He was very pleased.

Dr. Martin Luke came to the house to tell us that the Luke family was having a farewell mumu feast for us on Christmas Eve at 6:00 P.M. All of the people living in the Mission Station were also invited. The Luke family decorated the grounds outside their home with garlands of tropical flowers and greenery. Bill and I were seated in two chairs behind a small table covered with a white and green checkered cloth and a bouquet of fresh flowers. Doctor brought us a large platter which held our food wrapped in banana leaves and cooked separately from the other food in the mumu. He opened the leaves to show us the yam, kaukau, sliced onion, pumpkin and a half chicken which his wife had prepared especially for Daddy and Mom. He cut the chicken in half and served it and the vegetables on separate plates. Bill's portion of chicken was very rare; the blood ran freely as he tore the leg apart from the thigh. My two pieces of chicken were well done. I noticed that Bill consumed his chicken quickly before he ate the vegetables. After the meal Doctor gave a talk about our work with the Barai and then he gave Bill a wall hanging of black velour painted with the headdresses of seven different tribes and the inscription "Greetings From Papua New Guinea". Sister Dorcus gave me a shoulder bag she had made with tapa cloth decorated with Job's tears and cuscus fur. We had given our gifts to the Luke family a few days ago. Father Daniel was sitting on the ground on a pandanus mat near our chairs and he called to us," Sorry Bill and Margel that I had no money to buy a gift for you."

"Father you gave us a priceless gift the first Sunday that we attended your church. You told us that you regarded us as being just as black as you were. That meant to us that you accepted us as your equals. Thank you very much," I told him. He wiped a tear.

It was a lovely party and another event that we will always remember. As we walked to our house after the mumu I told Bill that I had marveled at how quickly he had consumed the partially raw chicken. "I hope it doesn't make you ill."

I was awakened about 10:30 that night by loud knocking and someone called, "Margel!" It was William Suremo. "I am sorry to wake you but I heard a message for you over the Popondetta radio this evening that asked you to call for an emergency message. They gave two different telephone numbers, but I was only able to write down one of them. I hope it is not bad news." I knew it was a Port Moresby telephone number.

I thanked William and went to the bedroom to waken Bill. Our first thought was that my son-in-law might have had another heart attack. It was too late to try to radio the Port Moresby telephone operator. That radio-phone service closed at 6:00 P.M. Tomorrow was Christmas and perhaps there would be no service over the holidays. We dressed and walked to Dr. Lukes and awakened him to see if he could call by radio through the Popondetta Hospital. "They are closed until Monday morning," he told us.

We walked back to the house and talked for a while and then we began to pack our artifacts, books and other belongings. We didn't sleep that night. At 7:30 A.M. I began trying to radio the Port Moresby operator. She answered at 8:00 and placed my call. The Assistant Peace Corps Director answered. "I'm sorry to tell you the bad news. Bill's son , Bill Jr., has died of a sudden heart attack. We have chartered a plane to fly you to Port Moresby so that we can fly you home for his funeral. Bring all of your belongings because you will not return to Itokama. The plane will arrive in Itokama about 2:00 today. Can you be ready.?"

"We will be packed." I replied.

"Either the Director or I will come with the plane," he said.

I repeated the message to Bill and put my arms around him and hugged him. He kept shaking his head and mumbling, "I don't know. I don't know what happened!" How terrible! What could I say? Bill is a very strong person and somehow he was able to go through the preparations to leave. I knew he was suffering silently. Young Bill had no health problems to our knowledge and the last time we saw him shortly before we left for Papua New Guinea he looked the picture of health. Bill continued packing and I ran to Nahara to tell William that we must leave today.

At 11:00 A.M. we heard a plane circling and then it landed. Soon the Peace Corps Director and his wife knocked on our door. After offering their sympathy, the Director told us that a storm front was moving in fast and so we needed to leave at once. The porch was filled with people and some came inside. Sister Dorcus and Wende were crying. They said that they would clean out the refrigerator and sweep the house after we were gone. We gave away all the things that we had not yet packed to the people. Some had asked to buy towels, sheets, tupperware, etc. "Take them, We give them to you. No money, please." Boys came to carry our luggage and boxes to the airstrip. We walked slowly out of our house for the last time and started saying our goodbyes!

The people filed off the porch and formed a line toward the airfield. They clung to us, shaking their heads in disbelief, their eyes filled with tears. Over and over we repeated, "We will miss you dear friend and we will never forget you. Thank you! Thank you!" The line of people continued down the center of Itokama. We were amazed to see people from other Barai villages. How did they know we were leaving? But then they have some type of jungle communication because we had experienced this same phenomenon many times when news of happenings seemed to reach the other Barai villages immediately after it was known in Itokama. Was it transmitted by ESP or whispers or by runners? It certainly was not sent by drums.

Emmanuel, who had worked with Bill building the trade store, sat on his front stoop sobbing loudly because his friend Bill was leaving. They had managed to communicate well with signs and eye contacts because neither spoke the other's language. His son ran to comfort his father and then he pushed into the line of people to tell us his papa wanted a towel, anything, to remember his friend. "Run to the house and take a towel from the bathroom. You can wash it and give to him," I told Lester, who was the manager of the walk-about saw. The line was endless. Suddenly we realized that we had already said our goodbyes to several people that were waiting in line. They had said farewell, then ran ahead and stood in line again. "Not to worry; not to worry!" They didn't want us to leave and we were sorry to go! Not only the adults stood in line but the children, little children as well; children who ran to shake our hands as we walked to work or returned home in the evenings, or called to us as we passed their house, no matter the time of day, "Morning, Morning." Zacchaeus was under two years old when we had arrive in Itokama. For the first few months whenever we came near to him he would scream in fright at the "white-skins". Here he was in line offering his little hand to say goodbye to his two "white-skin" friends. Oh, how we will miss these children and the adults! The line continued all the way to the Nahara store next to the airstrip. Handshakes, smiles, tears, touches, goodbye, goodbye, goodbye.

At the far north edge of the Nahara Coffee storage, away from the line of people, stood William and his family. His head was bowed and he was sobbing. "William," I said, "We have lived two years with the Barai people and we have tried to obey your customs, but if I were to say goodbye to you in my country I would do it this way." I put my arms around him and kissed him goodbye on his left cheek." William you have learned well and you will do fine with the trade store and coffee business. You are a smart man. If you have a problem write to me; I will answer." He never raised his face, looked at me or replied. I walked to the line of people leading to the airstrip entrance. More goodbyes, more handshakes, hugs and tears. Wende and her small son said goodbye for the fourth time as we boarded.

Bill and I were seated in the plane, and before our Peace Corps Director entered he stood at the door of the plane and said, "Bill and Margel, don't ever say that you didn't make a difference in Itokama. These people love you two. I've watched more than three hundred of them bid you goodbye. I am so glad I came today and saw it with my own eyes!" There were tears streaming down his cheeks when he boarded the plane.

As the pilot taxied to the north end of the airstrip for take-off, Bill and I saw Brother James running up the path from Kuai towards the airstrip, waving his arms and he was wearing Sister Daus's new straw hat with the red silk band.

The normal flight time from Popondetta, which is one hundred miles north of Itokama, to Port Moresby is thirty minutes. This time the flight took one and one-half hours because the National pilot had to fly east to the coast and follow the coast line south and then fly north along the western coastline to Port Moresby to avoid the storm over the central mountains. The Director and his wife took us to their home and then the Director and the Assistant Director worked the rest of the day at the Peace Corps office to secure us two seats on an airline to Los Angeles on Monday morning. The trip via Guam, Honolulu, Los Angeles to Chicago took thirty-five hours of which twenty-two hours were actual flying time. We landed at Chicago at mid-night and our final flight to South Bend, Indiana was scheduled for 7:00 A.M. Neither of us felt like sleeping so we sat in the terminal all night. At 6:00 A.M. it began to snow and at 6:45 A.M. the flight was canceled because South Bend airport was closed due to a blizzard. We managed to catch a bus and five and one-half hours later we arrived at the South Bend terminal. The bus driver had radioed the terminal to page my son who was waiting there to drive us to our home at Akron to get warm clothing and drive us to the funeral. He had called the mortuary to tell them that we might arrive late. The funeral service was delayed for one-half hour until we finally arrived.

CHAPTER 15

"If the days grow dark, if care and pain press close and sharp on heart and brain, then lovely pictures still will bloom upon the walls of memory's room." - Charles Monroe Dickinson

We returned from the U.S.A. to Port Moresby on January 10, 1988 to complete the last two months of our three month extension. Bill was immediately sent to the Mendi/Kagua area for ten days to consult with the Peace Corps couple who had been sent to Kagua High School and to talk with the Headmaster of the school. I remained in Port Moresby to work in the Peace Corps office and to move our few belongings into the Peace Corps training house which was a twenty-two minute walk from the office. It was a comfortable furnished house; there were three bedrooms, a living/dining area, a kitchen and a laundry room equipped with an Australian semi-automatic washer and dryer and an ironing board and electric iron. For the first time in over two years I was able to iron our clothes. Every window of the house was covered with steel grid and both outside doors had a second steel grid bar door on the exterior and double locks on each door. There was a third steel grid door at the entrance to the hall leading to the three bedrooms and the bath. This was for the protection from "rascals" or thieves. We had in fact changed our safe surroundings in Itokama to an environment contaminated with crime. However we could buy fresh vegetables and meat, long-life milk and fresh bread, no more canned meat and rice. It was a drastic change in our life style.

When Bill returned from his trip to Mendi he repaired two burners on the electric stove at the Peace Corps training house, installed security lights on the four corners of the house and on the house of the APCD. Then the Director sent us to Menyamya in Morobe Province for two weeks to assist a senior citizen woman Volunteer who had been sent to work with agri projects at the Menyamya High School. She had phoned him that when she arrived the Headmaster had insisted that, in addition to managing the school gardens, she must also teach and she had no teaching credentials. She was very concerned; however the Headmaster said that he would get permission for her to teach from the proper authorities.

When we landed at the Menyamya sod airstrip a National showed us the way to the Guest House where we were to stay. Each unit was large enough for two bunk beds, a tiny table and storage shelves. There were two bath facilities at the far end of the row of rooms and a separate building to serve as a lounge, dining area and kitchen. We must cook our own meals. Millie, the Volunteer, was also staying here until her new house was finished. She had been in Menyamya about three weeks and so far no attempt had been made to connect the electricity, gas, water and sewage so that she could move into the house. We knew our first task was to get acquainted with the Headmaster so we could push him to finish the construction.

The next day we visited the Headmaster, Paul Rillion, to introduce ourselves and to volunteer to help him in any way. He told us that an Australian contractor was building the new high school to replace the present school and dormitories mostly made of bush materials. At the present time the contractor was concentrating on completing the classrooms so that the students could be moved to the new school as soon as possible. New houses had also been built for the teachers near the new school site; all except the house for the new Volunteer were completed and occupied. The Headmaster had purchased unassembled furniture, an LP gas stove and an automatic washing machine to furnish the house. Bill offered to assemble the furniture. Later we walked to the new house which was set on a hill overlooking a field of kunai grass, the new school and the Yapwoi river. The house had three bedrooms, a kitchen with built in cabinets and sink, a large living area, bath and laundry room and polished wood floors. This new development was about a twenty minute walk from the town.

Menyamya is a government station. All the houses and building are made of sawed timber. There are several well stocked trade stores, a daily produce market, a coffee buying station, a post office, two banks, a small hospital, a D.P.I station, a forestry station, provincial offices, the Anga Development office, a sawmill, a Lutheran Church and Mission School, a high school and an active, busy airstrip. Mail arrives three days a week. We felt Millie would be living in a city compared to our amenities in Itokama!

The following morning we visited the old school. The Headmaster and some of the teachers were organizing their classrooms for the opening of the new school year on Monday. Three sewing machines were broken so Bill remained at the school to repair them, a lawn mower and to sharpened all the school's bushknives and grassknives. He talked with Michael, the agriculture teacher, about his plans for the school poultry project. Michael had ordered one hundred broiler type chicks from Lae to use as meat birds in the cafeteria. "Last year there was a big problem. The students over-fed them and so they got too fat and couldn't walk," he said. Bill told him that the cause of the problem was that he had put too many birds in too small an area therefore they had no room to exercise.

This year the class gardens would be moved near the new school site. Headmaster Rillon said the school owned a Ford Model 6000 tractor, but neither he or Michael knew how to utilize it. "Bill can you teach us to plow? Next week I will borrow a two-bottom disc plow from D.P.I." Of course Bill was glad to help. Then Paul Rillon invited us and Millie to come to his house for dinner the next evening. He said that his wife, who was also a teacher, would prepare a special Filipino meal because their home was in Manila.

The dinner party gave us an opportunity to get better acquainted and to talk about the uncompleted house. He told us that the contractor needed to connect the septic tank to the bathroom soil pipes, the LP gas line and the electricity and then Millie could move in. "Let me do that," Bill said. The Headmaster agreed that Bill could start on Monday. Then he told us that he was taking a group of boys by school truck tomorrow, Saturday, to collect some long poles to repair the seventh and eighth grade boys' dormitory which had been damaged by fire. Bill and I were invited to accompany them to see the beautiful scenery. He must travel about sixty kilometers on the Lae road to reach the forests; the country side around Menyama is mostly rolling hills covered with grass and a few small trees and bushes. When he came to the forests, he dropped off the boys to cut the poles and then he drove us several kilometers further to a lookout point to show us the winding road ahead flanked by more forest and a view of the purple mountains in the distance. His wife had sent sandwiches for the three of us and as we ate our lunch we enjoyed the lovely view ahead. Then we returned to pick up the boys and the poles. They were waiting for us at a turnout along the road; some of had draped green vines around their neck and decorated their hair with sprigs of fern. Before they loaded the poles on the truck the Headmaster set a large kettle of cold rice, plus two cans of fish on the ground for their lunch. The boys quickly gathered banana leaves to serve as plates and three of the boys produced small woven mats of green pandanus leaves which they had made while they waited for us to return to drive them back to Menyamya.

The next day the Paul and Bill assembled the furniture and then Bill connected the gas line to the new stove and connected the electricity to the house. Monday morning Bill started digging the trench for the sewage pipes and soon three boys arrived to help him. Headmaster said that before the septic system could be completed he must drive to Lae to buy the six inch sewage pipe to connect the septic tank to the bath room drains, so he would have the boys build a small "liklik haus" for Millie to use until he needed to travel to Lae for school supplies. He had not planned to buy her a refrigerator, but after Bill insisted that she would be much happier if she had one, Paul agreed that he would purchase a refrigerator on his next trip to Lae. He had advised Millie that she must pay for her utilities. We told him that it was customary for the organization who had requested a Peace Corps Volunteer to pay the utilities. He promised to discuss it with the Board of Governors. We had been one of the few Volunteers who had to pay for LP gas and kerosene.

The new site for the school gardens, located on the side of a hill, covered an area of about three hectares. Years before the local Nationals had planted gardens here dividing the ground into small plots with shallow dug drainage ditches. The ground was covered with waist high kunai grass which would be difficult to plow under and, combined with having to drive across the numerous ditches, would be a demanding task for an experienced tractor operator. When the time arrived for Bill to teach Michael and Headmaster to plow, he discovered that the tractor switch was damaged; someone had tampered with it, so he wired the tractor direct to start it. While Bill was instructing Michael how to maneuver the equipment across the ground, the Headmaster and the thirty-two boys from grade ten arrived to watch. After Bill finished teaching Headmaster Rillon, he invited each of the boys to plow one or two rounds. None of the boys had ever driven a vehicle; they had no knowledge of operating mechanical equipment; they had never put their hands on a steering wheel or released a clutch with their foot. Each boy took his turn while his friends watched and cheered. When it was time for them to return to the school for lunch, they refused to go so Bill sent one boy to find me at the guest house with a note for me to bring some lunch to the field. I bought bread, peanut butter, pork luncheon meat, sweet biscuits and pop at a trade store and took to them. The boys were delighted. Later, after every boy had a turn, Bill finished plowing the field.

The only possible place for the tractor to enter the garden site was a narrow strip of ground at the top of the hill and even then the driver must guide the tractor over an abrupt stoney mound. Bill feared that neither Michael or Paul Rillon were capable of driving over this rough ground without the possibility of upsetting the tractor. It was more dangerous driving up the hill out of the garden because the front wheels of the tractor lifted off the ground. So Bill asked Headmaster to send two or three older boys with shovels to help him remove some of the larger stones to smooth the way for the tractor. Paul sent the same three boys who had helped Bill dig the trench for the septic pipe. Their names were Solomon Moses, William Mekeni and Foukawe Onafimo.

I didn't feel productive at Menyamya. My only accomplishments were talking with and encouraging Millie, helping her shop for bedding and kitchen items and helping her carry her belongings to her new house During the day I sometimes walked through Menyamya, visiting the stores and talking with the Nationals. Most days I would go to the village market to buy fresh vegetables and fruit for our evening meal. Each morning people from distant villages walked many kilometers to the Menyamya outdoor market carrying huge bilums of fruits and vegetables grown in their gardens to sell. It was amazing to see the variety of produce grown in this area. There was the usual kaukau, yams, taro, beans, corn, greens, bananas and pineapple, but there were also cabbages, carrots, sweet peppers, peas, chinese cabbage, oranges, English potatoes and green onions. The women wore grass skirts and a blouse and the men wore arse grass or shorts; if it was raining they wore a poncho or cape of tapa to cover their head and body.

One day as I was walking along the dirt main street, I approached a group of chanting marchers. Their faces were painted; they had greenery draped about their heads and shoulders; they were carrying axes, bushknives, bows and arrows and their faces were filled with anger. They were going to the provincial office to protest a death and demand that the doctor at Menyamya's small hospital be expelled immediately. A National from a nearby village had been bitten by a poisonous snake and was brought to the doctor for treatment. The doctor had no antitoxin serum and, and knowing that the man would surely die without serum, he refused to admit him to the hospital. The victim soon expired and so the people of his village were extremely angry. The doctor left Menyamya on the next commercial plane!

The school boys told Bill that a kilometer or two beyond the new school site was a swinging bridge which had been built by the Japanese during WWII. Bill asked the Headmaster if we could drive the tractor to the bridge. The narrow winding road on the opposite side of the river from the school was more like a path. We passed by giant clumps of bamboo before we approached a path leading to the right. Two Nationals were standing along the roadway evidently wondering what vehicle was approaching. We asked how much farther we must drive to see the swinging bridge. "Come. We will take you there," they replied. So we parked the tractor and followed them down a narrow twisting path several hundred feet until we came to a small village. The walls of the huts were made of pandanus leaves held in place by bands of small sticks and the roofs were of kunai grass. These huts sat on the ground and had dirt floors. The people were very friendly and eager for us to take their photos. Then they led us down a path to the bridge. The two hundred foot bridge was suspended from two 1 inch steel cables above and two 1 inch cables below which held the expanded metal flooring. The sides were woven wire. The village people told us that the bridge had been improved from the original bridge built by the Japanese.

We were to leave Menyamya on Saturday morning at 7:00. The evening before we were to depart Headmaster Rillon and his wife came to the guest house to say goodbye and he gave each of us an achievement pin from the school. "I wish you two people would come to Menyamya for one or two years and help me. Bill, you are an unbelievable man!" Very early the next morning the three boys, Solomon, William and Foukawe, came to the guest house while we were eating breakfast to say goodbye to Mr. Bill. Foukawe and William each gave Bill a bilum. "I wish my father could have met you, Mr. Bill," Foukawe exclaimed. "He is the Headmaster at Goroko High School in Eastern Highland Province." Then all three asked if we could find them a pen pal in the United States. We promised to try.

The three boys and Millie walked with us to the airport. Soon Michael, the agriculture teacher, came and then Headmaster Rillon and his wife Leti appeared. They promised that the next time they traveled to the U.S.A. they would come to Indiana to visit us. Then Leti gave us a cookbook from the Philippines. Millie was also from Indiana and lived about forty-five miles east of us. We had traveled half way around the world to meet. When the plane arrived at 7:00 A.M. the pilot told us that this plane would fly west to Kerema before continuing to Lae on the eastern coast which was our destination. He told us a plane flying direct to Lae would arrive at 1:00 but he would advise us to fly with him because often Menyama had fog by noon and so perhaps the afternoon plane would be unable to land. The pilot flew south west through country laced with jungle and limestone canyons. He landed at Kaintiba airstrip which was on the side of a hill and the steepest airstrip in Papua New Guinea. The plane landed on this very short runway going up hill and on takeoff the plane traveled down hill, reached the end of the short runway and fell into space before it gained flying speed. The next stop was at Karauwi airstrip and then the plane landed at Kerema on the western coast of Gulf Province. The Kerema airport is considered the most dangerous landing strip in Papua New Guinea because the sea is at the end of the runway, much like Hong Kong's Kai Tak Airport. Then our plane took off and landed again at Karauwi and Kaintiba airstrips to deliver passengers and supplies. It was mid-afternoon before we finally landed at Nadzab Airport, built by the Allies during WW11, forty-five kilometers northwest of Lae. About six months ago the Lae Airport had been closed by the Minister of Aviation because of cracked tarmac and the impossibility of securing additional land to lengthen the runways. We must find a ride to Lae to spend the night before continuing our travels to Kavieng in New Ireland Province the next day. Traveling in Papua

New Guinea is a challenge and endurance test. We asked our pilot if we would be safe to ride a PMV to Lae. "No," he replied. "Although the new PMV laws forbid us to carry passengers in our Talair van, I will make an exception because you two are foreigners." The Talair van delivered us to our reserved room at a hostel. Our first task was arranging for a ride early the next morning back to Nadzab Airport for our flight on Air Niugini airlines. Finally we hired a National, who lived next door to the hostel, to drive us to the airport the next morning. He charged us 39 kina.

We flew to Rabaul, at the eastern end of New Britain Province, the next day where we must spend a day before we could get a continuing flight to Kavieng, New Ireland. As our plane prepared to land at the Rabaul Airport, it passed over a chain of volcanoes which emitted clouds of steam and sulphur gases Rabaul is regarded as the only town in the world to be built inside the rim of an ancient volcano. About fourteen hundred years ago the caldera crumbled and fell and sea water rushed in to form Simpson Harbor. Matupit is the only remaining active volcano which poses a threat. It erupted in 1937 almost destroying Rabaul and again in 1984 the rumblings increased to such an extent that Rabaul was put on alert, but then Matupit quieted. We hired a taxi to take us on a tour of the area. The driver drove us along the coast to view the scattered relics of WW11, rusting aircraft, tanks and coastal guns. Then he drove on the Kokopo Road to the ruins of Queen Emma's home, Gunatambo; only the stairs to her once beautiful mansion remains and a magnificent view of the city. In the late 1800's Queen Emma, who was an American citizen from Samoa, established her own little empire comprised of plantations, a number of ships and many trade stores. The driver also showed us the Japanese War Memorial. The next day we flew Air Niugini to Kavieng where we would spend two weeks at Manggai High School with the new Peace Corps female Volunteer who had been sent there to work with the agriculture projects. She owned and had lived on a cattle ranch in Montana and had also taught school. Siniwin, the agri teacher, had told us before we left Manggai in November that he had just been informed by the Provincial Education Department that he would be transferred to Utu High School near Kavieng for the 1988 school year, therefore Manggai badly needed a Volunteer to head the agricultural activities.

As we approached the entrance driveway to Manggai High School, we saw Siniwin driving a Ford tractor along the road. When he recognized us riding in the school truck, he was so excited that he ran off the roadway into the grass. We were surprised to see Siniwin and to learn that he had remained at the Manggai School. Since Siniwin had returned, the Volunteer was assigned to teach classes in agriculture and Home Economics and she would help with the class gardens. She was very worried that Peace Corps would be unhappy with her for the change in her work, but we reassured her that they would understand.

Bill and Siniwin spent a lot of time together looking at the cattle and poultry and discussing ways to improve and enlarge the operation. Siniwin was eager to learn about animal husbandry methods which Bill used on his farm. With the change in the work assignment for the Volunteer, we must find some other way to be productive. Bill found that none of the twelve sewing machines in the Home Economic department functioned so he began repairing them. Some were beyond repair, because of missing parts and rust; others were out of adjustment, dirty and needed to be oiled. Sometimes he asked me to sew with one that he had fixed to see if I thought it was satisfactory. Doris, the teacher in charge of the Home Economic Department, asked me if I would help her re-arrange the sewing room and organize the bolts of material, the patterns and the sewing accessaries.

She told us that this year her students were baking rolls for the mess. We watched them mixing the dough and making out the individual rolls. It was quite time consuming. Bill suggested that bread would be much faster using his recipe which requires no kneading. So he taught Doris and Susan, the teacher in charge of the mess hall, how to bake bread. He also taught them to make scotchbread cookies for the teachers' tea time. Then he noticed that the screen on the bread/roll storage cupboard had big holes in it; rats often got inside. He replaced the old screen with new.

Next he repaired and cleaned three school typewriters, worked on a VCR, a duplicating machine, a slide projector, two weed sprayers, a pump and helped to re-arrange the science room.

The Headmaster told us that the school needed supplies from Kavieng; the school driver was taking the truck the next day to town. "Would you like to ride along?" We always provided more than our share of food when we stayed with a Volunteer and so we were eager to ride along and buy more supplies. It also gave us the opportunity to explore Kavieng. After we bought groceries, we walked along the seashore to the Kavieng market and viewed the vegetables and fruits offered for sale. Here the produce was carried in bilums of woven green pandanus. Later, as we retraced our steps to town, we passed a Catholic church and decided to go inside. The Father, an American, showed us the facilities and told us of his wonderful years in Kavieng administrating to the Nationals. On our return trip to Manggai we put our purchases in the rear of the truck. As we traveled down the Boluminski Highway, the driver would frequently stop to pick up people walking along the road and later drop them off at their village. When we reached Manggai High School and collected our sacks of food, we found one containing bread and crackers was missing. Evidently one passenger had taken more than he had purchased. "Slowly, slowly. Not to worry."

When one of the teachers, Josephine, saw me sewing, she showed me her blouse and asked if I knew how to make patterns. "I'll cut a pattern if you will allow me to take some measurements and the blouse to the Volunteer's house. I will need some large sheets of paper," I replied. While I was cutting the pattern the wife of a school laborer came to bring some fruit to give to the Volunteer. Soon she came back with a dress.

"I heard that you can sew on the sewing machine. I have material for a dress. Can you make me a dress just like this one?" she inquired.

"Yes," I replied. And soon I was asked by another woman to make her a similar dress. Then Selma, another teacher, asked me to cut her a pattern for a meri blouse. Another day I taught Doris and Susan to bake banana bread and also gave them the recipe to make kaukau bread.

Each evening some of the teachers came to visit. One evening the Volunteer invited Siniwin for dinner and later she invited David, a teacher, to eat with us. One night teacher Oinikai came. She told us that each Sunday evening the students were entertained with some type of program in the mess hall. She was in charge of the next program. "Will you talk to the student body on the topic, U.S.A Government,

Customs and Education?" she inquired I had given several talks to schools and church groups and always the audiences were quiet and attentive. This time the students often raised their hands while I was speaking to ask a question. They were so interested in learning about the U.S.A., especially how young people married and about our school system.

One day Siniwin told Bill that some of his students were going to butcher a steer and a pig for a school feast, a school holiday in observance of the founding of the New Ireland Provincial Government. Bill and I walked to where they were butchering the steer. The carcass was hung from a rope and the boys were skinning the animal by cutting off small patches of skin. Then, rather than dissecting the animal in the normal way, they simply cut off huge chucks of flesh. Bill offered to show them how he would cut up a carcass, but they were not interested. The next evening the celebration dinner was held in the school mess hall. The beef and pork were delicious, the best we had ever tasted in Papua New Guinea.

Most of the women in New Ireland Province have a small tattoo in the center of their forehead which looks like spokes of a wheel. I had asked Josephine, a teacher who often came to the Volunteer's house in the evenings to visit, where I could get a tattoo and she told me she knew how to do it. "Bill would you mind if I asked Josephine to put a tattoo on my ankle like the women have on their forehead?" I asked. He didn't care. Josephine said that before she could make the tattoo she must first go to the jungle to collect a special leaf and she would come to the house the next evening. First she crushed some of the leaves and rubbed them over my ankle. She said the juice from the leaves would prevent any infection or soreness. Then she mixed some black soot, from the burner of her kerosene refrigerator,with a bit of water to make a paste and dipped a sewing needle into it and repeatedly pricked my skin. It took two hours to make the design. When she finished she again crushed more leaves and rubbed over the pricked area and told me to keep my ankle dry for ten days. My ankle never got a bit sore and now I have the tattoo of the New Ireland women.

The last day we were at Manggai the Headmaster, Wilson Tsapan, asked Bill if he would repair his wife's sewing machine. Later he came to thank Bill and me for our congeniality and help. "I wish you two would stay at Manggai to work on repairs and act as consultants," he told us. Many of the teachers and neighbors came to the house our last evening to say goodbye and to get our address so that they could write to us in the United States. We had made a lot of new friends. Tomorrow we would fly to Port Moresby, give our reports to the Peace Corps office and prepare to depart on our return trip to the U.S.A. on March 7, 1988.

When we left Papua New Guinea from Jackson Airport to fly around the world so that we could visit some other countries on our trip home, we didn't realize that we would soon face the greatest challenge of our term in Peace Corps. We visited Manila, Hong Kong, Macao, China and the Republic of South Africa. On April 17th we arrived at our home to resume our farming operation. And then we experienced cultural shock. Suddenly we felt so lonely because for two and one-half years in Papua New Guinea we were constantly surrounded with Nationals. We had lived in a simple society where time was unimportant and there were no deadlines, routines, pressures or competition. Now we must learn to live again by our watches; there were so many cars; the houses were larger than we had remembered. The super markets sold all kinds of foods. The shopping malls contained an abundance of expensive items. Everyone was in a hurry. So we preferred to stay home on our farm, but few came to visit us. Our wonderful U.S.A had changed. Or was it that Bill and I had changed? We found that we must fasten our seat belts in contrast to being grateful to get a ride to town traveling in a 4-wheel truck over a rugged road in Papua New Guinea. The television programs told us that we must watch our cholesterol, eat more bran, avoid red meat. We had learned to be content with whatever type of food was available. Evening news told us of conflicts, drugs, crime and acid rain. We were engulfed with pressure and negative news. Now we understood that the most difficult task we would face in Peace Corps was learning to leave it.

We have adjust ; we have settled into our former routines, but it took nearly nine months to accomplish. Yes, we have both changed. Material possessions are not paramount to us any longer because we lived in Papua New Guinea with only the bare necessities and were extremely happy and content.

Our early morning pattern remains similar to when we sat in our kitchen/family room, drank coffee and dreamed about going to Peace Corps. Now we reminisce about our wonderful time in Papua New Guinea. The walls of the room are decorated with artifacts and memorabilia, a story board from the Sepik, three hunting spears from Barai land, a kundu drum, a shield, three spirit masks, a yam mask, an ancient ceremonial axe, bow and arrows, a lime pot, wood carvings, bilums, bilias, Bill's bushknife and our four killing stones.

" Bill, do you remember the time you saw Joe's wife and her son Zacchaeus walking along the road near Tama and you asked them if they would like to ride back to Itokama? She started to get into the back of the truck but you insisted that she and Zacchaeus ride in the front seat with you. She thanked you when you arrived at Itokama. It was a great honor for a woman to be allowed to ride inside a truck."

"During our Peace Corps training in Wau, remember how our favorite Tok Pidgin teacher, John Kaulo, would come to our bedroom in the evenings to visit? After he left you would spray the room with your perfume because his "udi", body odor, was so strong. He taught me to make a fire with a piece of green bamboo rubbed over a hard stick layed over dried moss. After about ten minutes the moss would start to smoke and then we blew on it and it began to blaze. He coaxed me to chew a betal nut."

I remember when he came to Lae to attend the All Volunteer Conference that on the way to Lae the PMV he was riding in was stopped by rascals and John was robbed of all his money. You gave him 20 kina and John said, "Bill, I don't know how soon I can repay you." You replied, "John, this is a gift to my friend, not a loan."

"I'll always remember the time John told us that he had been born in the stone age and now he must learn to live in a space age," Bill replied. "He was well educated and had taught at the university."

"I think about our Barai friends. I miss them so much. Someday we must return to Papua New Guinea for a visit."

We continue to dream; we reflect. Our most prized possessions are the killing stones because they are symbols of a pristine sosiety who still believe in close family relationships, past heros and myths. Brother Jame's words echoes in our ears, "Yumi brata; tumbuna olsem."

CHAPTER 16

"The images of myth are reflections of the spiritual
potentialities of every one of us. Through contemplating
these, we evoke their powers in our own lives." - Joseph
Campbell

The Nationals love to story about the past. It is one of their main sources of entertainment and their method of passing unwritten history and legends from generation to generation. The following pages contain copies of two stories written in English by Barai men, a story by a man from Southern Highlands Province and other material that we collected in Papua New Guinea. The three stories are reprinted exactly as they were originally written using their grammar and punctuation. Since English is actually their third language, which is used in government and schools, these men show linguistic aptitude.

A YAM STORY
By
Brian Kasira - 1980-81
From Neokananee Village

This book has been produced in remembrance of the big yam feast held in Itokama village in 1981. Information was collected from the elders in the village and a survey was conducted during the preparation of this big feast.

In 1980, the people of Itokama and Neokananee villages dug yams and gave them to one another and to their in-laws. While this was going on, they dug some yams from Itokama which they named. An elder named Mark Akove from Itokama dug two big yams and named one Isekube and the other he named Niuvani. One yam was named Varovaro by Tinari from Neokananee village.

Small feasts have taken place around Itokama for some time and the lawyer from Itokama named Abel Anama thought about it for a while and then called all the village elders together to talk about having one big general feast which would then be the last feast for the people with tattoos on their bodies. So he called a meeting and talked about the matter. All the village elders agreed and said that they would do it and told everybody about the feast which was to be held in 1981.

So early in 1981, the people talked and thought about this feast and went around in the bush in groups helping each other making new gardens. When all the new gardens had been cut down to dry, the elders then went around displaying sticks and strings for tying yams to the people during the planting time. Then the elders met together again and called every one to their meeting. They told them all the rules they would have to follow while making yam gardens. When the gardens were dried up, the people then went around and burned them and cleared up the rubbish from the gardens. The people then offered sacrifices to their dead ancestors while dividing the gardens among themselves and planting the first yams. They went around in groups doing that until the gardens had all been planted. When the planting season was over, the people met together again and talked about the feast they were going to have in 1981. Early in 1981, the people went back to the gardens and cleared up the weeds and made sure the yams were growing properly. In May 1981, it was time for harvesting yams and so the people went around and dug up yams in their gardens. When all the yams had been dug up and were ready for the people to view them, the people then went around in groups and viewed the yams being put away in the yam houses by the owners. After this was done, the people then agreed in a meeting to have a feast in Itokama village.

While this was going on at Itokama there was a very big feast down in a village called Mafuanama which the people from Itokama had been invited to. The people of Mafuanama village cut a mango tree and planted it in the middle of the village and stuck all their yams around that mango tree until it reached the top of the tree. They killed 35 pigs during that feast. It was on the 18th of May that the people of Itokama arrived at Mafuanama village for that feast. The Itokama people sat and watched while the Mafuanama people gave yams and pigs away to each other and to their in-laws. On the afternoon of the 18th the Mafuanama people then killed pigs, cut them up and got them ready to be given away. When everything was ready, they gave yams and pig meat to the Itokama people. It was a very big heap of yams and pig meat. The Itokama people baked the yams and pig meat on stones and shared among themselves. On the next day, the 19th of May, the Itokama people took their yams and pigs away to their village. It was a very big feast and so the rope that the Mafuanama people used to measure their yams was given to the Itokama people through the Itokama councillor.

When all the yams and pig meat had been carried from Mafuanama to Itokama, the people baked yams and meat on the stones and shared with everyone and in the afternoon they had a meeting and all agreed to have a feast in Itokama village and invite the Tama people to that feast. After agreeing on the idea, they went back to their garden and dug yams and set aside some yams for the feast and some for new gardens. When everything was ready in the gardens, the people came to Itokama and built small shelters for the feast. The people from Umuate, Neokananee and Kuai all agreed to have the feast together so all these people came to Itokama and built shelters. While the men gathered fire wood, the ladies went around in groups and carried all the yams to Itokama. Sometimes the Youth Club was paid to help with the yams and fire wood. The preparation for the big feast went on for 3 months.

When all the preparations were nearly complete, the people the got the big yams and tied them on to display racks and painted them with mud. Also all the yams were painted with blue and red mud. When the tying and painting was over, they cut forks and sticks and made a yam pile right through the center of the village from one end to the other.

Then they stood all the yams which had been tied on display racks against the supporting sticks they made and laid all the other yams on the ground beside the yams tied on sticks. The yams were lined up by clans or villages right through the village. Starting from where the Nahara store stands were the Kuai peoples' yams, then the Itokama peoples's, then the Ufia peoples', and then the Umuate people laid the yams at the other end of the village.

While this was going on, the people went around and told their in-laws to come and dance at the feast. The feast was about to begin when the pigs were tied under the houses. There were 19 pigs ready to be killed during the feast.

Then on the 16th day of October 1981, the Itokama people had their feast. Early in the morning the stones were burned and the ladies started to pile up yams and taro that were going to be baked on the stones. There were 21 stone fires going at once. While the ladies were piling the yams, the men started to put the yams in heaps according to whom they were going to give the yams. There were too many to name the people to whom the yams were given but the heaps of yams counted were 77. The rope which the Itokama people used to measure their yams was tied from where the Nahara store stands right to the end of the village. But Nafuanama peoples' rope went only from where Nahara stands to where Amos' house was. While young people were tying the rope, the older people danced and sang songs which made people remember the past days and cry.

Most of the heaps of yams were quite big but two heaps of yams were the biggest ones of all. These two heaps were for Aron Akove's family and for Margret's parents. At about 3 pm. the mumus were taken off and people started to place baked food beside the heaps of yams for their in-laws to eat. When everything was prepared, they called their in-laws to eat. After they had enough, they put the cooked food away safely and covered the bananas and betalnuts and cleared up the place for the dancers. The first group of dancers were the Afore people who danced the Sisive dance. The second group was the Kuaruvo people who also danced the Sisive dance. The third groups of dancers were the Musa people who preformed two Kikia dances. The Musa peoples' first dance was called Garea and the second one was called Gegea. The fifth group of dancers were the Tama people who danced Ujau. So there were 5 groups of dancers during the feast.

The people of Itokama, after showing the dancers where to stand and dance, went back and brought firewood and made fires for them and then started giving them food. They kept the dancers going by giving them smokes, betelnut, and keeping the fires going until daybreak.

Both the dancers and the Itokama people really enjoyed that night. There was no fighting or arguing because everyone had held Simon's Bible and James Noble's badge before the feast. The dance went on until daybreak. It was Saturday morning and the dancers had a rest. The Itokama people got down and broke down the heaps of yams and shared among themselves. At about 4pm on Saturday, the councillor got down and blew the horn. When the Itokama people heard the horn blowing, they thought it was time for them to give yams, meat, betelnut and ran up and down the village to show how proud they were to pay back the yams they had brought down from Tama village. After running around, they came and put the yams in a heap in front of Amos's house where the Tama people were staying. They did that several times and after that they brought firewood, banana leaves, stones, dry bamboo, and axes for the Tama people to make a mumu. This heap of yams was the biggest one of all. When the Itokama people moved back to their houses, the Tama people made stone fires and baked their yams and meat. When it was cooked they opened the mumu and ate it.

The next day was Sunday, so everyone attended the service and after the service, they came back and had a rest and cooked food and ate until at about 1pm when the Itokama people went down again to give yams to people who came from different places. So they gave food to the Musa people, then to the Kuaruwo, then to the Ajari people, then to the Anatua people, then to the Afore people, then to the Ubuvara people and then to the Itokama staff members. After that they went back and gave yams to the Tama people, then again they got yams tied on sticks plus rice, fish, pig meat and gave them to the Tama people. Everyone really enjoyed that day until it got dark and they slept.

The next day was Monday so everybody got all their yams and went home. Everyone really enjoyed themselves during the feast. The Tama people were carrying yams in string bags and the Itokama people felt sorry for them so they told them to use the truck and load their yams down to their village. On Tuesday, the Tama people came back to carry their pigs down. When they came back, the Itokama people went down and gave them another heap of yams with the pigs. But they took only the pigs and went and left the yams behind. So the Itokama people got the yams back and shared among themselves and ate them. They did that while the Musa people killed their two pigs and mumued them. While waiting for their mumu they gave presents to the owner of the pigs and the owner also gave them some presents. In the afternoon they opened up their mumu and ate it. The next day they all went to their places.

The rope that they used to measure the yams was tied for the Tama people but they did not untie it so the Itokama people untied the rope and kept it for their own. That was the biggest feast ever held in that area. So the older people were really sad to see such a feast like that go by. They also said that, this was the last feast and that they will never have one again in the future.

There were many people who attended the feast and it was so crowded that we couldn't count the people to get the right number, so we estimated the number to be eight or nine hundred people. The feast was over and everyone went back to his/her place and are working hard in their new life.

That is about all for the big general feast held at Itokama village in 1981.

****

KAJAEDO VUA (The Story of Kajae)
By
Simon Savieko, Itokama Village

This book is written about Mr. Kajae. To read this book, we well see how Kajae has changed all of his life from the old ways to the new life with God.

To start with, we will see the birth record of Mr. Kajae and then we shall see how God worked through Kajae throughout his whole life. Mr. Kajae's father was Amegi and Amegi is from Birare. Birare is a place in Itokama village. Amegi got married to a woman named Ikievo who was from a clan named the Sanaeko clan, in Neokananee village. Ikievo's mother is called Damua and Amegi's father is called Amako. Amako and Dumua were known to be the grandparents of Kajae. The grandparents of Kajae used to kill their friends and eat them. Ao Amegi and Ikievo are the parents of Kajae. When Kajae was born, the people from Tama village and the people from the Dafarie clan named him Kajae. Amegi and Ikievo did not only have Kajae, but had four more children as well. Their names are: Rumui, Iduka, Bakoe and Gaeki. There were five of them in the family, but all of them died.

Some got married and had children, but both the parents and children passed away and only Kajae is still alive.

Mr. Kajae was a small boy when his father Amegi died. When his father passed away, his mother, Ikievo, got married to another man named Agae. Agae and Ikievo stayed together and looked after Kajae well and he grew up quickly.

When Kajae was about 6 or 7 year old, his mother Ikievo died. When his mother passed away, Kajae was looked after by Mr. Maejaru and Nanamo throughout his life until the two men died. Before the two men died, it came time for Kajae to go through the tattooing ceremony. Mr. Nuniari and Vuvone took Kajae and made the traditional initiation ceremony. In the past, every single man has had to go through the initiation ceremony before he got married. Mr. Kajae's initiation took place near Itokama village, and because Kajae went through that ceremony, he is known to be one of the people with tattoo designs on his body.

When the traditional ceremony was over, Kajae was a single boy and so he thought it was time for him to get married. So he found a girl named Ajiamo and made friends with Ajiamo and when those looking after him found out about this, they were happy too. Then after some time, Kajae got married to Ajiamo in Itokama village by agreement of Ajiamo's parents and the people looking after Kajae.

Kajae was just newly married and stayed in a bush place named Furuarane when Mt. Lamington erupted. After the eruption, Kajae and Ajiamo came back to Itokama where they stayed and Ajiamo gave birth to their five children. There were seven altogether, but two died and they were left with five. There are three sons and two daughters in Kajae's family.

The children grew up and the first born girl named Kinio married a man from Orokaiva. The other girl, Soso, married a man in Tama village, Suagi Aseto. Kajae's three sons are still living with him. Their names are Irevara, Kisia and Gaguae. Kajae advises his sons and he is happy to have them with him. The children also love their parents and do whatever they are told.

Kajae was a "bigman's" son. His father was a lawyer and a man who worked hard in the garden, who went hunting in the bush. So Kajae was taught by his father to do all these things. Kajae carried out his father's advise when he was a small boy up to the stage where he changed his whole life to God's way. Kajae was doing all the things taught by his father when a patrol officer came to Itokama.

The patrol officer was looking for people wandering in the bush to get them living together in one village. The patrol officer chose some people in the villages who could speak Hiri Motu to look after the village people. Those people were called the Tusirini councilors. These councilors' duties were to make sure the villages were tidy and everyone slept in the village houses. They also stopped fights in the villages and brought any troublemakers to report to the patrol officers in the patrol posts. The councilors were also good speakers of Hiri Motu so they helped village people who cannot speak Motu to stand before the patrol officers if they were found guilty of any crime.

Kajae was a good Motu speaker because he had traveled a long way away to various towns to see people, to help people and also to take his children to the hospitals. He has been to Tufi, Pongani, Kokoda and Sahio hospital. Kajae went to the above mentioned places with his wife, but there are some places that he traveled himself. It was during the Second World War that he traveled by himself. He traveled to Samarai and helped the Australian soldiers to carry their cargo during the fighting.

Kajae saw and did many new things while he was in other places away from his own place. Ao when he returned to Itokama, he was told by the village people to become a Tusirini councillor and look after his people. The former councillor was Mr. Orari who did not speak Motu well, so the badge was given to Kajae because he spoke Motu well and he was a man who talked a lot. So Kajae was the Tusirini councillor who looked after the Ilokama people and advised them to live a good and peaceful life.

Kajae was doing the government's work in the village when the missionaries arrived at Itokama village in 1958. The missionaries were the people who brought God's messages to the people. When they arrived at Itokamam, they stood a cross in the middle of the village and went back. The one who stood the cross up was Bishop David Hand. He was the head of the Anglican Church so he stood the cross to show other denominations that the Bari area had been found by the Anglican church already. The Bishop also told Kajae to be the church councillor. However, Bishop Graydon was with Bishop David when he came to Itokama on that day, so they both did that work in Itokama village.

It was on that day that Kajae became the church councillor of Itokama church. He told the people to come to church to hear the Good News about the Lord Jesus Christ. God was working in Kajae's heart so he began to get the village people to build a church and name it St. Matthias Church.

Kajae also told the people to clear a site for a mission station. In only five years, everything seemed to change quickly in Itokama. In 1964 there had been a big development in Itokama area in which three school houses were built plus a hospital. Three teachers were told to come to Itokama and to start a mission school there. In the same year, the airstrip was built by the village people with the assistance of the teachers. The older people were really surprised to see the new things and so they did all the work in only five year's time. They wanted to see what would come next so their work was quick and smart.

Kajae had taken his son Kusia and his daughter Kinio to big hospitals and had seen some new things. He had been to a big hospital called Sahio and had seen how hospitals were built and run. After gathering information from the doctors and medicals at Sahio Kajae returned to the village and decided to build a hospital at Itokama. The doctor at Sahio promised to help him with a medical worker for his new hospital. But after building three houses for the hospital, there was no one to work for them. Kajae fought hard for one medical and finally Parminas Ogome was sent to Itokama to look after the hospital. The people were happy to have a medical in Itokama village.

Mr. Kajae is a man with tattoos on his body and had not been to school, but God really worked through him so he could think and do the right things for his people. Being a thoughtful man, Kajae remembered what he had been told by one of the medicals at the Dea mission station while he was there to pick up medicines for Itokama hospital. He remembered the medical advising him to make the strip, and with the help of the village people, the strip was made soon afterwards. When it was ready, a mission plane was the first plane to land. But when the plane landed, the pilot told the people that the strip was not long enough. However, the older people wanted to see new things, so with Kajae's supervision a new airstrip was made and that's the airstrip we have now at Itokama.

Having a mission is a good thing because the schools, hospitals, airstrip and businesses will always come after the mission station has been set up in any place. They got these things and now you can find many new things happening at Itokama.

Kajae saw that many new things were happening so he praised God for that. Whenever a visitor came to Itokama Kajae was the man to meet them and take them to his house for meals. He wanted to learn new ideas, so he talked with the visitors and asked many questions about how to live a new life. After the visitors had gone, Kajae sat down with his people and told them what he had heard. The people listened carefully and do what he says because everyone wants to see new things come to their place. All the new happenings really changed Kajae's life, so he forgot all about what he had been taught by his father about how to make big gardens, hunt, fight and do other old ways.

He does follow some old ways when there is a need for him to do so, but now he can think and do new things in Itokama village.

Kajae has not been to school, doesn't read and write, but by God's power working through him, he thinks properly and talks to people about the messages about the Lord Jesus Christ. He sits at night in the village talking to people about what he heard in church on Sundays about the Good News.

Kajae got the missionary to his place while he was a young man. Since then he has not gone back to the bush for anything. The village people sleep in garden houses in the bush, but Kajae stays in the village. Now he is growing old, but by his strength in words and actions, you can see many good things happening in Itokama village. Kajae really fought hard to get all the Barai language speaking people to where they are now. If he was not here with us now, then maybe the Barai people would still be fighting each other and doing all the old things our ancestors were used to doing.

It was God who really appointed Mr. Kajae to work for His people in Itokama village and so we thank and praise God for giving the Barai people the kind of man who can think and do good things. This book will show us in the future how Kajae did a great thing for us.

Kajae's story ends here!
(Footnote: Amos Kajae died in August 1983. His passing was a great loss for the Itokama people, but they are happy for the good example he set for them.)

****

BIRTH OF A TRIBE
by
Samuel Sigam
Sowa Village, Southern Highland Prov.

Once upon a time there lived two brothers. The eldest was called Yul Yako and the younger was Kipira Olum. They were alone because their parents had died when they were very young. Everyday Tul Yako tried to gather enough food to feed the both of them.

One bright morning, the two brothers got up early to go in search of food as usual. Soon they came to a muddy track and decided to follow it. This led them to a clearing. In the middle of the clearing was a small hut which stood under a bush of casuarina trees. Not far from the hut was also a small stream. From the hut they could see a ring of smoke rising. When they saw that the two boys quickly hid among the kunai grass. The two boys were very curious to find out who lived in the hut. So they hid and waited patiently. Not long an old man came out of the hut. The two boys could tell that he was going off to his gardens.

Yul told his younger brother to wait while he checked out the inside of the hut. In the hut he found a taro baking in the charcoal at the fireplace. He took this out to where his brother waited and they both ate it up. Then Yul told Kipira to go further down stream and wait for him. He also told Kipira to collect anything that floated down the stream. "Collect everything except human hair," Yul told his younger brother.

When Kipira went down stream, Yul climbed up the tallest casuraina tree that towered over the little hut. There he sat and waited for the old man to return from his garden. Not long the old man returned home. Yul watched him go into the house and heard him search for the taro he had left on the ashes at his fireplace. The old man was very angry when he found the taro missing. He screamed out,"Who stole my taro?"

From the tree top Yul screamed in reply, "I did!"

The old man was so cross he completely went out of his mind and pulled all the things in his house down and out of his garden and threw them all into the stream. Included among these things were two of his daughters whom he always imprisoned. Always, in between throwing the things into the river, the old man said the name of each item. And each time Yul from above in the tree would call back in reply and say,"I did!" Eventually the old man had nothing more to throw into the stream except himself. By now he was beyond himself with anger. He screamed,"Who stole my beard?"

And Yul from the top of the tree said, "I did." The old man then pulled all his beard from his face and threw these into the stream. Then he too threw himself into the stream.

From down stream Kipira did as his brother had told him and did not touch the beard that flowed past him in the stream. And when the old man followed, that too he did not touch.

When Yul saw the old man throw himself into the stream and drown he came from the tree and joined his younger brother and the two girls. The two brothers then divided all the things in two, one brother got one of the sisters and the other one got another. Each of the brothers married his girl and they all lived happily ever after.

The tribe Aim Enja Oparep in the Southern Highlands is made of people who descended from the two brothers and their two wives. The stream Kaso Ipa still exists and continues to flow down from Yar hill through the middle of Sowa village.

****

PAPA BILONG MIPELA
(The Lord's Prayer in Tok Pidgen)
Papa bilong mipela yu stap long heven
Mekim nem bilong yu i kamap bikpela.
Mekim kingdom bilong yu kam.
Stongim mipela long behainin laik bilong yu long graun
Olsem ol i behainin long heven.
Givim mipela kaikai inap long tude.
Pogivim rong bilong mipela,
Olsem mipela i porgivim ol arapela i mekim rong long mipela.
Sambai long mipela, long taim bilong traim.
Na rausim olgeta samting nogul long mipela.
Amen

****

Boarding information in both Tok Pidgin and English as posted in the Jackson Airport terminal:

TOKSAVE LONG OL MAN/MERI
Air Nuigini itoksave olsem man/meri husat igo long balus. I mas soim olgeta pikinin sapos krismas bilong ol ino winim 2 yia pastaim long kisim balus. Dispela tok save ibihainim lo ikamap yet long opis bilong gutpela lukaut bilong man/meri na ron bilong balus.
Husat man/meri ino bihainim dispela toksave em bai inopop go long balus.

Translation:

PUBLIC NOTICE

Due to OAC saftey requirements, the members of traveling public are advised to declare any infants under 2 years to the check-in staff when checking in. Failure to do so could result in the airline denying your boarding if flight is full.

Coffee cherries

Butchering a pig

Stuck in the muck on the Pongomi-Afore highway after a tropical rain.

Simon Savaiko carries his small son in a bilum.

Natius weaving a pandanus mat

Men weaving bamboo siding

Lelia cooking over open fire. Food is cooked in this manner.

L to R: Doctor Martin Luke, Kingsley, Sister Dorcu and Iloi

EPILOGUE

We remember Papua New Guinea
And the dear friends we made in that land.
Take a peek at this Stone Age culture;
Visualize it if you can.

It is a land of fuzzy hair, dark skin people
Composed of seven hundred languages, tribes and more.
A land that time nearly forgot
And some civilized people might deplore.

There, family ties are of the utmost importance.
The culture and rituals are complex, and yet,
It is the land where lives our very dear friends;
The country we will not soon forget.

Sing Sing is the name for ceremonial dancing
Where the participants are decorated with feathers and shells.
Their dancing continues all night long
Accompanied by kundu drums, chantings and yells.

There the word kaikai means food.
Kaukau, yams and pitpit are cooked in a pot.
The houses are built of bamboo and sticks,
And time and competion means not a tot.

Their life style may be primitive, but it is uncluttered
By the civilized standards we place.
The simplicity overpowers progress;
We long to return to that pace.

We dream of Papua New Guinea
And the experience of their undeveloped ways,
Where life means only to survive
And the ecology has unlimited days.

We have travel to many far distant countries
And enjoyed the culture and beauty of all,
But of all the places we have encountered
PNG is the most beautiful we can recall.

By Margel Lee Craig

BIBLIOGRAPHY

Connolly, Bob & Anderson, Robin: *First Contact*, Viking Penguin, Inc. N.Y. 1987.

Smith, Hollie G.: *Information For Visitors And Intending Residents*: PNG Chamber of Commerce & Industry: 1985.

GLOSSARY

APCD - Assistant Peace Corps Director. Peaces Corps had two APCD, an American man and a National. Shortly before we left Papua New Guinea they hired a third APCD, a National woman, to be in charge of the health workers.

asi - a spirit which has no ancestoral connection; one of the Barai spirits.

asi giama - a person that can see and communicate with an asi spirit.

Bailey bridge - a portable bridge consisting of a series of prefabricated steel sections in the form of lattices.

barome - the name given to the spirit of a recently dead ancestor by the Barai tribe.

betal nut - The small fruit of the Areca palm. The outer husk is removed and the inside fruit chewed with lime and mustard producing red saliva. It acts as a stimulant similar to nicotine; it acts on the mucous membrane and central nervous system, lessening hunger and fatique.

bigman - the chief or head man of a village or tribe; the leader.

bilas - (Tok Pidgin) - finery, ornaments, jewelry, decoration or fancy dress, shells and feathers.

bilum - string bag or net bag woven from native fibers, plastic or yarn; used to carry items, babies, food, etc. by the people of Papua New Guinea. Sometimes refers also to baskets or pouches woven from pandanus or other plants.

brata - (Tok Pidgin)- brother.

bride price - the settlement in kina, pigs, yams or anything of value paid by the bridegroom to his father-in-law as payment for the daughter/bride. The amount paid depends on the talent, education and ability of the woman to generate income.

bubu - (Tok Pidgin) - grandparent or respected old one.

bushknife - machete, a heavy bladed knife used to cut underbrush, etc.

cordial - (pronounced cord-e-al) - a non alcholic drink made of imitation or natural fruit juices.

cuscus - a small marsupial, about the size of a possum. There are many colors from grey, brown and snowy white. They are valuable as food and their skin is used to decorate headdresses and other bilas.

DPI - Department of Primary Industry, a government organization to aid in rural and small business development

Europeans - a term used by the Nationals for people of western countries.

expiates - slang name for people of other races living within PNG.

firebox - a place to light a fire for cooking or warmth usually located inside the bush house. Small logs are laid in a square to form a framework of about 3 ft x 3 ft. The center is covered with sand to prevent the small fire from burning through the floor.

furufuru - another Barai spirit which has a human-like body, very tiny feet and wears a special feather in its hair.

grassknife - a double edged knife used to cut grass - approx 36 inches in length and curved at the cutting end.

Headmaster - the administrator or principal of a school.

hectare - metric measure; 2.47 acres.

kaukau - a type of sweet potato which is one of the main staples in PNG diet. The plant vines along the ground and produces a tuber with white, cream, pink or purple colored meat. There are over 300 varieties.

kava - another member of the Barai spirits which cause people to act irrationally.

kavene - indwelling spirit of a live Barai person.

killing stone - a ball shaped or disc shaped stone mounted on the end of a strong stick and used to kill or stun the enemy; a war club.

kilogram - metric measure; 2.2 pounds.

kilometer - metric measure; 0.62 miles.

kina - currency - approx. $1.00. The name comes from the kina shell originally used for barter.

kine - a Barai spirit; a barome who excells in wisdom may become a kine who aids and instucts the shaman, the medicine man.

kulau - a green coconut; the inside liquid is used as drinking water.

laplap - wearing apparel; a straight length of material or tapa wrapped around the body to form a skirt. It may also refer to a waistcoat, a loincloth, any piece of material or rag.

laulau - Malay apple; a pear shaped fruit with bright pink skin and a white interior.

liklik haus- (Tok Pidgin) translation = little house; usually refers to an out door toilet.

loliwara - (Tok Pidgin) a soft drink; ex: orange pop.

meri blouse - a short sleeve or sleeveless blouse gathered at the neckline to produce a very loose fitting blouse similar to a maternity blouse.

mission station - an area apart from the village which may include a church, school and medical facility.

nappies - diapers; usually a square of terry cloth.

National - a born citizen of Papua New Guinea.

OIC - Officer In Charge of a national or provincial governmental department.

pandanus - a family of trees found throughout Papua New Guinea. The leaves are used for matting and thatching and the nuts of some varieties are eaten.

petrol - gasoline.

private mail bag - a means of distributing mail in a locked pouch or bag to remote villages.

PMV - a privately owned bus, van or truck used to transport passengers for a small fee.

rubber - a sling shot.

rainmaker - a man thought to possess super natural powers to call the rain clouds to come to an area or village.

shaman - a medicine man; tribal doctor.

SIL - Summer Intstitute of Linguistics, a division of the Wycliffe Bible Translators, Inc. Their principal objective is to translate the Bible into the tribal language and to teach the translation process to some of the members of the tribe.

sista - (Tok Pidgen) a sister.

sister - (Tok Pidgen) a nurse; a nun.

solicitor - attorney; lawyer.

story - to tell a story; to tell a legend.

tapa cloth - a cloth-like material made from the inner bark of the mulberry tree. The inner bark is soaked with water, laid on a flat surface and pounded with a paddle until it resembles cloth. Later it may or may not be painted with dyes made from plants and berries found in the jungle.

taro - a tuber bulb; they are a lily-like plant with broad smooth, spear or heart -shaped leaves. Polynesia "poi" is made from fermented ground taro.

tato - Barai name for grandparent or respected old person.

toea - PNG coin currency equivalent to a cent. The name comes from the toea shell originally used for barter.

torch - flashlight.

trap specialist - a man possessing supernatural powers to trap animals and fish.

tumbuna - (Tok Pidgin) dead ancestor; also used to refer to grand parents and great-grandparents.

ubaibogi - Another Barai spirit, an ancient ancestor; they have large bodies and are very quick and agile.

udi - body odor.

vaiai - the Barai name for the phyical body.

wantok - (Tok Pidgin)-one who speaks the same language; one who is of the same nationality; a compatriot; a neighbor; one who is from the same country.

wantok system - means what you have is mine and what I have is yours. For example: you are my wantok, therefore if I own something such as clothing or an item which you wish to have, I would be expected to give it to you.

waswas - (Tok Pidgin) to wash; to bathe.

wokabaut somil - (Tok Pidgin) a portable saw mill.

yam - a tuber; a spreading climbing vine which has heart-shaped leaves. The root tuber varies in color, shape and size but generally have a thin hairy brown skin and pink, purple or white starchy interior. The Barai tribe was named after the baro yam which has a purple meat and if from 9 to 18 inches long. Some varieties grow to enormus size and may measure 30 to 36 inches in length.